*Religion in Public Life*

# Religion in Public Life:
# A Dilemma for Democracy

Ronald F. Thiemann

A Twentieth Century Fund Book

GEORGETOWN UNIVERSITY PRESS / WASHINGTON, D.C.

Georgetown University Press, Washington, D.C. 20007

© 1996 by The Twentieth Century Fund, Inc. All rights reserved.

Printed in the United States of America

10   9   8   7   6   5   4   3                    1996

THIS VOLUME IS PRINTED ON ACID-FREE ∞ OFFSET BOOK PAPER

**Library of Congress Cataloging-in-Publication Data**

Thiemann, Ronald F.

Religion in public life : a dilemma for democracy / Ronald F.
Thiemann.

   p.     cm.

"A Twentieth Century Fund book."

Includes bibliographical references.

1. Democracy—Religious aspects—Christianity.   2. Religion and
state—United States.   3. Religion and politics—United States.
4. United States—Politics and government.   5. United States–
–Politics and government—1993-   6. United States—Religion.
7. United States—Religion—1960-   I. Title.

BR115.P7T475   1996

322'.1'0973—dc20

   ISBN 0-87840-609-3 (alk. paper).

   ISBN 0-87840-610-7 (pbk.: alk. paper)

*For my daughters*
*Sarah Elizabeth and Laura Kristen*
*With love,*
*Pop*

# Contents

# Foreword

The founders of the American Republic, although remarkably similar in background, ethnicity, and religion, were very aware that religious toleration and freedom could not be taken for granted. Because the dangers of religious persecution were fresh in their minds, these new leaders of a new nation took extraordinary care to separate the state and politics from faith and sectarianism. Madison, Jefferson, and their colleagues debated these issues with great intellectual seriousness and with a minimum of sloganeering or pandering, leaving us a remarkable record of their substantive arguments about these issues in their letters, speeches, and public documents.

The re-emergence of religion as a potent force in politics in the 1990s is very different, taking the form of news reporting and public discussion that is overwhelmingly characterized by two approaches: how does it affect whatever political "horse race" is in progress and how does it reflect the tactics and strategy of the political participants involved? In place of the Federalist Papers or Madison's "Memorial and Remonstrance Against Religious Assessments," we are offered the latest polling results or fund-raising statistics. The great compromises that knitted the infant nation together are replaced, in this simplistic view, by base alliances of convenience and plain dealmaking.

We recognize that questions at the intersection of religious beliefs and political actions, especially when they are specific—for example, supporting or opposing federal funding of abortion—raise, for many Americans, very complex moral issues. We know, too, that the public policy implications of these debates inflame real passions and set in motion powerful political forces. But we find little guidance about how to think through constructive responses in the familiar rhetoric of most politicians or the superficial reporting of most of the media. The former, with some notable exceptions such as ex-Governor Mario Cuomo, usually avoid public explication of the moral reasoning behind their conclusions—perhaps because an elected official who agonizes out loud about even the most vexing aspects of morality arouses suspicions of either insincerity or, perhaps worse, waffling. When it comes to reporting, the imperatives of the media business—the need to attract our attention—usually trump sober analysis and good journalism. The formula applied to these political and moral issues is to emphasize conflict and contests. Few are willing to risk low ratings by walking their audience through the complex reasoning that underpins all serious efforts to balance religious conviction, community values, and pluralistic democracy.

One can rationalize about the sterility of public discourse: perhaps this treatment is merely the free market giving us what we are willing to pay for; and perhaps as well, these reports do provide a fair characterization of the shallow motivation of many of those involved. But surely this way of discussing the place of religion in public life does not provide the sustenance necessary for a healthy democratic process. Relying on slogans and labels ignores the complexity of the issues debated two hundred years ago; they are still serious and intellectually challenging subjects once again in need of thoughtful public discourse.

Therefore, the Trustees of the Twentieth Century Fund commissioned Ronald Thiemann, dean of Harvard's Divinity School, to write about the deeper moral, constitutional, and political issues that lie beneath the current surface discussions about the place of religion in public life in America.

Thiemann grounds his exploration in the constitutional foundations of the republic. The framers, in his view, recognized the dilemma inherent in protecting religious expression and yet limiting the influence of any particular religion. The political dynamic involved in pursing these two principles simultaneously ensures, in a sense, that the place of religion in public life will often seem skewed. Yet, the alternative—some sort of rigid set of rules that reflect neither the shifting wishes of a democratic majority or the competing claims of various minorities—is simply unrealistic and probably not even desirable. Of course, when the pendulum has swung to one extreme or another, it is small consolation to the aggrieved parties to be told that such exaggerated outcomes are occasionally inevitable given the nature of the delicate balancing act involved.

The difficulties inherent in that balancing act are reflected in the zig-zag historical record on these issues. Indeed, despite the persistence of a liberal American tradition, as Thiemann says, of "liberty, equality, and toleration," religion often has been exploited for political purposes. For example, candidates like William Jennings Bryan fused religion to political causes directly and overtly. A generation ago, of course, it was considered crucially important for candidate John F. Kennedy to separate his public persona from his personal adherence to the Catholic Church. Today, the Republican party deems it necessary to shoehorn adherence to traditional Christian values into one's sales package for the voters.

One of the real strengths in the pages that follow is that Thiemann returns to the central questions of the debate, offering answers of real substance to basic questions about what the interaction of religion and politics should look like in the United States. While his observations and conclusions will not satisfy everyone (an impossible task given the subject), he supports them with closely reasoned argument, incorporating all the richness of his experience and intellect. He does not simplify; he does not underestimate the difficulties involved. In a debate that can never really be settled, we can ask for no more. Indeed, in a real sense, Thiemann's work reminds us that, when it comes to those in the media and in public life, we would do well to insist that they should do no less.

On behalf of the trustees of the Twentieth Century Fund, I thank him for his efforts.

The Twentieth Century Fund          Richard C. Leone
August 1995                                      President

# Preface

This book has been nearly ten years in the making. I came to Harvard University as Dean of the Divinity School in 1986 planning to write a book on the role of communities of faith in American public life. Though many might have thought such a plan foolhardy for a full-time administrator, I received the full support and encouragement of Harvard president Derek Bok. Not only did he encourage me in the role of scholar-administrator, he also approved a one semester leave which allowed me the time to begin the research and writing on this volume. Harvard's current president, Neil Rudenstine, has been equally supportive of my work on this project. I owe them both a debt of thanks, not only for their help in sustaining my work but also for the way in which they have epitomized the role of university president as public intellectual.

A project as broad as this one inevitably involves the advice and counsel of many people in a wide variety of fields. I have profited immensely from conversations about the character of public speech in democracy with Michael Dyson, Kent Greenawalt, Martha Minow, John Rawls, Michael Sandel, and Michael Walzer. I regret that Professor Greenawalt's *Private Consciences and Public Reasons* did not appear in time for inclusion in my discussion of "criteria of publicity" in chapters four and five. Many scholars have given generously of their time to read and comment on portions of this manuscript, among them: Derek Bok, Angela Carmella, Mark Edwards, Francis Fiorenza, David Hollenbach, David Little, Ernie Monrad, John Noonan, Bill Placher, Mike Root, Dennis Thompson, Bill Werpehowski, and Cornel West. The critical reading offered by my doctoral seminar was invaluable as was the response received from two scholarly groups, the Boston Theological Society and the Yale-Washington Theology Group. It is literally the case that this book could not have been written without the extraordinary help of my two research assistants, Charlene Galarneau and Brent Coffin. Charlene assisted me with the early research and served as a reliable guide through the thicket of materials on first amendment jurisprudence. Brent Coffin worked closely with me in the revising of the early material of the book and in the writing of the final chapters. I want to express my gratitude not only for their diligence and insight, but also for their unwavering belief in the value of this project.

The Twentieth Century Fund has for more than seventy-five years supported projects which address crucial issues of American public life. I am grateful for the support provided by the Fund and for the assistance of their staff members, particularly Roger Kimball and Greg Anrig, Jr. I especially appreciate the patience and understanding shown for the rather deliberate pace of research and writing necessitated by my administrative responsibilities. The staff of Georgetown University Press, under the direction of John Samples, has been unfailingly helpful in bringing this book to publication.

The past ten years have witnessed not just the development of this project but the growth and maturation of my two daughters, Sarah and Laura, from childhood into young adulthood. The joys of parenting are manifold but the personal and intellectual blossoming of one's children is a gift especially to be treasured. From their earliest years these young women have conspired to keep their father honest, humble, and of good humor. I delight that we can have spirited discussions about literary theory, affirmative action policies, and democratic politics and still laugh ourselves silly over someone's bad joke, or share the pain of being Red Sox fans. To "my girls," Sarah Elizabeth and Laura Kristen—women of faith, character, and compassion—I dedicate this book.

Cambridge, Massachusetts                               RONALD F. THIEMANN

# 1

# *Religion in Public Life: An American Dilemma*

The question of the proper role of religion and of religiously based moral convictions within American public life has been hotly debated during the past fifteen years. The rise of the Moral Majority immediately prior to the first Reagan presidential campaign and the presidential candidacies of ordained ministers Pat Robertson and Jesse Jackson directed the media spotlight to the issue of religion and politics. These years have been a time of aggressive Christian politics, as evangelicals entered the political fray seeking to mold public policies that would conform to their own religious convictions. On issues ranging from abortion to prayer in the public schools, evangelicals sought to use the instruments of the American political system to forward their interests and values. Since their agenda fit snugly with that of conservative politicians, advocates for "public religion" were generally associated with conservative political causes. During the 1980s the Moral Majority targeted "liberal politicians" for defeat in congressional elections. Alliances of evangelical Christians and conservative politicians introduced bills into state legislatures mandating silent prayer or moments of silence at the beginning of the school day in the hope of reversing a trend they viewed as increasingly hostile to religion. Abortion became the litmus test for evangelical Christian politics, and the pro-life movement gathered an increasingly diverse group of religious folk under its banner.

During the decade of the 1990s overt evangelical politics became less prominent in our national political life. The scandals in the evangelical community involving such important figures as Jim Bakker, Jimmy Swaggert, and Jerry Falwell drove Christian politics somewhat into the background, and the decisive defeat suffered by Pat Robertson in the 1988 Republican primaries indicated the limits of support

1

for such candidates within the American electorate.[1] The national gathering of evangelicals in Houston, Texas, following the 1992 Republican convention revealed the darker side of Christian politics, as speakers like Pat Buchanan viciously attacked homosexuals, welfare mothers, and any whose lifestyles contributed to the "moral decay" of American culture. The backlash against this divisive political stance contributed in part to George Bush's defeat in that fall's presidential election. Consequently, in the succeeding years of the decade religious conservatives have focused more on local elections, using a well-organized grassroots movement called the Christian Coalition to support school board candidates and other other local officials who endorsed the Coalition's platform for moral and political reform. The substantial success of this movement in the congressional elections of 1994 has shown that evangelical politics remains a significant force in American public life.

Despite the considerable attention given to recent Christian politics the issues raised by the evangelical movement remain unresolved. What role should religion and religiously based moral convictions play within American public life? Should religious beliefs be allowed any voice in a pluralistic democracy with a constitutionally mandated "separation between church and state"? How does our official policy of "separation" square with the fact of congressional and military chaplains paid from public funds; of tax exemptions for churches, synagogues, and their auxiliary institutions; of currencies inscribed with the motto "In God We trust?" Why is prayer permitted in the Supreme Court and the U.S. Congress but not in American public schools?[2]

"We are a religious people whose institutions presuppose a Supreme Being."[3] These words, written by Supreme Justice William O. Douglas in 1952, point to an inescapable fact of American life. Every statistical analysis of the religious beliefs and practices of the American people demonstrates the robust religiosity of our citizenry, and so it is not surprising that our public institutions have come to reflect some of these beliefs. Compared with the populace of any other industrial or postindustrial free market democracy, the American people are remarkably and resiliently religious. Fully 93 percent of Americans identify themselves as "professing" religious persons, and nearly 77 percent of the population characterize themselves as "practicing" some form of organized religion.[4] Among practicing American Christians more than half report they are "regular" in their church attendance. While Christianity remains, by some considerable margin, the majority religion in the United States, the last two decades have witnessed a sharp increase in genuine religious diversity within the American populace.[5]

While statistical information on religious groups other than Christians and Jews is notoriously difficult to gather, the best analyses indicate that growth patterns among Muslims, Buddhists, and Hindus are particularly striking.[6] While the Jewish population has remained relatively stable during the past twenty years (approximately 3.2 percent of the population), the number of Muslims has nearly quadrupled during the same period. It is estimated that there are currently 3 million practicing Muslims in the United States; in 1970 there were fewer than 800,000. While growth among Buddhists and Hindus has been somewhat slower, both groups now constitute significant religious minorities within the overall population (700,000 Hindus and 250,000 Buddhists). Despite the clear evidence of robust religious practice in the United States, however, the single fastest growing segment of the population is the "religious nones," those who characterize themselves as nonreligious. While in 1952 the nonreligious comprised only 2 percent of the population, today they represent anywhere from 8 to 10 percent.[7]

Clearly "we are a religious people," and our institutions, shaped in the Protestant culture of the late eighteenth century, reflect to some degree that culture's belief in a Supreme Being. But to what extent should the religious convictions of the American people influence the development of public policies? Should the majority religion of the republic have a privileged role in the shaping of public institutions, programs, and policies? How should the diversity within Christianity and Judaism and the growing religious pluralism within the nation affect religion's role in public life? Can public decision makers possibly be responsive to the myriad and often conflicting religious voices of our culture? What public role should be assigned to those religious traditions that do not affirm a Supreme Being or those persons who understand themselves as agnostic, nonreligious, or atheistic?

Public religion presents a dilemma for American democracy. The reasons why some would encourage a religious voice in our public life can be easily identified. Given the pervasiveness and importance of religious convictions within the American populace, it would indeed be odd to deny such profound sentiments any role in public life. Given the historic significance of religion in shaping our national political culture, the removal of religion from the "public square" would seem to violate our most ancient traditions.[8] Given the deep connection between religion and morality, the elimination of religious symbols from public discourse at a time of perceived moral crisis would appear to be self-defeating. Nonetheless, the relation between religious convictions and public life remains deeply problematic, and the arguments opposing a role for religion in public life are also at hand. When a single religious tradition like Christianity is so numerically dominant, support for a public religion can quite easily yield preferential treatment for the majority religion. A single religious tradition can so dominate public life as to threaten the dissenting beliefs of other religions and of the nonreligious. At the same time the growth in religious pluralism might portend a renewed period of religious tension or even conflict.

Religious beliefs and practices are notoriously particular. Christian prayer in the name of Jesus, Buddhist spiritual meditation, and Moslem invocations of Allah grow out of distinct religious and cultural traditions. While these spiritual practices may share some common characteristics, their differences are equally profound. The values, convictions, and virtues of these traditions occasionally coincide, but more often they conflict, often decisively, with one another. How can such conflicting values be coherently reflected in public policy decisions? How can public officials be expected to decide which of these diverse and clashing convictions should be introduced into the public square? Given the historical tendency of religious disagreement to spawn violent conflict, the introduction of religion into public life may contribute as much to divisive political discord as to moral renewal.

The question of the proper role for religion and religiously motivated convictions in American public life remains unanswered. Despite countless articles in the popular press and numerous scholarly tomes, we have gained neither conceptual clarification nor political consensus. We remain confused about the meaning and application of the phrase "separation of church and state," particularly in a time of growing religious pluralism. We are divided on the issue of whether government ought to be scrupulously secular and neutral, neither favoring nor disfavoring religion, or benevolently disposed toward religion, seeking to encourage the flourishing of all communities of faith. While we proclaim the theoretical separation of religious and political institutions, we often encourage their intermingling in practice. In the absence of either national consensus or coherent practice in these matters, public decision makers are left to their own devices in seeking to resolve the many dilemmas cast up by the presence of religion in the

public sphere. Unfortunately, their decisions often represent conflicting and contradictory solutions to the problem of religion in American
public life, thereby contributing to our current aporia. Consider the
following examples drawn from three diverse public institutions. In
each of these cases, different but equally problematic solutions are offered to the dilemma of religion in American public life.

## RELIGION, VALUES, AND POLICY DECISIONS

*RELIGION, VALUES, AND THE JUDICIARY.   Should the religious beliefs of the
majority of Americans determine the moral framework within which legal decisions are made? What is our legal responsibility to those who disagree or
dissent from those majority beliefs? When are religious convictions relevant
to judicial decision making?*[9]

On June 30, 1986, the Supreme Court of the United States, by a
5 to 4 margin, sustained the felony conviction of Michael Hardwick,
thereby upholding the constitutionality of the Georgia statute that
criminalized the practice of sodomy between consenting adults. In its
argument before the Court, the state of Georgia had appealed to what
it called "traditional moral values" to support the moral repugnance
and thus the criminality of such acts.[10] The Court, in the opinion written by Justice White, agreed that the Western moral tradition overwhelmingly prohibited homosexual acts and ruled further that such
"private sexual conduct between consenting adults" is not "constitutionally insulated from state proscription."[11] In a concurring opinion
Chief Justice Burger made the moral argument more explicit by stating
that the "condemnation of those practices is firmly rooted in the
Judeo-Christian moral and ethical standards."[12] The "presumed belief
of a majority of the electorate in Georgia that homosexual activity is
immoral and unacceptable," Justice White concluded, provides an adequate basis for sustaining the statute, since "the law . . . is constantly
based on notions of morality."[13]

On the following day, July 1, 1986, six defendants—including
priests, nuns, and lay workers—were sentenced to prison, having
been previously convicted of conspiracy to smuggle illegal aliens from
Central America into the United States. In a crucial decision made
early in the trial, the presiding judge of the U.S. District Court of Ari-
zona ruled that the defendants' religious beliefs were irrelevant to the
case and thus inadmissible as evidence.[14] Since the defendants understood their actions as motivated by religious convictions, the judge's

ruling precluded the defense from presenting the primary moral and legal rationale for their activity—the long-standing religious and legal tradition that allowed religious communities to offer refuge to those fleeing persecution. That rationale was stated in a letter from the Reverend John Fife, pastor of Southside Presbyterian Church of Tucson, shortly after church members had voted to harbor illegal aliens. "We believe that justice and mercy require that people of conscience actively assert our God-given right to aid anyone fleeing from persecution and murder."[15] The presiding judge refused to acknowledge the relevance of that religious and moral right, asserting that the law does not recognize religious convictions as justifications for committing a crime, no matter how pious the motive may be. That opinion was confirmed by the Ninth Circuit Court of Appeals when on March 30, 1989, it sustained the defendants' conviction. "So long as defendants intended to directly or substantially further the illegal presence of aliens, it was irrelevant that they did so with a religious motive."[16] In its final opinion, the Court also denied the appellants' claim that the conviction violated their right to exercise their religious beliefs freely. "It seems clear," the Court stated, "that a religious exemption for these particular appellants would seriously limit the government's ability to control immigration. . . . The government's interest in controlling immigration outweighs appellants' purported religious interest, and an exemption would not be feasible."[17]

Despite the temporal proximity of these two cases, they offer strikingly different resolutions to the issue of the role of religion and religiously based moral convictions in American public life. In *Bowers* v. *Hardwick,* the justices invoked what they perceived to be a broad religious and moral consensus concerning homosexuality and based their judicial decision primarily on moral/religious grounds. In their judgment, the religious and moral beliefs of the majority of the citizens of Georgia were valid grounds on which to base their decision. In *U.S.* v. *Maria del Socorro Pardo Viuda de Aguilar* the Federal Courts ruled religious convictions as inadmissible, despite their evident role in the defendants' motivation. The defendants' moral/religious beliefs were characterized as mere *interests* either irrelevant to the Court's deliberations or outweighed by the government's superior interests. Consequently, the moral and religious issues were never given serious consideration by the Courts. Ironically, religiously based moral convictions were granted a role in the judicial process when they were only vaguely and indirectly related to a case (the state of Georgia did not explicitly appeal to the Judeo-Christian tradition) but were excluded when they appeared both clearly and directly relevant.

In neither case, however, were the moral/religious questions given adequate attention. In *Bowers* v. *Hardwick* the justices appealed to majority moral opinions and an ancient legacy of moral proscription as the basis for their decision. In so doing, however, they neither analyzed nor evaluated the moral arguments offered in the literature they so briefly referenced. For example, in the course of his opinion, Justice White invoked a distinction between procreative and nonprocreative sexual activity. Since "no connection between family, marriage, or procreation on the one hand and homosexual activity on the other has been demonstrated," he asserted, homosexual activity cannot enjoy the privacy protection afforded by the Constitution. Though he invoked the distinction, he provided no moral argument to justify the distinction or its relevance to this case. Had he inquired further of his sources, he would have discovered that the arguments proscribing homosexual activity on the grounds that it is nonprocreative apply equally to heterosexual activity, including in many cases any use of contraception within marriage. But since the Court had previously protected the right of privacy within marriage in *Griswold* v. *Connecticut* (381, U.S., 484) the simple distinction between procreative and nonprocreative sex cannot be invoked in support of his decision in *Bowers*. There may be a moral distinction that justifies Justice White's position, but he does not cite it in his opinion. Consequently, his appeal to majority beliefs and a legacy of moral teaching appears nonprincipled and arbitrary.

This uncritical use of majoritarian moral/religious teaching as justification for a legal decision offers the unhappy implication that moral principles are presumed valid simply by virtue of their longevity and preponderance. But such reasoning begs the essential question raised by the litigant in this case, namely, is the right to privacy of a person who dissents from majority moral beliefs protected by the Constitution? Is the mere invocation of majority religious beliefs sufficient to decide the moral and legal issues in such a case? How does one adjudicate, morally and judicially, a conflict between majority beliefs and minority dissent? These complicated questions deserve careful scrutiny and analysis. Once the justices introduced moral considerations into their deliberations, they assumed the obligation to engage in careful moral reasoning. Their failure to do so serves to exacerbate the current confusion concerning the proper role of religious and moral principles in judicial deliberations.

In a vigorous dissent from the decision in *Bowers*, Justice Blackmun (joined by Brennen, Marshall, and Stevens) raised serious questions about the quality of the moral reasoning employed in the Court's final opinion.

> I cannot agree that either the length of time a majority has held its convictions or the passions with which it defends them can withdraw legislation from this Court's scrutiny. . . . That certain, but by no means all, religious groups condemn the behavior at issue gives the State no license to impose their judgments on the entire citizenry. The legitimacy of secular legislation depends instead on whether the State can advance some justification for its law beyond its conformity to religious doctrine. . . . A State can no more punish private behavior because of religious intolerance than it can punish such behavior because of racial animus.[18]

In offering this argument, Justice Blackmun recognizes the important fact that religious legitimation can function both to sustain and to undermine proper moral reasoning. While religious beliefs may be relevant to judicial deliberation, they cannot be decisive within a pluralistic constitutional democracy. The simple invoking of majority religious convictions runs the risk of denying the legitimacy of dissenting beliefs simply because they are held by a minority of the population. The use of religious convictions for the purpose of abridging the rights of minorities is particularly abhorrent. Whether the Court is guilty of such an offense in this case cannot be easily determined, since the authors of the majority opinion engage in such faulty moral reasoning. Thus a divided Court gives us little guidance concerning the question of the proper use of religious and moral convictions in judicial reflection.

The Supreme Court's failure in *Bowers* makes the Appellate Court's refusal to address the moral issues in *Aguilar* all the more distressing. By construing the religious convictions of the defendants as mere interests, the Court both misrepresented their beliefs and threatened to trivialize the issues at stake.[19] Surely an act of civil disobedience grounded in religious and moral principle deserved to be treated as more than a conflict between individual and governmental interests. By avoiding any semblance of moral reasoning, the Appellate Court simply sidestepped one of the most important issues of contemporary public life. Once again the moral and religious beliefs of a dissenting minority were rebuffed without adequate legal justification.[20]

These two cases illustrate the current tendency of the judiciary either to avoid all consideration of moral and religious matters or to engage in faulty moral reasoning based on majoritarian assumptions. If Justice White is correct in asserting that the law is "constantly based on notions of morality," then the Courts have an obligation to tackle these complicated issues with a greater degree of care and responsibility. But the lack of political consensus on basic moral issues and the lack of conceptual clarity regarding the role of religion in public life will make that task daunting indeed.

RELIGION, VALUES, AND HEALTH CARE POLICY. *Should religious beliefs about the nature of human life be employed in the development of health care policies? Can public policies properly be based on moral principles derived from religious premises? Must the government justify its policy decisions in a pluralistic democracy solely through rigorously secular arguments?*

Early in 1984, the Department of Health and Human Services adopted new regulations for the treatment of severely handicapped newborns.[21] The federal government developed those guidelines following the famous "Baby Doe" case in which an infant born with Down's Syndrome and a digestive system blockage was allowed to die, in accordance with the parents' wishes, without receiving corrective surgery. Following that incident the government issued its controversial directives requiring hospitals to give the same life-preserving care to handicapped infants as they would to the non-handicapped. The standards specifically prohibited any consideration of "quality of life" in determining whether and how to treat handicapped infants:

> Section 504 requires that health services be provided to the handicapped "on a basis of equality with those not handicapped" in order to assure "the evenhanded treatment of qualified handicapped persons. . . . It is only when nonmedical considerations, such as subjective judgments that an unrelated handicap makes a person's life not worth living are interjected in the decision-making process that the Section 504 concerns arise. . . . A judgment not to correct an intestinal obstruction or repair the heart of a Down's syndrome infant because the infant suffers the handicap of Down's syndrome is . . . not a medical

judgment. . . . Beneficial care may not be withheld from an individual infant because of a subjective judgment that such infants as a class possess an insufficient quality of life.[22]

These regulations raise important questions about government intervention into private familial decisions and about the appropriate limits for extraordinary or heroic care, matters that remain unresolved in the present public debate. I do not, in this context, want to offer my own assessment of those important issues; rather, I want to use the controversy surrounding these regulations to show that the disagreement about this matter of public policy is a dispute about the deepest principles and convictions that define the kind of society we want to be, and ultimately about the role of religiously based moral principles in public decision making.

Philosophers Peter Singer and Helga Kuhse have developed an extended and vigorous argument opposing the government's position on the basis that the guidelines are religiously motivated. These critics are not primarily concerned to raise the standard objections about governmental intervention or heroic care. Rather, they oppose the underlying principle that they think motivated the government's position, namely, the belief that "all human lives are of equal worth." The authors state their conclusions straightforwardly. "We cannot coherently hold that it is all right to kill a fetus a week before birth, but as soon as the baby is born everything must be done to keep it alive. The solution, however, is not to accept the pro-life view that the fetus is a human being with the same moral status as yours or mine. The solution is the very opposite: to abandon the idea that all human life is of equal worth."

The principle of the equality of human life ("equal regard") has played an indispensable role in the quest for justice in the United States. It has been invoked in the fight against slavery, in the struggle for women's suffrage, in the civil rights movement, and in efforts for ratification of the Equal Rights Amendment. Singer and Kuhse oppose not just a particular application of this principle; they oppose the principle itself. And their rationale is extremely important, precisely for the question of the degree to which religious beliefs ought to influence public policy decisions. The authors argue that the belief in the equal worth of all human life is a particular Christian conviction that is not shared by all participants in American public life. To organize federal guidelines around a specific religious belief is to introduce "a special brand of ideological or religious zeal" into the public sphere. The principle of "equal regard," Singer and Kuhse argue, is not a belief expressing the consensus of American citizens but a particular Christian conviction masquerading as a commonly held national conviction.

The Singer/Kuhse argument is representative of a larger class of positions which assert that the introduction of religious principles into policy discussions violates the rules of public discourse in a pluralistic democracy. The authors assume that religious beliefs are essentially private, subjective interests that will inevitably distort policy debates if introduced into the public discussion.[23] Consequently, they offer a purely procedural argument against the principle of "equal regard," branding it as "religious" or "ideological" and thereby declaring it unfit for forming public policy in a diverse democracy. They fail either to analyze the content of the principle or to evaluate its contribution to the development of just public policies.

Not only is the authors' argument historically, philosophically, and ethically flawed, but it also functions to deflect our attention from the important moral and political issue that is at stake in the discussion of the federal government's guidelines, namely, how shall we understand equality in contemporary America? If equality is not to be understood as based in equal regard, then what should its basis be? If equal regard is indeed an essential Christian moral principle, should that fact alone disqualify its role in the shaping of public policy? As we shall see in a later chapter, confusion about the role of this principle has also bedeviled the attempt to develop universal health coverage in the United States.[24] By eliminating religious convictions *tout court* from public policy considerations, Singer and Kuhse seek to avoid rather than engage the question of the proper role of religion in public life. In so doing, they make it impossible for us to engage in debate about the most basic moral convictions that should govern the development of public policies. But such political and moral debate is essential if we are to create policies that reflect the deepest aspirations of the American populace to be a virtuous people. To inquire concerning the moral basis of public policy is inevitably to engage the question of the role of religion in public life. Our dilemma is that we are not prepared either conceptually or politically to engage in such discussion. The historical ambiguity in our attitude toward religion in public life and our uncertainty about contemporary religious pluralism conspire to rob us of the ability to carry on intelligent and civil conversation about a matter of great public import.

RELIGION, VALUES, AND PUBLIC DECISION-MAKING.   *Should the personal religious beliefs of politicians influence their role as public officials? When the personal beliefs of a public official conflict with the policies he or she is charged to administer how should this dilemma be resolved? What role, if any, should the particular moral principles of a religious community play in the formation of policies in a pluralistic democracy?*

On September 13, 1984, at the height of the controversy surrounding religion's place in public life, Governor Mario Cuomo of New York addressed the Department of Theology at the University of Notre Dame on the topic "Religious Belief and Public Morality."[25] In a courageous but controversial address, Governor Cuomo, a Roman Catholic layman, spoke to the issue of abortion and his responsibilities as a Catholic public official. Just three months earlier John Cardinal O'Connor, Archbishop of New York, had indicated publicly that the church could exercise disciplinary measures, including the ban of excommunication, against public officials who failed to conduct themselves in accord with Catholic moral teaching. Since Geraldine Ferraro, a Catholic laywoman and supporter of abortion rights, was then a candidate for vice president, Cuomo's speech had significant political and religious implications.

Cuomo begins his address by describing the dual responsibility demanded of the religiously committed public official. On the one hand, the politician is a loyal child of the church, committed "to the essential core of dogmas that distinguishes our faith" and engaged in "a lifelong struggle to understand [that faith] more fully and to live it more truly." On the other hand, as an office holder in a pluralistic democracy "he or she undertakes to help create conditions under which *all* can live with a maximum of dignity and with a reasonable degree of freedom; where everyone who chooses may hold beliefs different from specifically Catholic ones—sometimes contradictory to them."

The freedom inherent in the constitutional tradition allows religiously motivated arguments to enter the public sphere as long as they are "not just parochial or narrowly sectarian but fulfill a human desire for order, peace, justice, kindness, love, any of the values most of us agree are desirable even apart from their specific religious base or context." Acknowledging his own personal belief that "the whole community . . . should agree on the importance of protecting life—including life in the womb," Cuomo then asks, "When should I argue to make my religious value your morality? . . . What are the rules and policies that should influence the exercise of this right to argue and promote?" In his answer to those questions Cuomo appeals to the notion of communal consensus.

> Our public morality then—the moral standards we maintain for everyone, not just the ones we insist on in our private lives—depends on a *consensus view of right and wrong*. The values derived from religious belief will not—and should not—be accepted as part of the public morality unless they are shared by the pluralistic community at large, by consensus (italics added).

Having made this point about moral consensus, Cuomo then immediately asserts that the problems with religion in public life begin when "religious values are used to support positions which would impose on other people restrictions they find unacceptable." "The community must decide if what is being proposed would be better left to private discretion than public policy; whether it restricts freedom, and if so to what end, to whose benefit."

While Cuomo's position is nuanced and subtle, his line of reasoning still presents some genuine difficulties. The argument seems to go like this: Our constitutionally guaranteed freedom allows the use of religious arguments in the public realm as long as those arguments appeal to values embraced by a significant portion of our pluralistic population. Purely sectarian arguments, that is, arguments that can only appeal to religious grounds, have no place in the persuasive forum of a constitutional democracy. Moreover, those values that guide public morality are established by a "consensus view of right and wrong" and religious values are appropriate only *insofar* as they "are shared by the pluralistic community at large." The use of religious arguments to impose restrictions on the freedom of others is particularly reprehensible and is unacceptable in a democracy.

But surely there is an element of circularity in this position. Religious arguments are welcomed in public debate as long as they are already accepted by communal consensus. But how then can religious arguments ever play a role in *forming* that consensus? It appears that religiously based arguments are acceptable only after they are no longer relevant to one of the most basic forms of political debate, the discussion which seeks to shape a consensus about our public morality. Ironically, Cuomo's argument eliminates religious argumentation from the very sphere in which its expertise would seem most relevant, the formation of communal values. On Cuomo's interpretation, it appears that religious arguments against slavery would have been unacceptable as long as the legal and political consensus supported slavery. Consequently, religious arguments cannot function to overturn a consensus that religious people find morally objectionable. Moreover, any religious argument which functions to restrict the freedom of others is, on Cuomo's reading, inappropriate in a pluralistic democracy. But surely some moral arguments ought to be used to restrict the freedom of others if that freedom violates a value that the community ought to hold dear. Arguments against slavery, in favor of minority civil rights, and in support of equal opportunity for women are designed to overturn a political and moral consensus through the use of moral persuasion. It is odd, indeed, for religious arguments to be eliminated from such vital moral debate simply because they begin from religious premises.

The instability of Cuomo's position becomes even more obvious when he applies it to his own role as a public official motivated by religious convictions. "As a Catholic," Cuomo admits that he accepts the church's teachings on abortion "as the right ones for myself and my family. . . . As a governor, however, I am involved in defining policies that determine *other* people's rights in these same areas of life and death." The question of whether one's personal religious beliefs should become the basis for public policy is "not a matter of doctrine; it is a matter of prudential political judgment." Since the Catholic position on abortion "is in the minority," "political realism" dictates that a legal prohibition of abortion is not appropriate, given the lack of consensus on this issue among the general populace.

Cuomo then proceeds to offer an eloquent account of the steps Catholics might realistically take to offer support to those women and children, particularly among the poor, who are victimized by current social policies.

> We should understand that whether abortion is outlawed or not, our work has barely begun: the work of creating a society where the right to life doesn't end at the moment of birth; where an infant isn't helped into a world that doesn't care if it's fed properly, housed decently, educated adequately; where the blind or retarded child isn't condemned to exist rather than empowered to live.

"We can be fully Catholic," Cuomo concludes, "leading people to truth by love. And still, all the while, respecting and enjoying our unique pluralistic democracy. And we can do it even as politicians."

Cuomo's final remarks are an important reminder of the inadequacy of slogans like "pro-life" and "pro-choice" to capture the complexity of ethical reflection in the formation of social policies. And yet the moral distinctions he seeks to draw between private and public, between personal conviction and political judgment remain troubling. It is striking that Cuomo never subjects the "Catholic position on abortion" to careful scrutiny. He simply acknowledges that as a loyal Catholic he accepts the church's teaching. But on what grounds? By appeal to what moral principles? Cuomo gives the impression that he accepts the teaching simply because it is taught by the Catholic hierarchy, but that is a surprising position for one so well versed in moral reasoning to adopt. The subtlety Cuomo demonstrates in applying Christian moral principles to questions of social policy for the poor (or in another context on the issue of capital punishment) is lacking when it comes to the issue of abortion. Here he seems content to accept a teaching in his private or personal behavior but to disregard it in his public or political behavior. But since this teaching asserts that abortion is the taking of innocent life, it is difficult to imagine that a morally sensitive person could accept that moral verdict in the private realm but somehow disregard it in the public realm. Garry Wills certainly seems correct when in a review of the Governor's Notre Dame speech he asserts "that Cuomo claims to believe the Church's teaching on abortion, but acts as if he does not."[26]

Cuomo has two escape routes available, if he wishes to avoid Wills's critique: he can develop the moral components of his political argument into a critique of the reasoning of the Catholic bishops, or he can apply the moral reasoning of the bishops to the public realm and thereby revise the political position he has taken. But as long as he keeps the two positions separated by an appeal to privacy, or moral consensus, or political prudence, he will appear to be entrapped in a contradictory position. Thus we look in vain to one of the most articulate of American politicians for clarity on the vexing problem of the relation between religiously motivated convictions and the development of public policies.

This review of three cases, drawn from diverse public institutions, illustrates the confusion that characterizes our current reflection on the place of religion in American public life. Our corporate bewilderment on these matters is so deep and pervasive that it yields incoherent decisions and contradictory policies. This tangled web of issues has created a knot so snarled that it resists the efforts of our best public figures to untie it. To understand how we have come to this bewildering state it is necessary to view our contemporary dilemma in historical perspective. To that task we now turn.

## NOTES

**1.** In a recent study of Americans' views on religion and politics 21 percent of the persons surveyed indicated that they would be unwilling to vote for a candidate who has been a minister of a church. On the other hand, fully 62 percent indicate that they would be unwilling to vote for an atheist for President. *The Williamsburg Charter Survey on Religion and Public Life* (Washington, D.C.: The Williamsburg Charter Foundation, 1988), p. 2.

**2.** "Perhaps," former Chief Justice Burger once ironically remarked, "the historic practice of the Congress and this Court is justified because members of the Judiciary and Congress are more in need of Divine Guidance than are schoolchildren." Chief Justice Burger in his dissenting opinion in *Wallace* v. *Jaffree*, 472 U.S. 38 (1985) at 85.

**3.** Justice William O. Douglas, *Zorach* v. *Clauson*, 343 U.S. 306, at 313. Justice Douglas made this claim in 1952 in his majority opinion as the Supreme Court upheld as constitutional a New York State law that allowed "released time" for students to engage in "religious observance and education." Ibid., at 308, footnote 1.

**4.** Edwin Scott Gaustad, *Historical Atlas of Religion in America* (New York: Harper & Row, 1976), p. 711.

**5.** Eighty-eight percent of Americans (approximately 200,000,000) identify themselves as Christian, 40 percent Protestant (90,000,000) and 30% Roman Catholic (68,000,000). More than 80% of the Protestants are practicing (74,000,000) as are nearly 75% of Roman Catholics (50,000,000). Wade Clark Roof and William McKinney, *American Mainline Religion* (New Brunswick and London: Rutgers University Press, 1987), p. 83.

**6.** A recent study on American religious pluralism recently begun at Harvard University holds promise of providing, for the first time, accurate information on the growth and development of non-Christian and non-Jewish communities of faith.

**7.** Statistical surveys differ on the exact number of nonreligious persons in the United States. The most recent study, done in 1988, suggests that their number might be as high as 2.3 million. See *The Williamsburg Charter Survey on Religion and Public Life* (Washington D.C.: The Williamsburg Charter Foundation, 1988), p. 35.

**8.** This argument has been made most forcefully by Richard John

Neuhaus, *The Naked Public Square: Religion and Democracy in America* (Grand Rapids: W. B. Eerdmans, 1984), and *America Against Itself: Moral Vision and the Public Order* (Notre Dame: University of Notre Dame Press, 1992). See also, Robert Benne, *The Pardoxical Vision: A Public Theology for the Twenty-first Century* (Minneapolis: Fortress Press, 1994) and Michael Novak, *The Catholic Ethic and the Spirit of Capitalism* (Grand Rapids: W.B. Eerdmans Publishing Co., 1993).

    **9.** The importance of the following two cases was first pointed out to me by my colleague Bernadette Brooten, the Kraft and Hiatt Professor of Christian Studies at Brandeis University.

    **10.** *Bowers v. Hardwick* 106 S. Ct. 2841 (1986)

    **11.** Ibid.

    **12.** Ibid.

    **13.** Ibid., p. 196.

    **14.** *U.S. v. Maria del Socorro Pardo Viuda de Aguilar,* 871 F. 2d 1436.

    **15.** Douglas L. Colbert, "A Symposium on the Sanctuary Movement: The Motion in Limine: Trial Without Jury: A Government's Weapon Against the Sanctuary Movement," in *Hofstra Law Review* 15 (1986), p. 5, at footnote 204. The letter was sent to U.S. Attorney General William French Smith and to the Director of the INS.

    **16.** *U.S. v. Aguilar,* 1439.

    **17.** *U.S. v. Aguilar,* 1470.

    **18.** Ibid., pp. 211-213.

    **19.** The best discussions of the conflict between the free exercise claims of churches and the interests of government are Bruce N. Bagni, "Discrimination in the Name of the Lord: A Critical Evaluation of Discrimination by Religious Organizations," 79 *Columbia Law Review,* 1514 (1979), and Douglas Laycock, "Towards a General Theory of the Religion Clauses: The Case of Church Labor Relations and the Right to Church Autonomy," 81 *Columbia Law Review,* 1373 (1981). While neither of these articles addresses the question of civil disobedience, they do offer proposals regarding the limits of church autonomy under the first amendment religion clauses. Cf. also Note, "Developments in the Law: Religion and the State," *Harvard Law Review,* 100:7 (1987) 1750-1781.

    **20.** In the Williamsburg Charter survey cited above, only 24 percent of the respondents approved of religious protection of immigrants whom the government defines as illegal.

    **21.** "Final rules" were issued on January 12, 1984 (*Federal Register,* 49(8): 1622-1654). Relevant materials prior to issuance of final rules are "interim final rule" (*Federal Register,* 48(45): 9630-9632) and "proposed rules" (*Federal Register,* 48(129): 30846-30852).

    **22.** "Proposed rules," 30846-30847.

    **23.** Ironically, the federal guidelines that Singer and Kuhse are criticizing also share the view that moral premises are essentially "subjective."

    **24.** See Chapter 7, "Beyond the Wall of Separation: Reconceiving American Public Life."

    **25.** *New York Review of Books* 21 (October 23, 1984): 32-37.

**26.** "Mario Cuomo's Trouble with Abortion," *New York Review of Books* 27, 1 (June 28, 1990): p. 11. While Wills' critique of Cuomo is particularly ungenerous it does point to a fundamental moral tension in Cuomo's position. For my own attempt to resolve this tension see Chapter Seven.

# 2

# Our Contemporary Dilemma In Historical Perspective: Religion, Values, and the Framing of the Constitution

The ambivalence shown to religion by contemporary decision makers reflects an ambiguity built into the very foundations of the American republic. The question of the place and function of religion in American society was at the heart of the deliberations that led to the framing of the American Constitution, particularly the Bill of Rights. The framers were determined to devise a distinctive "experiment" in constitutional democracy.[1] Influenced by the theory and practice of previous republican and federalist governments, they sought to design a superior republic, freed from the flaws of those earlier undertakings. Recognizing the despotism that often characterized traditional civic republicanism, they fastened on freedom of conscience as the moral centerpiece of their democratic experiment.[2] Drawing broadly and creatively on various Enlightenment philosophers, the framers saw religion as the essential expression of conscience and as the greatest threat to its flourishing.[3] These two concerns: to protect the free expression of religion in all its variety and to delimit the influence of any particular religion animated the founders' thinking about the role of religion in American society.

Of the many contributions to late eighteenth-century thinking about religion's place in the new republic, those of James Madison are of signal importance. He has been called "our greatest constructive legal statesman" in the field of church-state relations.[4] Indeed, his "Memorial and Remonstrance Against Religious Assessments" has been described as "the most pungent of all American argumentative documents on this subject, the rhetorical equivalent, one might say, of

*Common Sense* in this field."[5] Written in opposition to the use of Virginia public funds to pay teachers of the Christian religion, this brief statement captures the complexity of Madison's view of religion.

At the outset of the "Remonstrance," Madison identifies the essential link between freedom of conscience and the exercise of religion. "The Religion then of every man must be left to the conviction and conscience of every man; and it is the right of every man to exercise it as these may dictate."[6] This right is "unalienable" both because human opinions should be formed "only on the evidence contemplated by their own minds" and "because what is here a right towards man, is a duty toward the Creator. It is the duty of every man to render to the Creator such homage, and such only, as he believes to be acceptable to him." Since the duty to the Creator is "precedent . . . to the claims of Civil Society . . . in matters of Religion, no man's right is abridged by the institution of Civil Society. . . . Religion is wholly exempt from its cognizance." While in other spheres of society the will of the majority holds sway, with regard to religion the free exercise of all must be defended lest the majority "trespass on the rights of the minority."

Religion, Madison argues, is the great test case for a genuinely free republic. "The preservation of a free government" demands that no governmental department or public official "overleap the great Barrier which defends the rights of the people." The defense of those rights is "the first duty of citizens, and one of [the] noblest characteristics of the late Revolution." To allow public funds to be used to support the teaching of the Christian religion would deny the very principle for which the revolution was fought: freedom of conscience. "We revere this lesson too much, soon to forget it. Who does not see the same authority which can establish Christianity, in exclusion of all other Religions, may establish with the same ease any particular sect of Christians, in exclusion of all other Sects?"

Religion is also the great test case for the principle of equality within a genuinely free republic. The bill before the Virginia General Assembly not only denies the free exercise of religion, it also "violates that equality which ought to be the basis of every law." Madison's argument on this point is so clear and eloquent that it deserves to be quoted at length.

> If "all men are by nature equally free and independent" all men
> are to be considered as entering into Society on equal conditions;
> as relinquishing no more, and therefore retaining no less, one

than another, of their natural rights. Above all are they to be considered as retaining an *"equal* title to the free exercise of Religion
according to the dictates of conscience." Whilst we assert for ourselves a freedom to embrace, to profess and to observe the Religion which we believe to be of divine origin, we cannot deny an
equal freedom to those whose minds have not yet yielded to the
evidence which has convinced us. If this freedom is abused, it is
an offense against God, not against man.[7]

The bill before the Virginia Assembly would, if adopted, be the
first step toward the establishment of Christianity as the official religion of the commonwealth. This bill "implies either that the Civil Magistrate is a competent Judge of Religious truth; or that he may employ
Religion as an engine of Civil policy. The first is an arrogant pretension
. . . the second an unhallowed perversion of the means of salvation."
Such an establishment would be a denial of "the *equal* right of every citizen to the *free exercise* of his Religion according to the *dictates of his conscience.*"[8] To deny this right would make vulnerable all those rights
which serve as the "basis and foundation of Government."

Madison's arguments in the "Remonstrance" capture the essential principles that undergird the religion clauses of the first amendment. The basic principle animating the Bill of Rights is the "freedom
of conscience." Since religious conviction, on Madison's reading, is the
primary expression of a free conscience, the defense of religion's free
exercise becomes a primary duty of the republic. If persons are genuinely *free*, then they must be considered *equal* participants in the
goods of society; therefore, the free and equal right of every citizen to
exercise his religion "according to the dictates of his conscience" must
be defended. If citizens are to be free and equal in the exercise of religion, then it follows that no particular faith or creed can be the preferred religion of the republic. The establishment of religion denies the
freedom of some and the equality of all, and thereby denies essential
freedom of conscience. Genuine freedom implies pluralism; pluralism
demands equality; and equality cannot be maintained under an ecclesiastical establishment.

Given the relative homogeneity of Colonial society, Madison's
reflections on pluralism and the dangers of majoritarian dominance of
minorities are truly remarkable. The defense of freedom requires
particular vigilance against the potential tyranny of the democratic
majority. While in the "Remonstrance" Madison makes this point as

an implication of his primary argument concerning freedom and equality, two years later in *The Federalist* (no. 10), he develops this theme into a theory concerning human nature and factional politics. The defense of minority rights, he now argues, is required because human beings are by nature prone to the kind of self-interested behavior that creates factions that act against the public interest.

> By a faction I understand a number of citizens, whether amounting to a majority or minority of the whole, who are united and actuated by some common impulse of passion, or of interest, adverse to the rights of other citizens, or to the permanent and aggregate interests of the community.[9]

If factions were to take root in the majority of the nation, they would be particularly worrisome, for popular support could combine with self-interested behavior to justify the violation of the rights of minorities. While Madison identified "the most common and durable source of factions" to be "the various and unequal distribution of property," he also identified religion as a major cause of factionalization.[10]

> A zeal for differing opinions concerning religion, concerning government, and many other points . . . have, in turn, divided mankind into parties, inflamed them with mutual animosity, and rendered them much more disposed to vex and oppress each other than to co-operate for their common good.[11]

Since "the latent causes of faction are thus sown in the nature of man," it is impossible for any government to eliminate the causes of factionalism; the only hope of success is to address the effects. Only through the establishment of an "extensive republic" in which power is delegated to representatives elected from a variety of districts can factionalism be controlled.

> Extend the sphere and you take in a greater variety of parties and interests; you make it less probable that a majority of the whole will have a common motive to invade the rights of other citizens. . . . A religious sect may degenerate into a political faction in a part of the Confederacy; but the variety of sects dispersed over the entire face of it must secure the national councils against any danger from that source.[12]

This more sober, perhaps even cynical, view of human nature and religion stands in some tension with Madison's argument in the "Remonstrance." How are we to reconcile his positive conception of human beings as free and equal bearers of natural rights with his pessimistic assessment of human beings as "more disposed to vex and oppress each other than to co-operate for their common good"? The difference appears to lie in Madison's belief that individuals lose their natural disposition toward virtue when they associate with others in social groups. In a memorandum entitled "Vices of the Political System of the United States," written between the "Remonstrance" and *The Federalist* (no. 10), Madison states his position on the vices characteristic of corporate human behavior. In speaking of the natural tendency of individuals to respect the character of other persons, Madison writes,

> However strong this motive may be in individuals, it is considered as very insufficient to restrain them from injustice. In a multitude its efficacy is diminished in proportion to the number which is to share the praise or the blame. . . . The conduct of every popular assembly acting on oath, the strongest of religious ties, proves that individuals join without remorse in acts, against which their consciences would revolt if proposed to them under the like sanction, separately in their closets.[13]

In adopting this position on the vicious behavior of social groups, Madison reflects an assumption widely accepted among Enlightenment thinkers. As David A. J. Richards has shown, Madison's argument in *The Federalist* (no. 10) bears an uncanny similarity to David Hume's position in his essay "Of the Independency of Parliament."[14] Hume writes:

> In contriving any system of government, and fixing the several checks and controls of the constitution, every man ought to be supposed a *knave*, and to have no other end, in all his actions, than private interest. . . . Men are generally more honest in their private than in their public capacity, and will go to greater lengths to serve a party, than when their own private interest is alone concerned. Honour is a great check upon mankind: but where a considerable body of men act together, this check is in a great measure removed.[15]

Freedom and equality, those natural and inalienable rights of human beings, are easily distorted and violated by the stronger passions of corporate self-interest. Religion, that most pristine expression of freedom of conscience, can become the foe of freedom when joined to the party spirit of political factions. While individual religious belief and practice are to be honored and vigilantly protected, corporate or institutional religion, particularly the religion of the majority, is to be viewed with suspicion. The religion of the individual is to be protected from all corporate incursions, either from the state or from the majority religious institution. Thus Madison develops a second rationale against "established religion," the tendency of majority religions to "vex and oppress" the religious views of minorities or dissenting individuals.

Madison employs this theory of factionalized politics primarily to argue for a balance of powers within the new republic, but the theory of political psychology he adopts reaches beyond the pragmatic end for which it was intended. Nothing in Madison's position regarding freedom and equality requires the pessimistic view of corporate human behavior he developed in *The Federalist* (no. 10). Indeed, he could have presented a plausible argument against the accumulation of power in any one branch of government simply by relying on premises regarding freedom, pluralism, equality, and the rights of minorities. By introducing the argument about self-interested factionalized behavior, however, Madison threatens to undermine one essential aspect of his own political philosophy: the conviction that the primary purpose of republican government is to pursue the common good. How is it possible for passionate self-interested factions to cooperate for the public welfare? How can competing political interests be encouraged to collaborate for the sake of the common good? Can the public *vices* of selfishness, avarice, and party spirit be countered by correlative public *virtues*? Madison's position regarding the balance of powers only indicates how these vices can be neutralized; it tells us nothing of how public virtue can be nurtured in the populace.

Madison was clearly aware of this issue, for in *The Federalist* no. 45 he argues that "the public good, the real welfare of the great body of the people, is the supreme object to be pursued; and that no form of government whatever has any other value than as it may be fitted for the attainment of this object."[16] In the final days of the Virginia ratifying convention, he expressed his views on this matter with typical eloquence. "Is there no virtue among us? If there be not, . . . no form of government can render us secure. To suppose that any form of government will secure liberty or happiness without any virtue in the people, is a chimerical idea."[17] But what are the sources of such public virtue? And how, given the theory of factionalized politics, is that virtue to be nurtured? What role, if any, should government play in fostering "virtue in the people"?

Having engaged in a careful critical study of the classical republics, Madison and the other founders became convinced that these governments encouraged public virtue by enforcing a single view of human flourishing that flouted the demands of freedom and equality within a pluralistic populace.[18] Moreover, classical civic virtue was equated with blind patriotism and a desire for national glory fostered by a system of internal violence and war against foreign enemies, qualities that the founders adjudged to vices not virtues.

> The civic virtue of the ancients *legitimated* not only slavery and the subjection of women . . . but also a rampant imperialism of military adventure and glory. The civic virtues of classical republicanism were—as both Montesquieu and Hume had taught the founders—often masks for political manipulation and tyranny, an elitist ideology that blinded people to the moral demands of equality.[19]

If classical civic virtues were not to be pursued in the American republic, what sort of public virtue was appropriate to this new experiment in representative democracy? We look in vain to the writings of Madison to discover an account of the public virtues appropriate to the new nation. Madison seems rather to have lodged his hope for a virtuous government in the character of the representatives whom the people would elect. Elected representatives would "refine and enlarge" the unreflective and factionalized views of the public

> by passing them through the medium of a chosen body of citizens, whose wisdom may best discern the true interest of their country and whose patriotism and love of justice will be least likely to sacrifice it to temporary or partial considerations. Under such a regulation it may well happen that the public voice, pronounced by the representatives of the people, will be more consonant to the public good than if pronounced by the people themselves, convened for the purpose.[20]

Indeed, Madison believed that the distinctive advantage of the American representative system was that it made possible *"the total exclusion of the people in their collective capacity,* from any share in" governing.[21]

Madison and the other founders looked to the elected representatives for the wisdom, virtue, and sense of justice that would serve the common good. But why should these leaders be immune from the vices that characterize the general populace? If the authority to govern is derived from the people, and the people are, in their corporate political behavior, a vicious lot, how will their representatives escape the vices of factionalism and party spirit? The only answer forthcoming from the founders is that safeguards built into an "extensive republic" will maximize the possibility that persons of good character will be elected. "As each representative will be chosen by a greater number of citizens in the large than in the small republic, it will be more difficult for unworthy candidates to practise with success the vicious arts by which elections are too often carried; and the suffrages of the people being more free, will be more likely to center on men who possess the most attractive merit and the most diffusive and established characters."[22]

Madison's confidence that the electoral process would produce virtuous public officials appears almost naive in light of his persuasive account of factionalized politics.[23] While the founders acknowledge that good character, virtue, and a sense of justice are essential to republican government, they neither identify the sources of those values nor tell us how they are to be protected against the acids of factionalized self-interest. Instead they propose a government designed to protect freedom of conscience and the inalienable rights inherent in such freedom. Arguing that freedom implies pluralism and pluralism demands equality, they look to the *processes* of government to protect the rights of all citizens. While the processes of a constitutional republic might provide a bulwark against the violation of rights, they cannot provide the positive incentive for people to seek justice and equality.

The founders' argument is conceptually incomplete and thus politically flawed, since they fail to provide an account of those virtues that will enable free persons to make equality a political reality. That failure becomes a near fatal flaw, because they furnish such a powerful account of the political vices that undermine the pursuit of freedom, justice, and equality. Consequently the "ethics of equal respect" which was "the motivating public morality of American republicanism" lacks the theory of virtue necessary for an effective political ethic.[24]

This defect in the founders' political ethic is further reflected in their limited view of religion's role in the republic. Religion, understood as the free individual expression of conscience, is to be protected against every incursion by corporate institutions ("free exercise of religion"). Institutionalized religion, like all forms of corporate human activity, can contribute both to the oppression of minority views and to the factionalization of society. Consequently, no particular form of religion should receive the endorsement of the state ("no establishment"). Religious sects should be allowed to proliferate as the inevitable result of free exercise and as a bulwark against the concentration of power in any single sect. This rationale undergirds the language finally approved for the religion clauses of the first amendment to the Constitution: "Congress shall make no law respecting an establishment of religion or prohibiting the free exercise thereof."

While these clauses address many of the founders' concerns about the role of religion in public life, they are silent on the question of whether religion might function to foster the virtues requisite for the pursuit of justice and equality in the nation. Is the role of religion, in both its individual and corporate forms, in shaping the public values and virtues of the people allowed, encouraged, or prohibited by the Constitution? Since the founders failed to address the question of the sources and function of public virtue in American society, it is not surprising that they remained silent on the place of religion in that larger scheme. But their failure to address the matter did not impede religious figures, symbols, and institutions from playing just such a role in our nation's history. Indeed, the constitution's silence on this issue may well have encouraged the development of an unofficial "established piety" during the first two centuries of the republic's life.

## CIVIC PIETY AND AMERICAN PUBLIC LIFE.

Supreme Court Justice Joseph Story, writing a scant forty years after the ratification of the first amendment, offered the following analysis of the place of Christianity in American society.

> It is impossible for those, who believe in the truth of Christianity, as a divine revelation, to doubt, that it is the especial duty of government to foster and encourage it among all the citizens and subjects. . . . There will probably be found few persons in this, or any other Christian country, who would deliberately contend,

that it was unreasonable or unjust to foster and encourage the Christian religion generally, as a matter of sound policy, as well as of revealed truth. . . . Probably at the time of the adoption of the constitution . . . the general, if not the universal, sentiment in America was, that Christianity ought to receive encouragement from the state, so far as was not incompatible with the private rights of conscience and the freedom of religious worship.[25]

That such sentiments could be expressed by American's premier constitutional scholar less than two generations after Madison's "Remonstrance" is truly remarkable. Madison had argued that the right to conscience and the freedom of religious worship *prohibited* government from fostering or encouraging any particular religion through the use of civil policy. Yet Justice Story could argue that the first amendment not only permitted but countenanced governmental support for the majority religion of the nation. Madison's concern about majoritarian oppression of minority religious views seems to have disappeared from view only four decades after the ratification of the first amendment.

The failure of the founders to address the question of the role of civic virtue and public religion in providing the moral context within which policy decisions are made created a vacuum that was quickly filled by a civic piety derived from Christianity. While Madison and others addressed the question of the *legal* establishment of Christianity, they neglected to ponder fully the consequences of Christianity's *cultural* establishment as the majority religion of the republic. Since the founders' vision provided no means by which civic virtue was to be encouraged in the populace, a modified version of Protestant Christianity came to provide both symbolic and institutional support for a new American civil piety.

Although the founders did not explicitly anticipate the significance of this civil piety, one of the Enlightenment thinkers whose work influenced the framers of the constitution did describe the "classical conditions" for the emergence of such piety. Jean Jacques Rousseau coined the term "civil religion" in his *Social Contract* to identify an alternative mode of believing for those whose traditional faiths had been shattered by the skepticism bred in the Enlightenment. While Rousseau had significant disagreements with many of the *philosophes* of his native France, he shared their antipathy to historical positive religion. True religious sentiment, he believed, could not be captured in the particular beliefs of a historical tradition, for in such traditions truth is identified with the revealed dogmas of a specific faith rather than with the universal principles available to all "men of reason." Such a view of truth was, according to Rousseau, inherently intolerant, for if a particular belief encapsulated the truth, then conflicting beliefs of other traditions must by definition be false.

This view of religious truth, Rousseau believed, encouraged the kind of religious warfare that had plagued Europe in the century following the Reformation. If, in the era of enlightenment, society was to avoid such sectarian conflict, governments would have to be founded on rational principles. But in contrast to other eighteenth-century philosophers, Rousseau did not believe that religion must be eliminated altogether from the public realm. If government was to gain the true allegiance of the populace, then it must find a way to engage the deepest passions of the people, passions that could be turned to peaceful civil purposes. Since sectarian religion inevitably bred factionalism, only through the emergence of a nonsectarian civic piety could a peaceful social contract be maintained. A civil religion could provide an understanding of religious belief that would allow it to become the common possession of all members of a society. In addition, civil religion would overcome the intolerance of positive religions, for it would forge a bond between religions and the *polis* in support of the common good of the society.

> The dogmas of civil religion ought to be simple, few in number, precisely fixed, and without explanation or comment. The existence of a powerful, wise, and benevolent Divinity, who foresees and provides the life to come, the happiness of the just, the punishment of the wicked, the sanctity of the social contract and the laws: these are its positive dogmas. Its negative dogmas I would confine to one—intolerance.[26]

This form of piety would be independent of both church and state, and yet would serve as the bond that defined the common commitment of both institutions. Like the social contract itself, civil religion was to be the expression of the general will of the people and would function to legitimate the beliefs and actions of the civil society. Rousseau envisioned a fully developed civil religion that would create its own institutional structures, while cooperating or co-existing with ecclesiastical and governmental institutions. In order for such an independent institutionalized religion to exist, it would be necessary, Rousseau argued, for ecclesiastical personnel to give up their monopoly on religious discourse and for political officials to be willing to adopt a modified form of that discourse. Only when such a sharing of religious ideas became a reality could a true civil religion become manifest.

Clearly the first amendment of the constitution prohibited the development of Rousseau's institutionalized civil religion on American soil. From the founders' point of view a fully developed civil religion would simply be a form of religious establishment that had no appropriate place within the new republic. But the forms of civic piety that did emerge in eighteenth- and nineteenth-century America reflected many of the characteristics Rousseau had identified, particularly the sharing of religious ideas and rhetoric within ecclesiastical and political institutions. The passage already quoted from Justice Story illustrates the extraordinary dominance of the nation's majority religion, Protestant Christianity. Not only was Christianity the de facto religion of the republic, it also provided powerful images and symbols for politicians seeking to persuade the public to follow some course of action.

Examples of the peculiar mixing of politics and Christianity abound. One of the first acts taken by the initial House of Representatives (May 1, 1789) was to appoint the Reverend William Linn, a Congregational minister, as Chaplain to the House. The resolution which the House approved was forwarded to them by a committee on which James Madison served.[27] On September 24, 1789, the House voted to recommend the First Amendment to the States for ratification; the following day, they began debate on a resolution requesting that President Washington issue a Thanksgiving Day Proclamation. That resolution also passed the House, the members apparently seeing no conflict between their actions and the provisions of the first amendment. Every President, except Jefferson, has, since the founding of the Republic, issued a Thanksgiving Day proclamation urging citizens to give thanks to the Creator for manifold gifts of freedom and prosperity. James Madison reestablished the practice during his Presidency, though he later expressed his opinion that such proclamations violated the First Amendment.[28] The language of Madison's 1815 proclamation provides a useful look at the peculiar rhetoric of American civil piety.

No people ought to feel greater obligation to celebrate the goodness of the Great Disposer of Events and of the Destiny of Nations than the people of the United States. His kind providence originally conducted them to one of the best portions of the dwelling place allotted for the great family of the human race. He protected and cherished them under all the difficulties and trials to which they were exposed in their early days. Under His fostering care their habits, their sentiments, and their pursuits prepared them for a transition in due time to a state of independence and self-government. . . . And to the same Divine Author of Every Good and Perfect Gift we are indebted for all those privileges and advantages, religious as well as civil, which are so richly enjoyed in this favored land.[29]

Practitioners of American civil piety have traditionally been quite selective in their use of the symbolic resources of Christianity. They have employed those images most likely to gather the broadest degree of support from a religiously diverse population. The theological notion of "providence" has been a particularly prominent concept, because its generality—both in the sense of general acceptability and conceptual vagueness—served the nonsectarian purposes for which the idea was employed. The peculiar version of "civil religion" that grew up in American soil was a form of nonchristological theism that relates the history and destiny of the nation to divine providence. The images of this civic faith were derived from the Bible's storehouse of images; thus, the language of providence, election, covenant, and destiny have predominated in the rhetoric of American "civil religion." Deeply influenced by this country's Calvinist and Puritan heritage, in its bolder moments this piety has declared the United States to be the "New Israel," a chosen people with a manifest destiny. Even in its more modest expressions, however, this civil faith expressed America's abiding conviction that the republic is a divinely "favored land."

The conviction that America stood under the guidance of a "favoring providence" has often encouraged arrogant misuses of political power, particularly in the area of foreign affairs.[30] American Presidents, emboldened by the promise of divine assistance, have used the biblical heritage of the Puritans to justify the Spanish-American war, the annexation of the Philippines, and the inexorable westward expansion that resulted in the slaughter of many native Americans and the displacement of the rest.[31] But in the hands of America's greatest public theologian, Abraham Lincoln, that same heritage could be invoked in judgment over the acts of a blood-stained nation.

If we shall suppose that American slavery is one of those offenses which, in the providence of God, must needs come, but which, having continued through His appointed time, He now wills to remove, and that He gives to both North and South this terrible war as the woe due to those by whom the offense came, shall we discern therein any departure from those divine attributes which the believers in a living God always ascribe to Him? Fondly do we hope, fervently do we pray, that this mighty scourge of war may speedily pass away. Yet, if God wills that it continue until all the wealth piled by the bondsman's two hundred and fifty years of unrequited toil shall be sunk, and until every drop of blood drawn with the lash shall be paid by another drawn with the sword, as was said three thousand years ago, so still it must be said, "the judgments of the Lord are true and righteous altogether."[32]

America's nonchristological theism functioned for nearly two centuries to provide a common rhetorical and ideological context for the development of public policies. Notions of citizenship, civic virtue, and public service were derived from the images and symbols of America's "civil religion." Consequently, this loose network of ideas borrowed from America's majority religion provided the raw materials from which a sense of public virtue emerged. This civic piety was most effective at a time when a modest diversity, comprising various Christian sects, characterized the republic. But as Madison saw so clearly, a republic that institutionalizes even modest religious pluralism could easily be torn apart by the factionalism bred of sectarian strife. Any nation that attempts to unite people into common action for the sake of a common good must find some vehicle for the expression of those common aspirations.

Since the institutionalized religious plurality precluded any particular tradition from playing that unifying role, it is not surprising that a substitute system arose, one that could bind together persons from diverse backgrounds for the sake of common action. But this common civic piety could function effectively and equitably only as long as Christianity remained the culturally established religion in the United States. As Christianity began to decline in cultural influence and secularism and religious pluralism began to increase, the American civil piety lost its ability to shape civic virtue within the republic. The fragmentation of American civil religion had a dual effect: it al-

lowed the emergence of voices that had long lay silent under the sti-
fling influence of the majority tradition, and it exposed the founders'
failure to articulate a vision by which civic virtue could be nurtured in
a truly diverse population.

## THE CURRENT DILEMMA: AMERICA'S UNRESOLVED TENSION.

It is clear that from the earliest days of the nation public officials used
the images and rhetoric of Christianity to evoke a sense of loyalty and
commitment to the new experiment in democracy. The establishment
of congressional chaplains, the custom of presidential thanksgiving
proclamations, the invocation of the divine name on the currency are
examples of the important function of religious rhetoric in the governing of the nation. Christianity's role in the nurturing of public
virtue was clearly seen by Alexis de Tocqueville during his travels
across the United States in the 1830s. De Tocqueville was so im-
pressed by Christianity's ability "to purify, control, and restrain that
excessive and exclusive taste for well-being" that dominated the
American character that he identified religion as "the first of their
political institutions."[33] Despite the fact that religion "never inter-
venes directly in the government of American society," it still functions, he claimed, to encourage the "sacrificing [of] private interests"
for the sake of "God's plan . . . this great design . . . this wondrous ordering of all that is." Religion could function in this fashion in early
America because "Christianity reigns without obstacles, by universal
consent."[34]

Protestant Christianity provided the primary symbols for our
common political culture throughout much of our nation's history. As
long as Protestantism remained the culturally established religion of
the republic its hegemonic power rendered most voices of dissent quiescent. Among the republic's founders, Madison was most acutely
aware of the dangers of majoritarian tyranny over the rights of minorities, but he focused most of his arguments on the dangers of a legally
established institutionalized religion. Only later in his life, after he had
left the presidency, did he recognize the dangers of a culturally established symbolic religion. Thus, in his "Detached Memoranda," Madison expanded his views on the dangers of establishment by arguing
that the "Constitution of the U.S. forbids everything *like* the establishment of a national religion," including the appointment of chaplains
and the issuing of presidential thanksgiving proclamations.

The establishment of the chaplainship to Congress is a palpable violation of equal rights. . . . The tenets of the chaplains elected [by a majority] shut the door of worship against the members whose creeds & consciences forbid a participation in that of the majority. To say nothing of other sects, this is the case with that of Roman Catholics & Quakers who have always had members in one or both of the Legislative branches. Could a Catholic clergyman ever hope to be appointed a Chaplain? To say that his religious principles are obnoxious or that his sect is small, is to lift the evil at once and exhibit in its naked deformity the doctrine that religious truth is to be tested by numbers, or that the major sects have a right to govern the minor.[35]

Madison also argued that "religious proclamations by the Executive recommending thanksgiving and fasts are shoots from the same roots. . . . Altho' recommendations only, they imply a religious agency, making no part of the trust delegated to political rulers."[36]

Madison's important reflections on the consequences of these quasi-established practices emerged too late to have any significant impact on the effective power of cultural Christianity. The observations of Joseph Story and Alexis de Tocqueville indicate that by the 1830s civic Protestantism had become the de facto established religion of the republic. For nearly 200 years this "common religion"provided the primary symbols that staked out the common ground between the political and religious spheres.[37] As long as this common religion functioned effectively "everything in the moral field [was] certain and fixed."[38] Once that religion began to fragment, however, the moral context for public decision making became fluid and ambiguous.

Numerous studies have documented the fact that America's historic civil religion no longer functions to provide the symbols for our common public life.[39] Sociologists now regularly refer to America's "three disestablishments." The first, the *legal* disestablishment, is represented by the religion clauses of the first amendment. While the constitution prohibited the establishment of a national church, this legal prohibition had little effect on the symbolic power of our culturally established religion, Protestant Christianity. The second or *religious* disestablishment occurred with the fragmentation of America's civic piety. With the rise of sizable Roman Catholic and Jewish minorities and the emergence of the distinctive witness of the black churches, the predominance of cultural Protestantism began to wane.

Initially these minority communities appeared to be compatible with and supportive of American civil religion. The remarkable cooperation among communities of faith during the civil rights movement encouraged many to believe that America's civic faith could incorporate these diverse religious traditions.[40] But the fragile bonds that held these groups together burst asunder during the divisive political debates that began during the late 1960s. Traditional religious differences combined with political disagreement to spawn the third *moral* disestablishment. Divisions within the American body politic rendered America's civic faith incapable of providing the common principles for personal and public morality.

During the 1950s and early 1960s it appeared that America's civic piety would have sufficient resilience to incorporate these newly influential communities of faith. Indeed, in his influential study *Protestant-Catholic-Jew*, published in 1955, sociologist Will Herberg sought to identify the "American faith" that had become the nation's new "common religion," a faith that transcended the doctrinal divisions that had traditionally separated these communities.[41] The growing popularity of the phrase "Judeo-Christian" to describe the common heritage of those two distinct traditions signaled a typical American confidence in the ability of the "melting pot" to blend even the most divisive disagreements into a bland civic mixture.

This confidence was hardly well placed. Newly emergent religious groups began to emphasize their particular and distinct identities. Jewish scholars demonstrated that the phrase "Judeo-Christian" functioned primarily to repudiate the distinctiveness of Jewish faith by assimilating its beliefs to those of the dominant Christian tradition.[42] Not only did this practice hide the characteristic emphases of Judaism from public view; it also encouraged Christianity's historical tendency to deny Judaism's continuing religious validity. By distancing itself from the dominant tradition, Judaism could both preserve its own heritage and protect itself from the persecuting tendencies of Christianity. Among African Americans, the black power movement spawned black theologies that rejected the influence of the Anglo-European tradition and sought to articulate the particularity of African and African American culture.[43]

The feminist movement encouraged women to extricate their distinctive religious experience from the male dominated patriarchal heritage within which it had been submerged for centuries.[44] Indigenous revolutionary movements in third world countries emerged from communities of faith that stressed the uniqueness of the experience of the oppressed.[45] As liberation theologies offered increasingly sophisticated methods for the analysis and critique of the structures of oppression, the dominant traditions of American Protestantism became the target of an emerging "hermeneutic of suspicion." American civic piety, so its critics argued, could provide the symbols for our common culture only by systematically silencing the voices of minority communities.[46] With the empowerment of those communities, the pretence of commonality was finally revealed.

The divisions that emerged during the 1960s and early 1970s shattered any illusion of political and religious unity within the American populace. The emergence of divisive battles over issues like Vietnam, affirmative action, the equal rights amendment, nuclear weapons, and abortion spread the hermeneutic of suspicion throughout American life. Political opponents no longer assumed that they shared a common set of values or principles by which to adjudicate their differences. Moral and political options were presented as incompatible alternatives, and the art of compromise appeared to wane. Interest group politics began to dominate the public sphere, and notions of the common good and the public welfare seemed to fade from public consciousness.

It is now clear that America's historic civic piety has disintegrated and that no new public philosophy has arisen to take its place. Consequently we live among the fragments of shattered moral and religious traditions, no one of which has yet shown its ability to provide a basis for our common public life. Some commentators—most notably Alasdair MacIntyre, a philosopher at the University of Notre Dame—have suggested that our moral disagreements are so profound that we will never reach consensus on the most basic policy issues.[47] Since our political arguments begin from "rival and incommensurable moral premises,"[48] we are doomed, so the argument goes, to interminable and irresolvable moral and political disagreement. In such a situation, politics becomes "civil war waged by other means," as force, deception, and manipulation dominate the political atmosphere. If contending parties argue on the basis of incommensurable premises, then they have no hope of reaching rational agreement. Consequently neither has any stake in the use of rational argument as the means of political persuasion. Politics thus becomes a mere clash of wills, as each party, interest, and faction seeks to gain the upper hand in the struggle for political control.

MacIntyre's description of contemporary political life sounds like Madison's nightmare come true. While he has undoubtedly exaggerated the hopelessness of our current situation, MacIntyre has certainly captured something of our current cultural ethos.[49] Given the divisiveness of public life today, it is hardly surprising that there should also be widespread confusion concerning the place of religion in American society. Religious communities are themselves deeply divided by the controversies that tug at the fabric of our common public life.[50] Whether these communities can contribute to the renewal of our sense of the common good remains to be seen. But clearly, without some clarification of religion's role in public life, we will be unable to make significant progress toward addressing the moral divisions that plague our society. Religion has been intimately intertwined with the political life of this nation since its founding. But the failure of the founders and their successors to define the proper public function of religious symbols and the proper role of religious communities in nurturing a sense of public virtue has contributed to the current crisis. We must take up the task of seeking to define an appropriate place for religion within a pluralistic democracy. Our failure to do so will leave us caught in the grip a paralyzing and destructive predicament.

In chapter 1, I argued against three common strategies for defining the role of religion in public life: appeals to an imagined moral consensus provided by our historic civic piety (White and Burger in *Bowers*), attempts to remove religion altogether from public life (Singer and Kuhse), and efforts to divide personal religious commitments from public decision making (Cuomo). All fail to provide adequate solutions to our current dilemma. If we are to gain genuine clarity on these matters, we need to look anew at the constitutional principle and the cultural metaphor that influences every discussion of the role of religion in public life: the so-called separation of church and state. If we can come to a clearer understanding of that much maligned and often misunderstood principle, we will have taken a significant first step toward resolving our current dilemma.

## NOTES

1. At the Virginia ratification convention, James Madison commented, "I can see no danger in submitting to practice an experiment which seems to be founded on the best theoretic principles." *Debates in the Several State*

*Conventions on the Adoption of the Federal Constitution*, vol. 3 edited by Jonathan Elliot (Philadelphia: Lippincott, 1836).

2. For a discussion of this issue see, David A. J. Richards, *Foundations of American Constitutionalism* (New York: Oxford University Press, 1989), p. 18-77. Cf. also Thomas L. Pangle, *The Spirit of Modern Republicanism* (Chicago: University of Chicago Press, 1988) and Jean Bethge Elshtain, *Women and War* (New York: Basic Books., Inc., 1987). We will return to this issue when we analyze contemporary communitarian versions of civic republicanism.

3. The best study of the philosophical roots of the founders' view of religion is David A. J. Richards, *Toleration and the Constitution* (New York: Oxford University Press, 1986). I am indebted to Richards's thorough and illuminating study.

4. Anson Phelps Stokes, *Church and State in the United States*, 3 vol. (New York: Harper & Brothers, 1950).

5. William Lee Miller, *The First Liberty: Religion and the American Republic* (New York: Alfred A. Knopf, 1986), pp. 96-97.

6. "Memorial and Remonstrance Against Religious Assessments, 1785," *The Mind of the Founder: Sources of the Political Thought of James Madison*, edited by Marvin Meyers, revised edition (Hanover-London: University Press of New England, 1981).

7. Ibid., p. 8-9.

8. Italics added.

9. *The Federalist Papers*, edited by Clinton Rossiter (New York: NAL Penguin, 1961), p. 78.

10. Ibid., p. 79.

11. Ibid.

12. Ibid., pp. 83-84.

13. Robert Rutland, et. al. eds. *The Papers of James Madison, 1786-1787*, (Charlottesville: University of Virginia, 1984) pp. 355-356.

14. David A. J. Richards, *Foundations of American Constitutionalism*.

15. David Hume, "Of the Independency of Parliament," *Essays Moral, Political, Literary* (Oxford: Oxford University Press, 1963), pp. 40, 42, 43. Quoted in Richards, *Foundations of American Constitutionalism*, p. 35.

16. *The Federalist Papers*, p. 289.

17. Jonathan Elliot, *The Debates in the Several State Conventions on the Adoption of the Federal Constitution*, vol. 3 (Philadelphia: Lippincott, 1836), pp. 536-537.

18. In *The Federalist* (no. 9) Hamilton writes, "It is impossible to read the history of the petty republics of Greece and Italy without feeling sensations of horror and disgust. . . . If momentary rays of glory break forth from the gloom, while they dazzle us with a transient and fleeting brilliancy, they at the same time admonish us to lament that the vices of government should pervert the direction and tarnish the luster of those bright talents and exalted endowments for which the favored soils that produced them have been so justly celebrated" (pp. 71-72).

Similarly John Adams, reflecting on the Spartan republic, writes: "Separated from the rest of mankind, they lived together, destitute of all business, pleasure, and amusement, but war and politics, pride and ambition; . . . as if fighting and intriguing, and not life and happiness, were the end of man and society; as if the love of one's country and of glory were amiable passions, when not limited by justice and general benevolence. . . . Human nature perished under this frigid system of national and family pride." *A Defense of the Constitutions of Government of the United States of America*, vol. 4, *The Works of John Adams* (Boston: Little, Brown, 1851), p. 554.

19. David A. J. Richards, *Foundations of American Constitutionalism*, p. 49. Similar arguments against classical republicanism are offered by Jean Bethge Elshtain, *Women and War*, and Susan Moller Okin, *Justice, Gender, and the Family* (New York: Basic Books, 1989).

20. *The Federalist Papers*, p. 82.

21. Ibid., p. 387 (italics in original).

22. Ibid., pp. 82-83.

23. The 1994 election campaigns illustrate this problem in ever more graphic ways. Many candidates conducted largely negative media campaigns in order to undermine public confidence in their opponents. The further effect may be a continuing erosion of public confidence in public official and the electoral process itself.

24. Richards, *Foundations of American Constitutionalism*, p. 28.

25. Joseph Story, *Commentaries on the Constitution of the United States*, vol. 2 (Boston: Gray Hilliard, 1833), pp. 722-724.

26. Jean Jacques Rousseau, *Social Contract*, edited by C.M. Andrews (New York: William H. Wise, 1901), pp. 123-124.

27. We do not know how Madison voted on this resolution either in committee or in the House, though some years later in his "Detached Memorandum" he clearly condemned the practice of appointing Chaplains as a violation of the establishment clause. His reasons for opposing the Chaplaincy are completely consistent with his arguments in the "Remonstrance." "The establishment of the chaplainship to Congress is a palpable violation of equal rights, as well as of Constitutional principles: The tenets of the chaplains elected [by the majority] shut the door of worship against the members whose creed & consciences forbid a participation in that of the majority. To say nothing of other sects, this is the case with that of Roman Catholics & Quakers who have always had members in one or both of the Legislative branches. Could a Catholic clergyman ever hope to be appointed a Chaplain? To say that his religious principles are obnoxious or that his sect is small, is to lift the evil at once and exhibit in its naked deformity the doctrine that religious truth is to be tested by numbers, or that the major sects have a right to govern the minor." "Madison's 'Detached Memoranda,'" *William and Mary Quarterly*, 3 (1946): p. 558. For a discussion of the role of the memorandum on the chaplaincy in Madison's overall position on religion in the republic, see Robert L. Cord, *Separation of Church and State: Crisis in the American Constitutional System* (Boston: Northeastern University, 1982) pp. 29-36. Cord's discussion provides a useful overview of the question of Madison's consistency on these topics, but I find Cord's ultimate conclusions on this matter to be unpersuasive.

28. "Detached Memoranda," p. 560.

**29.** James D. Richardson, *A Compilation of the Messages and Papers of the Presidents, 1789-1897,* vol. 1 (Washington, D.C.: Bureau of National Literature and Art, 1910), pp. 560-561.

**30.** Of the many studies of this topic see, especially, William H. Hutchison and Hartmut Lehmann, editors, *Many are Chosen: Divine Election and Western Nationalism* (Minneapolis: Fortress Press, 1994).

**31.** Religious justifications for these political initiatives can be found in President McKinley's War Message to Congress and Senator Beveridge's Speech to the U.S. Senate (January 9, 1900).

**32.** Abraham Lincoln, Second Inaugural Address. Not only did Lincoln's public rhetoric demonstrate the power of religious symbols to invoke judgment on the failures of the nation. At its finest it also exemplified their power to redefine the fundamental values guiding the nation's identity and purpose. See Garry Wills, *Lincoln at Gettysburg: The Words That Remade America* (New York: Simon and Schuster, 1992).

**33.** Alexis de Tocqueville, *Democracy in America,* translated by George Lawrence, edited by J. P. Mayer, (New York: Doubleday, Anchor Books, 1969), p. 292.

**34.** Ibid.

**35.** Elizabeth Fleet, ed., "Madison's `Detached Memoranda,'" *William and Mary Quarterly,* 3 (1946): p. 560.

**36.** Ibid.

**37.** "Common religion" is a phrase used by John F. Wilson in his helpful article "Common Religion in American Society," in *Civil Religion and Political Theology* (Notre Dame: University of Notre Dame, 1986), pp. 111-124.

**38.** Tocqueville, p. 292.

**39.** See particularly Robert N. Bellah, *The Broken Covenant: American Civil Religion in Time of Trial* (New York: Seabury Press, 1975), and Robert N. Bellah et. al., *Habits of the Heart* (Berkeley: University of California Press, 1985). For a useful survey of the consequences of the breakdown of American's civil piety for the relation between Christianity and the state, see Christopher F. Mooney, *Boundaries Dimly Perceived: Law, Religion, Education and the Common Good* (Notre Dame: University of Notre Dame Press, 1989).

**40.** One of the greatest accomplishments of Dr. Martin Luther King, Jr., can be seen in the way he used the rhetoric of the founding documents to overcome the racism inherent in those very documents. The Preamble of the Constitution asserted the framers' intention to "secure the blessings of liberty to ourselves and our posterity," while Article I defined slaves as 3/5 of a free person, insured the continuation of the slave trade at least until 1808, and allowed a tax on imported "property" not to exeed ten dollars per slave. And yet Dr. King, sitting in a Birmingham jail cell in 1963, could write, "We will reach the goal of freedom in Birmingham and all over the nation, because the goal of America is freedom. . . . We will win our freedom because the sacred heritage of our nation and the eternal will of God are embodied in our echoing demands." "Letter from a Birmingham Jail," *The Writings of Martin Luther King, Jr.,* edited by James Washington, (New York: MacMillian, 1987), pp. 301.

**41.** Will Herberg, *Protestant-Catholic-Jew* (New York: Doubleday, 1955).

**42.** See Arthur Cohen, *The Myth of the Judeo-Christian Tradition* (New York: Harper & Row, 1970).

**43.** See *Black Theology: A Documentary History, 1966-1979*, edited by Gayraud S. Wilmore and James H. Cone (Maryknoll, New York: Orbis Books, 1979).

**44.** Of the many important books in this tradition see especially Elisabeth Schüssler Fiorenza, *In Memory of Her: A Feminist Theological Reconstruction of Christian Origins* (New York: Crossroad Publishing Company, 1983).

**45.** Despite many significant works in this tradition, the classic text continues to be Gustavo Gutierrez, *A Theology of Liberation* (Maryknoll, New York: Orbis Books, 1973).

**46.** For a particularly brilliant example of such analysis, see Cornel West's discussion of the "genealogy of modern racism" in *Prophesy Deliverance!* (Philadelphia: Westminster Press, 1982), pp. 47-68.

**47.** This argument has more recently been developed by the sociologist James Davison Hunter, *Culture Wars: The Struggle to Define America* (New York: Basic Books, 1991).

**48.** Alasdair MacIntyre, *After Virtue* (Notre Dame: University of Notre Dame, 1981), p. 8.

**49.** For an insightful criticism of MacIntyre that challenges his thesis about "incommensurable moral premises," see Jeffrey Stout, *Ethics After Babel* (Boston: Beacon Press, 1988).

**50.** Robert Wuthnow has argued that American denominations are moving toward a "religious realignment" based upon a political cleavage between conservative and liberal factions within each denomination. It is now common for conservatives and liberals to feel more closely connected to like-minded persons in other denominations than to the opposing party within their own faith tradition. See *The Restructuring of American Religion* (Princeton: Princeton University Press, 1988).

# 3

## The Constitutional Tradition: A Perplexing Legacy

### THE SEPARATION OF CHURCH AND STATE: A MISLEADING METAPHOR

"Congress shall make no law respecting an establishment of religion or prohibiting the free exercise thereof." These opening words of the Bill of Rights state what one scholar has called "the most distinctive concept that the American constitutional system has contributed to the body of political ideas," a principle commonly known as *the separation of church and state*.[1] That phrase is derived from a metaphor first used by Roger Williams in a letter to John Cotton[2] and then by Thomas Jefferson in a letter to the Baptist Association of Danbury, Connecticut,[3] but it became common constitutional parlance through a decision written by Justice Hugo Black in 1947.[4] Despite its somewhat obscure origins and its rather recent introduction into the legal tradition, this principle has come to shape our nation's understanding of the relation between the political and religious spheres in the United States. Not only has it guided constitutional interpretation of the first amendment; it has also molded the American public's understanding of the proper relation between government and religion.

Principles derived from metaphors have the advantage of capturing with vividness and felicity the essential elements of a complicated situation. They have the distinct disadvantage, however, of encouraging simplicity instead of precise analysis or fostering caricature when detailed portraiture is needed. At a time when our nation is struggling to define the proper role of religion and religiously based moral convictions within public life, the phrase "the separation of church and state" and its attendant metaphor "a wall of separation between church and state" serve not to clarify but to confuse.[5] While the phrases identify one aspect of government's relation to religion, they deflect our attention from other fundamental features of the first amendment guarantees. By focusing on religious and governmental institutions they obscure the essential concern for individual freedom and equality that undergirds both the "no establishment" and the "free exercise" clause. By speaking of "church and state," they seduce us into thinking of these complicated and textured organizations (communities of faith and governmental agencies) in singular and monolithic terms. By defining the relation between religion and government with the simple word "separation," these phrases conceal the variety of ways in which these two entities interact, and the phrase consequently constrains our ability to imagine new possibilities for their relationship. The slogan "the separation of church and state" impedes our understanding of the proper role of religion in American public life and, I will argue in this chapter, must be basically reconceived and perhaps even abandoned.[6]

---

"The First Amendment has erected a wall [of separation] between church and state. That wall must be kept high and impregnable. We could not approve the slightest breach."[7] The day Justice Hugo Black penned those fateful words, the U.S. Supreme Court was convened with the invocation, "God save this honorable court." A few hundred yards across the Mall from the Supreme Court building, the two houses of Congress opened their sessions with prayers offered by chaplains supported by public funds and paid with currency inscribed with the motto "In God We Trust." Some months later President Harry S. Truman would follow the custom of nearly every president since the founding of the republic by issuing a proclamation declaring a national day of thanksgiving, and urging Americans to engage in prayers of thanks to the Creator for his manifold gifts to the nation.

In light of these apparently contradictory sentiments about the role of religion in American public life it should not surprise the reader to learn that the decision which introduced the phrase "wall of separation" into the Court's lexicon actually *sustained* a New Jersey state statute that provided public funding for transportation of children attending Roman Catholic schools. Justice Black, having affirmed that the wall of separation must not be breached, then offered the puzzling opinion that "New Jersey has not breached it here," even though the state used public tax funds to support the busing of Roman Catholic schoolchildren.

The Supreme Court's record in adjudicating cases involving the religion clauses has been spotty at best. Court decisions since *Everson v. Board of Education* have been characterized by questionable logic and contradictory opinions. Supreme Court commentators have been virtually unanimous in their censure of the justices' reasoning in cases involving the religion clauses, particularly those dealing with the "no establishment clause." Critics representing the full spectrum of political ideologies have joined voices in characterizing the court's decision making in this area as "bizarre,"[8] "fatuous,"[9] "a hodgepodge . . . derived from *Alice's Adventures in Wonderland*."[10] Legal scholar Jesse Choper has argued that the current disarray in the adjudication of establishment cases "has generated ad hoc judgments which are incapable of being reconciled on any principled basis."[11] A summary of just some of the Court's decisions regarding state aid to education provides a useful illustration of the counterintuitive reasoning that seems to characterize Supreme Court opinions in matters of religion:

> The Court has held that the state may reimburse parents for the costs of public bus service to take students to and from nonpublic schools, but it may not pay for buses to take students on field trips. The state may furnish textbooks, but not other educational materials such as maps or film projectors. Publicly funded remedial teaching off the school premises is allowed, but remedial teaching on the school premises is not. The state may reimburse a sectarian school for administering state-created tests, but it may not fund tests created by the school's own teachers. Finally, the state may fund a wide variety of institutions and activities indirectly through tax subsidies that it may not fund directly.[12]

Howard Ball's suggestion that the Court is involved in "judicial meandering in search of the meaning and purpose of the establishment clause" seems correct.[13] Moreover, the Court's lack of clarity on these issues threatens both to polarize and politicize an already complicated situation. In his unprecedented attack on the Supreme Court in July 1985, then Attorney General Edwin Meese took aim at the Court's decision making regarding the religion clauses. Characterizing the Court's doctrine of "strict neutrality between religion and nonreligion" as "bizarre," Meese urged the justices to return to a "jurisprudence of original intent." He also questioned whether the Court's interpretation of the fourteenth amendment as mandating the application of the Bill of Rights to actions of the states could be maintained.

In making these arguments Meese relied heavily on political scientist Robert Cord's book *Separation of Church and State: Historical Fact and Current Fiction*, published in 1982 with a Foreword by William F. Buckley.[14] Consequently, criticisms of the Court's use of the "wall of separation" metaphor have become associated with a conservative political agenda.[15] The tendency to align a defense of "absolute separation of church and state" with political liberalism and the critique of that position with political conservatism can only serve further to confuse and confound the current discussion.

To understand these important but controversial issues we need a careful analytical unraveling of the many strands of judicial interpretation of the religion clauses of the first amendment. Instead of relying on slogans, metaphors, and political caricatures, we need to engage in a dispassionate evaluation of the various forms of reasoning that have characterized Court opinions since *Everson*. We need further to ask not simply about the *intentions* of the framers of the Constitution but about the *values* they sought to inscribe in the text. What political and cultural values are upheld by the Constitution's religion clauses? Are those values worth preserving in today's society? If so, what policies best uphold the values the founders sought to defend? How do the historical and cultural changes of the past two hundred years affect the way we apply those values to our current policy problems? By focusing on questions such as these we may begin to clarify the proper place of religion in judicial adjudication. But to gain such clarity, we must plunge into the midst of the perplexing legacy that the Court has created in the confusing and contradictory aftermath of *Everson*.

## THE CONFUSION DISPLAYED: ALLEGHENY COUNTY V. GREATER PITTSBURGH ACLU (1988)

One recent Supreme Court establishment clause case illustrates the complicated and contradictory pattern of reasoning that characterizes current judicial deliberations on issues of religion in public life. In *Allegheny County v. Greater Pittsburgh ACLU* the Court considered a case that involved the displaying of religious symbols on or near county property. The government of Allegheny County permitted the Holy Name Society, a Roman Catholic organization, to display a crèche on the grand staircase of the county courthouse. The crèche display, which included an angel bearing a banner with the words "Gloria in Excelsis Deo," was the sole holiday decoration within the main staircase of the courthouse. Another display, erected outside a building jointly owned by the county and the city of Pittsburgh, consisted of a 45-foot Christmas tree, an 18-foot menorah,[16] and a sign saluting liberty during the holiday season. The Greater Pittsburgh ACLU brought suit against the county seeking to enjoin the display of both the crèche and the menorah, arguing that they violated the first amendment establishment clause. While the Federal District Court held that neither display violated the first amendment, the Third Circuit Court of Appeals disagreed, holding that both symbols were violations of the establishment clause. The Supreme Court, in a truly Solomonic decision, finally held that the crèche was in violation of the first amendment while the menorah was not.

The opinions offered by the Supreme Court justices in this case present a crazy-quilt pattern of argument, but three major positions can be discerned within their presentations. The majority (Justices Blackmun, O'Connor, Brennan, Stevens, and Marshall) clearly uphold a "separationist" position, though they do so on different grounds. Blackmun and O'Connor argue that the crèche violates the establishment clause primarily because the display serves no clear "*secular purpose.*" Justices Brennan, Stevens, and Marshall take the stronger position of "*strict neutrality,*" arguing that the government is never permitted to display religious symbols of any kind; consequently, these justices argue that both the crèche and the menorah are in violation of the First Amendment. Justice Kennedy, joined by Justices Rehnquist, Scalia, and White, dissent from the majority opinion and argue that neither display is a violation of the establishment clause. Their position is aptly described as one of *symbolic accommodation.*

*Secular Purpose.* Justice Blackmun, writing for the majority, begins his opinion by confirming the principles adopted by the Court in three previous cases: *Everson* v. *Board of Education, Lemon* v. *Kurtzman,*[17] and *Wallace* v. *Jaffree.*[18] After quoting in full Justice Black's summary of the meaning of the establishment clause, Blackmun proceeds to reiterate the so-called *Lemon* test for determining whether a governmental practice is in violation of that clause. "Under the *Lemon* analysis, a statute or practice which touches upon religion, if it is to be permissible under the Establishment Clause, must have a secular purpose; it must neither advance nor inhibit religion in its principal or primary effect; and it must not foster an excessive entanglement with religion."[19] Finally, Blackmun invokes the notion introduced into establishment adjudication by Justice O'Connor: that government may not engage in practices that function to "endorse" religious beliefs. Thus any state action that serves to favor, prefer, or promote "one religious theory over another"[20] or "religious belief over disbelief"[21] is in violation of the no-establishment clause.

Since the Allegheny crèche display proclaimed a specifically Christian message, with no secular symbols to provide a broader cultural context, Blackmun argues that this action cannot be viewed simply as the acknowledgment of a "cultural phenomenon." "Government may celebrate Christmas in some manner and form, but not in a way that endorses Christian doctrine. Here, Allegheny County has transgressed this line. It has chosen to celebrate Christmas in a way that has the effect of endorsing a patently Christian message. . . . This display of the crèche in this context, therefore, must be permanently enjoined."

Despite the apparently straightforward reasoning reflected in Justice Blackmun's opening arguments, the complexity of this case emerges when he seeks to deal with the objections raised by his colleagues on the bench. Blackmun is forced to deal with the fact that the majority opinion appears to run counter to two earlier decisions rendered by the Court. In *Marsh* v. *Chambers* (1983),[22] the Court approved the Nebraska Legislature's practice of opening each day with a prayer offered by a chaplain paid by public funds; and in *Lynch* v. *Donnelly* (1984),[23] the Court upheld the right of the city of Pawtucket, Rhode Island, to erect a crèche as part of its observance of the Christmas holiday season. In light of these obvious "accommodations" to religious practice, Justice Blackmun takes particular care to answer the charges of the dissenting justices that the Court's action in this case is blatantly inconsistent with two of its recent precedents. This reversal of the Court's recent practice, the dissenters argue, represents not governmental neutrality but "an unjustified hostility toward religion."[24]

In reply, Blackmun states his position that the nonestablishment clause demands a "secular" government "precisely in order to avoid discriminating among citizens on the basis of their religious faiths." Legislative prayers, the national motto, and the Pledge of Allegiance contain acceptable "non-sectarian" references to religion. Indeed, Blackmun reminds his colleagues, "the legislative prayers involved in *Marsh* did not violate this principle because the particular chaplain had 'removed all references to Christ.'" By contrast governmental actions or practices "that demonstrate the government's allegiance to a particular sect or creed" must be prohibited if the nonestablishment clause is to be upheld. "The history of this Nation, it is perhaps sad to say, contains numerous examples of official acts that endorsed Christianity specifically . . . . Some of these examples date back to the founding of the Republic, but this heritage of official discrimination against non-Christians has no place in the jurisprudence of the Establishment Clause."

This interpretation of the first amendment, Blackmun argues, represents not hostility to religion but "a respect for religious pluralism, a respect commanded by the Constitution." The only way religious diversity can be appropriately respected is if "government is secular in its functions and operations." By permitting a display that proclaimed the religious, as opposed to the secular, meaning of the Christmas holiday, Allegheny County was clearly discriminating against the non-Christian population. Thus the majority decision permanently enjoining the display of the crèche represents not "a hostility or indifference to religion, but, instead, the respect for religious diversity that the Constitution requires." By contrast the Jewish menorah, surrounded as it was by various secular symbols, constitutes "not an endorsement of religious faith but simply a recognition of cultural diversity."

In her concurring opinion, Justice O'Connor offers some significant refinements of Blackmun's position. In particular she seeks to show the dissimilarities between the Allegheny and Pawtucket crèche displays, differences that justify the apparently contradictory decisions in *Allegheny* and *Lynch*. In *Lynch* the Court, employing the *Lemon* test, held that Pawtucket had a "secular purpose" for including a crèche in the city's Christmas display, namely, "to depict the origins of that Holiday." In addition, the display did not have the "primary effect" of advancing religion, since it was formally analogous to the "literally hundreds of religious paintings in governmentally supported museums." Finally, the display did not involve "excessive entanglement" between religion and government since there was "no evidence of contact with church authorities concerning the content or design of the exhibit." The Pawtucket display continued the common governmental practice of acknowledging the role of religion in American life. Practices like legislative prayers and invocation of the divine name in the national motto "serve the secular purposes of 'solemnizing public occasions, expressing confidence in the future, and encouraging the recognition of what is worthy of appreciation in society'." As long as a secular purpose is served, governmental acknowledgment of religion does not violate the nonestablishment clause.

Governmental acknowledgment is to be distinguished, however, from governmental "endorsement," for the latter "sends a message to nonadherents that they are outsiders, not full members of the political community, and an accompanying message to adherents that they are insiders, favored members of the political community." O'Connor's endorsement test thus seeks to differentiate discriminatory and nondiscriminatory governmental action in a religiously plural democracy. Practices like legislative chaplaincies and presidential thanksgiving proclamations are acceptable because they are "nonsectarian" in nature. Thanksgiving, for example, "is now generally understood as a celebration of patriotic values rather than particular religious beliefs . . . . Such long-standing practices . . . serve a secular purpose rather than a sectarian one and have largely lost their religious significance over time." Even the Christmas tree "whatever its origins, is not regarded today as a religious symbol," but the crèche, particularly as displayed in the Allegheny County Courthouse, is clearly a sectarian Christian symbol that conveys a message of marginalization to nonadherents of the Christian faith. By contrast the broader holiday display that included the menorah conveyed a "message of pluralism . . . [and] is not a message that endorses religion over nonreligion." Thus, the "combined holiday display had neither the purpose nor the effect of endorsing religion, but . . . [the] Allegheny County's crèche display had such an effect."

The attempt by Blackmun and O'Connor to define the proper relationship between religion and government is plagued by a number of serious difficulties. In seeking to preserve governmental neutrality within a pluralistic democracy, they characterize the state as "essentially secular" and mandate that its actions must always have a "secular purpose." Only a genuinely secular state, they argue, can avoid preference or favoritism among competing religious groups. State secularity is the guarantor of nondiscrimination on matters religious. This position, though internally consistent, entails a number of odd consequences.

If the courts are to have the responsibility of judging whether a governmental action has a secular purpose, judges will be placed in the uncomfortable position of being both theological and social critics. They must function as theological critics in order to determine the meaning of a symbol within a religious tradition's network of doctrines and practices; they must function as social critics in order to determine whether such a symbol has been sufficiently stripped of its inherent religious meaning to function in a nondiscriminatory way in the public realm. But such governmental activities run the risk of *violating* rather than *upholding* the no-establishment clause. Members of the judicial branch appear to be particularly ill-prepared to engage in even the minimal theological inquiry required to determine the meaning and function of a religious symbol within a religious community's vast network of beliefs and practices.[25] Moreover, such inquiry threatens to place the "civil magistrate" as a "judge of religious truth," a position Madison reckoned to be "an arrogant pretension."[26]

In addition, the "secular purpose" requirement mandates that public officials make the formidable social assessment that the religious content of a symbol has been sufficiently muted to make it acceptable in the public realm. Such judgments will be both difficult and controversial, but the requirement itself suggests that religious symbols are publicly acceptable only insofar as they are no longer religious. Justice Blackmun's approving observation that the chaplain whose prayers were the subject of adjudication in *Marsh* v. *Donnelly* acted appropriately because he had removed "all references to Christ" would sound abhorrent to the vast majority of Christian ministers who might be asked to serve in a similar capacity. The "secular purpose" argument as interpreted by Blackmun and O'Connor[27] would admit only the blandest symbols into the discourse of public life.[28] Not only would this requirement impoverish the already desultory rhetoric of contemporary politics, it would make religious people rightly suspicious of allowing their symbols into the public realm for fear that their meaning and significance would be lost through the homogenizing effect of our political culture.

*Strict Neutrality.* Precisely because the middle ground Blackmun and O'Connor seek to occupy appears so unstable, their concurring colleagues devise a different justification in support of their judicial judgment regarding the *Allegheny* case. Justice Brennan, joined by Marshall and Stevens, presents a *strict neutrality* argument as the basis for concurring with the majority decision. In finding both the crèche and the menorah in violation of the first amendment, Brennan takes issue with the Blackmun/O'Connor appeal to pluralism as a justification for the presence of religious symbols on governmental property. In so doing Brennan provides a different principled basis for his separationist position.

I know of no principle under the Establishment Clause . . . that permits us to conclude that governmental promotion of religion is acceptable so long as one religion in not favored. We have, on the contrary, interpreted that Clause to require *neutrality*, not just among religions, but between religion and non-religion (italics added).

In a clever bit of theological analysis, Brennan disputes the "secular purpose" requirement by showing that the argument for religious pluralism depends on the continuing religious significance of the symbols displayed in front of the jointly owned city/county building. Justice O'Connor approves of that display because it "conveyed a message of pluralism and freedom of belief during the holiday season." But Brennan points out, "the 'pluralism' to which Justice O'Connor refers is *religious* pluralism, and the 'freedom of belief' is freedom of *religious* belief. The display of the tree and the menorah will symbolize such pluralism and freedom only if more than one religion is represented. . . . Thus, the pluralistic message Justice O'Connor stressed *depends on* the tree possessing some religious significance." Consequently the "secular purpose" and "religious pluralism" arguments work at cross purposes with one another, and thus the Blackmun/O'Connor position cannot be consistently maintained.

Moreover, Brennan argues, by engaging in judgments about the religious significance of symbols like the menorah and the Christmas tree, the Court seeks to substitute its own judgments for that of the participants in the religious traditions. One may wonder why ministers across the nation read presidential thanksgiving proclamations from their pulpits if Thanksgiving Day has become "a celebration of patriotic values *rather than* particular religious beliefs." It may come as a surprise to millions of Christians who celebrate the Christmas season that the Christmas tree "is not regarded today as a religious symbol." So also religious Jews may be offended to learn the Court considers the menorah to be "primarily" a symbol of Jewish ethnic identity. Indeed, Brennan offers significant evidence to counter all of these judgments. The issue, however, is not which of the justices gets the best of the theological argument, but whether justices are competent to engage in such disputes. Such theological judgments, Brennan asserts, constitute "an interference in religious matters precluded by the Establishment Clause." As Justice Stevens states in his concurring opinion, "the Establishment Clause should be construed to create a strong presumption against the display of religious symbols on public property."

*Symbolic Accommodation.* The "softness" of the Blackmun/ O'Connor mediating position precipitated a sharply worded and strongly argued dissent from Justices Kennedy, Rehnquist, White, and Scalia. Writing for the dissenting minority, Justice Kennedy suggests that the majority opinion "reflects an unjustified hostility toward religion, a hostility inconsistent with our history and our precedents." This ruling continues the recent pattern of judicial interpretation that would require "a relentless extirpation of all contact between government and religion," a policy clearly at odds with "our political and cultural heritage." The time has come, Kennedy suggests, to consider "substantial revision of our Establishment Clause doctrine."

Kennedy rejects the notion that government can categorically maintain a position of "no assistance" to religion.

> As the modern administrative state expands to touch the lives of its citizens in such diverse ways and redirects their financial choices through programs of its own, it is difficult to maintain the fiction that requiring government to avoid all assistance to religion can in fairness be viewed as serving the goal of neutrality.

Rather the government should adopt a policy of *passive or symbolic accommodation* toward religion. Since "a vast portion of our people believe in and worship God and . . . many of our legal, political, and personal values derive historically from religious teachings,"[29] it is proper for government to encourage the flourishing of religion as long as the government does not coerce anyone to exercise religion or provide direct benefits to religious institutions.

> Absent coercion, the risk of infringement of religious liberty by passive or symbolic accommodation is minimal . . . Non-coercive government action within the realm of flexible accommodation or passive acknowledgment of existing symbols does not violate the Establishment Clause unless it benefits religion in a way more direct and more substantial than practices that are accepted in our national heritage.

Interpreting the establishment clause in this fashion, Kennedy argues, would be consistent with the Court's recent rulings in *Marsh* and *Lynch*. The majority's opinion, on the contrary, creates a pattern of hopeless confusion and contradiction and stands in opposition to the Court's most recent relevant precedents.

Kennedy reserves his sharpest criticisms for Justice O'Connor's "endorsement" test. "I submit that the endorsement test is flawed in its fundamentals and unworkable in practice. The uncritical adoption of this standard is every bit as troubling as the bizarre result it produces in the case before us." Kennedy zeroes in on the notion that the criterion for establishment clause violations ought to be "whether nonadherents would be made to feel like 'outsiders' by government recognition or accommodation of religion." By this standard virtually every accommodation of religion throughout our history would have to be ruled invalid including presidential thanksgiving proclamations, prayers offered at the opening of legislative sessions, the invocation of divine succor at the opening of the Supreme Court, the special prayer room in the Capitol building, the national motto, and the phrase "one nation under God" in the Pledge of Allegiance.

> Either the endorsement test must invalidate scores of traditional practices recognizing the place religion holds in our culture, or it must be twisted and stretched to avoid inconsistency with practices we know to have been permitted in the past. . . . In my view, the principles of the Establishment Clause and our Nation's historic traditions of diversity and pluralism allow communities to make reasonable judgments respecting the accommodation or acknowledgment of holidays with both cultural and religious aspects. No constitutional violation occurs when they do so by displaying a symbol of the holiday's religious origins.

Justice Kennedy offers some telling criticisms of the majority opinion in his carefully argued dissent. In particular he shows how the "neutrality" and "endorsement" criteria fail to provide a consistent standard for judicial judgments regarding public religion. In addition, he raises serious questions about the adequacy of the *Lemon* test as a general framework for establishment clause adjudication. His own position regarding "passive or symbolic accommodation" fails, however, to provide a defensible alternative. Kennedy simply sidesteps the issue that both Blackmun and O'Connor suggest stands at the heart of establishment clause adjudication, the question of religious pluralism. What are the appropriate limits of governmental accommodation of *majority* religious belief and practice within a pluralistic democracy?

At what point does proper accommodation of religion become improper aid or assistance to religion? When does accommodation of the majority religion become discriminatory toward religious minorities?

Justice O'Connor's "objective observer" theory is undoubtedly an inadequate guide to issues of discrimination, but Justice Kennedy's refusal to address the question hardly encourages a "substantial revision of our Establishment Clause doctrine." As James Madison clearly asserted, the no-establishment clause was designed to deal with the complicated issue of the relation between majority and minority religion.[30] Any reconsideration of the interpretation of that clause that fails to address the difficult issue of religious discrimination must be judged inadequate. Throughout his opinion, Justice Kennedy equates "religion" with "Christianity," so his appeal to "traditional practices recognizing the place that religion holds in our culture" is in fact a covert brief for the centrality of Christianity within American society.[31] Until Justice Kennedy addresses the issues of religious pluralism and governmental discrimination against religious minorities, "passive or symbolic accommodation" will continue to look like improper governmental support for the symbols of America's majority religion.

*Allegheny* illustrates the current confusion that dominates Supreme Court deliberations regarding religion in American public life. Religion clause cases are regularly decided by bare majorities, and those in the majority often disagree about the proper judicial basis for a decision. Thus, justices voting with the majority will both concur with and dissent from various aspects of the majority decision, and their concurring opinions often provide justifications that conflict with the rationale provided by the primary author. Cases like *Allegheny* and *Lynch* are decided in apparently contradictory fashion, and the justices' attempts to reconcile the antinomies appear facile and futile. Disagreements between majority and minority factions are being stated with increasing rhetorical sharpness, as justices trade charges of "Orwellian" distortion of the issues.[32]

The justices rarely acknowledge the validity of opposing viewpoints, and the very terms of the discussion have become clouded and imprecise. A Court so seriously divided against itself will hardly be able to provide the leadership needed for building consensus concerning religion's proper place in a pluralistic democracy. Yet given the decisive symbolic role played by the phrase "separation of church and state" in our national consciousness, continuing conceptual confusion within the Court could seriously damage efforts to address the broader issue. Thus, clarification of the Court's confusion becomes an essential first step in resolving our broader national dilemma.

## THE SUSPECT CONCEPTS:
## SEPARATION, ACCOMMODATION, AND NEUTRALITY

As the analysis of the *Allegheny* case shows, judicial interpretation of the religion clauses is constrained by the conceptual categories traditionally employed by the Court. The three key concepts—separation, accommodation, and neutrality—are present in all the opinions offered by members the Court, but they are used in quite different ways by individual justices. While the justices appear to be operating in the same conceptual world, they are in fact using the key terms in diverse and even contrary ways. Consequently their arguments and criticisms often fail to engage each other directly, and the observer gets a clear sense of the justices "talking past one another."

The primary concepts employed in religion clause adjudication were introduced into the judicial lexicon through Justice Black's fateful decision in *Everson*. In order to begin the process of conceptual clarification, we must return to that decisive 1947 opinion.

> The "establishment of religion" clause of the First Amendment means at least this: Neither a state nor the Federal Government can set up a church. Neither can pass laws which aid one religion, aid all religions, or prefer one religion over another. Neither can force nor influence a person to go to or remain away from church against his will or force him to profess a belief or disbelief in any religion. No person can be punished for entertaining or professing religious beliefs or disbeliefs, for church attendance or non-attendance. No tax in any amount, large or small, can be levied to support any religious activities or institutions, whatever they may be called, or whatever form they may adopt to teach or practice religion. Neither a state nor the Federal Government can, openly or secretly, participate in the affairs of any religious organization or groups and vice versa. In the words of Jefferson, the clause against establishment of religion by law was intended to erect "a wall of separation between church and State."[33]

A few paragraphs later in his decision, Justice Black explicitly equated the "separation of church and state" with government *neutrality* toward religion. "The First Amendment," he wrote, "requires the state to be neutral in its relations with groups of religious believers and non-believers."[34] In two opinions written during the following year (*McCollum* v. *Board of Education* and *Abington* v. *Schemmp*, 1948), Justice Black invoked his ruling in *Everson*, once again linking the "wall of separation" metaphor to the concept of judicial neutrality. "The breach of neutrality that is today a trickling stream may all too soon become a raging torrent"[35] unless the "wall between Church and State" is "kept high and impregnable."[36]

This fateful joining of the language of neutrality with the Jeffersonian "wall" metaphor has had a decisive influence on the contemporary judicial process. During the past four decades, the notion of "governmental neutrality" has attained doctrinal status equal to that of the separation principle itself. A sampling of the rhetoric from first amendment decisions will illustrate how the Court has sought to interpret the notion of church/state separation through the concept of governmental neutrality.

> The Government [must] maintain strict neutrality, neither aiding nor opposing religion.[37] . . . Government in our democracy, state and nation must be neutral in matters of religious theory, doctrine and practice. . . . The First Amendment mandates governmental neutrality between religion and religion, and between religion and non-religion.[38] . . . The Government must pursue a course of complete neutrality toward religion.[39]

Since *Everson* the notions of separation and neutrality have provided the conceptual baseline against which all other judicial concepts are measured. The Court has consistently asserted that "church and state" are to remain institutionally separate and that government must therefore adopt a position of neutrality with regard to religious belief and practice. Despite the apparent simplicity of this theoretical position, however, the Court has had to acknowledge that government and religion are in practice often deeply entangled with one another. Consequently, the Court has been forced to decide under what circumstances the state can appropriately "accommodate" religious belief without violating the nonestablishment clause of the first amendment. Thus a third concept, *accommodation*, has been developed in order to identify the sphere within which government and religion might properly cooperate. But the very term employed for this purpose indicates the exceptional character of such practical cooperation.

The logic of post-1947 religion clause adjudication thus proceeds as follows: The first amendment mandates the institutional separation of church and state. Government complies with this mandate by remaining rigorously neutral toward religion, though in certain exceptional cases the government is permitted to modify its normal behavior in order to accommodate some aspect of religious belief and practice. Two different problems emerge from the apparently simple logic of this position. First, while the demand for governmental neutrality has through the years remained relatively uncontroversial, the meaning of neutrality has been variously understood. Much of the conceptual confusion surrounding the interpretation of the religion clauses has resulted from the different, and often contradictory, construals of the meaning of neutrality. Second, while the Court has consistently allowed for governmental accommodation of religious belief, justices have differed decisively regarding the nature and scope of such accommodation. These problems have become especially acute in cases that require the Court to delve into the murky middle ground between the nonestablishment and free exercise clauses. In the next two sections of the chapter, we will examine in turn the conceptual problems surrounding the notions of accommodation and neutrality.

ACCOMMODATION AND RELIGION CLAUSE CONFLICT. "Congress shall make no law respecting an establishment of religion or prohibiting the free exercise thereof."

The confusion reflected in *Allegheny* and other establishment cases stems in part from a more basic tension inherent in the two religion clauses themselves.[40] Former Chief Justice Burger has characterized the problem in the following terms. "The Court has struggled to find a neutral course between the two Religion Clauses, both of which are cast in absolute terms, and either of which, if expanded to a logical extreme would tend to clash with the other."[41] Since the nonestablishment clause forbids any governmental assistance to religion, and the free exercise clause mandates governmental accommodation of religion, the two clauses can easily work at cross-purposes. The Court is primarily called upon to adjudicate cases that fall into the ambiguous gray area between the two clauses.[42] Questions such as the following arise when the Court examines the interaction between the free exercise and the nonestablishment clauses. When does proper *accommodation* of religion (permitted under the free exercise clause) become illicit *assistance to* religion (forbidden by the nonestablishment clause)? Under what circumstances can the government legitimately exempt individuals and institutions from responsibilities borne by the rest of the nation's citizens? How broadly or narrowly should "religion" be construed in determining whether an exemption is properly granted on the grounds of the "free exercise of religion?" In permitting institutional accommodations and individual exemptions, how does the government avoid discriminating against those not eligible for such special treatment?

One might have expected that the ambiguity created by the interaction of the two clauses would have forced the Court to seek the common judicial principles guiding the interpretation of both free exercise and establishment cases. On the contrary, the Court has responded to this situation by dealing with the two kinds of cases in isolation from one another. In the process, the Court has created two parallel and independent standards for the adjudication of cases dealing with religion.[43]

Free exercise cases provide the classic example of judicial accommodation. These cases typically arise when a religious practitioner requests exemption from facially neutral regulations on the grounds of religious belief and practice. Thus, in *Sherbert* v. *Verner* the Supreme Court permitted a Seventh-Day Adventist to receive unemployment compensation, even though she was fired for refusing to work on Saturday, her Sabbath.[44] So also in *Wisconsin* v. *Yoder* the Court rejected as unconstitutional the imposition of criminal penalties against Amish parents who refused to send their children to a public high school through age sixteen.[45] In free exercise jurisdiction, the Court has adopted a balancing test by which the interests of the state are weighed against the claimant's right of free exercise. The conflict between governmental regulation and individual free exercise is construed primarily as a contest of *interests*. The religious interests of the individual are to be abridged only if a state interest of the "highest order" can be demonstrated. "Only those interests of the highest order and those not otherwise served can overbalance legitimate claims to the free exercise of religion."[46] The government thus accommodates its interests in order to protect the individual's right of free exercise.

Governmental accommodation on the grounds of free exercise is well established and relatively uncontroversial; however, recent court decisions[47] have broadened the range of accommodation to include "public sphere accommodation of religion."[48] In these cases the court has upheld actions that not only "exempt . . . from generally applicable governmental regulation individuals whose religious beliefs and practices would otherwise thereby be infringed" but also create "an atmosphere in which voluntary religious exercise may flourish."[49] Among the various justifications offered for public sphere accommodation, the most controversial are those stressing the importance of religion among American cultural traditions[50] and the use of religion in providing shared symbols and values for the civil community.[51] These examples of accommodation occur not in the context of free exercise adjudication but under the aegis of establishment review. Despite the use of a common term, however, the Court has chosen to judge these two forms of accommodation by different standards.

Establishment jurisdiction has been decisively influenced by the principles enunciated by then Chief Justice Burger in his 1971 decision in *Lemon* v. *Kurtzman*. Following Justice Black's lead in *Everson*, the Court in *Lemon* adopted a three-pronged test to determine whether a governmental action violates the no-establishment clause. According to the *Lemon* test all government actions must (1) have a "secular purpose," (2) have a "primary effect" that "neither advances nor inhibits" religion, and (3) avoid "excessive governmental entanglement" with religion.[52] Decisions subsequent to *Lemon* have sought to refine and extend this standard, Justice O'Connor's "endorsement test" being the most recent attempt in this regard. All of these criteria seek to define the appropriate limits of the government's involvement in the institutional affairs of religion.

As the discussion in *Allegheny* illustrates, the *Lemon* test has come under increasing fire, from advocates of governmental neutrality and governmental accommodation. Note that the criticisms focus precisely on that murky middle ground created by the interaction of the two religion clauses. The disagreements focus primarily on the question of the appropriate limits for governmental accommodation of religion. The proponents of strict neutrality find that "secular purpose" and "primary effect" inquiries have the inevitable result of involving government in the kind of "excessive entanglement" that *Lemon* was designed to preclude. They argue that government should remain strictly separate from all symbolic and institutional accommodations of religion. Proponents of "passive accommodation" are equally sharp in their criticisms of *Lemon* and its successors, but they base their objections on the conviction that the test's rigid requirements are inherently hostile to religion and to the cultural traditions of the nation. As Justice Kennedy made clear in his dissent in *Allegheny*, the accommodationists would permit a much more supportive relationship between governments and the nation's majority religion.

By dealing with the free exercise and nonestablishment cases in this independent fashion, the Court has avoided the complex but important inquiry into the interplay between the two clauses. It is clear, for example, that if the "secular purpose" prong of the *Lemon* test were consistently applied to free exercise cases nearly every religious accommodation would be ruled unconstitutional.[53] The Court's exemption of conscientious objectors from military service and of Amish schoolchildren from compulsory public education could not withstand scrutiny from the point of view of "secular purpose." Clearly, in granting these exemptions the state is serving an evident religious purpose, namely, the right of persons of faith to live out their convictions, even when their actions conflict with laws applicable to all citizens. Instead of addressing this implicit conflict, however, the Court has been satisfied to continue the practice of separate traditions of jurisprudence for each of the religion clauses. By adopting parallel and independent standards for interpretation, the Court has not only impeded the attempt to develop a consistent set of criteria for first amendment cases; it has also created a heightened and artificial sense of the conflict between the clauses, thereby obscuring the unifying elements that hold them together.[54]

The entire conceptual framework within which the Court operates requires careful reconsideration and reform. The difficulties facing the Court are not sui generis; rather, they derive from fundamental problems in the liberal political philosophy on which the Court regularly draws. In particular, the notion of neutrality, a fundamental concept of liberal philosophy, bedevils every attempt of the Court to develop a consistent and coherent judicial framework for interpretation of the first amendment religion clauses. In the remaining section of this chapter, I will analyze the use of the concept "neutrality" in the Court's adjudication. Then in the subsequent chapter I will broaden my perspective by subjecting the larger liberal tradition to critical scrutiny.

NEUTRALITY: A PROTEAN CONCEPT.   Since 1947 the Court has consistently interpreted the principle of church/state separation through the doctrine of governmental neutrality. It is striking to note that for all of their pointed disputes, the justices writing in Allegheny are clearly agreed that state neutrality toward religion is mandated by the Constitution. While they differ decisively on the meaning and application of the concept, they nonetheless frame their arguments in a fashion that allows them all to remain advocates of governmental neutrality. Clearly, a concept so significant and yet malleable deserves our close attention.55

If we were to recast the three positions identified in *Allegheny* with reference to the justices' stance on neutrality, they could be analyzed as follows: strict neutrality (Brennan, Marshall, Stevens), nondiscriminatory neutrality (Blackmun, O'Connor), benevolent neutrality (Kennedy, Rehnquist, Scalia, White).

*Strict neutrality* mandates governmental *noninvolvement* in religious matters by requiring a consistent *no-aid to religion* policy.56 As Philip Kurland has argued, strict neutrality implies that "government cannot utilize religion as a standard for action or inaction because these clauses prohibit classification in terms of religion either to confer a benefit or to impose a burden."57 On the basis of this doctrine Justice Brennan argued in *Allegheny* that the Constitution requires "neutrality, not just among religions, but between religion and non-religion."

*Nondiscriminatory neutrality* softens the doctrinal purity of the previous position by allowing some public sphere accommodation, providing the symbols or practices supported by government are nonsectarian and nondiscriminatory. This position reads the Constitution as mandating a *no-aid to religion* (or *noninvolvement*) policy whenever sectarian practices are at issue, and an *equal aid to religion* (or *impartiality*) policy when the practices are generally cultural or have a discernible "secular purpose." Advocates of this position are particularly alert to possible discrimination against nonadherents, particularly when the symbols and beliefs of the majority religion are under consideration. Justice O'Connor's "endorsement test" seeks to provide criteria by which the doctrine of nondiscriminatory neutrality can be applied.

*Benevolent neutrality* explicitly seeks to broaden the framework within which religion might be freely exercised by expanding the doctrine of accommodation to include public sphere accommodation. This position interprets the strict neutrality and the no-aid to religion doctrines as implying government hostility toward religion, a policy at odds with "our political and cultural history." Benevolent neutrality proscribes only "governmentally established religion or governmental interference with religion."58 Beyond the "two limiting principles," namely, that government may neither coerce religious belief nor provide direct benefits to religion, government is free to encourage an atmosphere in which the free exercise of religion might flourish. This position further rejects the notion that government must be neutral between religion and nonreligion. Neutrality simply implies governmental *impartiality* in its dealing with various religious groups.

While all three of these positions offer important insight into the complex relation between government and religion, each is subject to serious and perhaps debilitating criticism. The strict neutrality position, while logically consistent, is finally unworkable in practice. The *no-aid to religion* doctrine is simply unfeasible in a democracy in which government regulation affects virtually every aspect of individual and corporate life.[59] Applied consistently, strict neutrality would render government services like fire and police protection unconstitutional. Nothing in the text of the Constitution, or in its interpretive tradition, suggests that religious institutions should be disadvantaged by being denied the benefits available to the general populace. At the same time the strict neutrality position, demanding as it does that government be blind to religious considerations, would prohibit virtually every free exercise claim of religiously motivated litigants.[60] To consider exemptions from facially neutral regulations on the grounds of religious belief, the courts cannot conceivably decide such cases without carefully examining those beliefs. Inevitably the courts will have to make value judgments, for example, concerning the sincerity with which the beliefs are held, but such judgments are unavoidable in free exercise cases. Even if the strict neutrality position worked within the confines of the nonestablishment clause (and I have argued it does not), its limitations in the area of free exercise render it inoperable as a working judicial principle.

It is not clear that benevolent neutrality is really a theory of neutrality at all. This position is most notable for its criticisms, often telling, of other church/state views, but its advocates have focused more on defending the notion of benevolence than explicating the concept of neutrality. Consequently, we know more about what benevolent neutrality is not than what it is. Proponents of this view have been primarily concerned to justify public sphere accommodation and to defend religion against the unwarranted hostility they believe is implied by strict neutrality. While benevolent neutrality clearly rules out governmental coercion and direct government support, it is difficult to discern whether any other limits to public sphere accommodation would be acceptable to its supporters. In particular, defenders of this position have failed utterly to address the question of the possible discriminatory effects of a broadened view of accommodation. If the notion of neutrality is, in part, an attempt to define the conditions for governmental *fairness* in the realm of religion, then it must deal with the question of religious pluralism and the possibility of discrimination. Until the advocates of benevolent neutrality take up this challenge, their position will remain insufficient as an account of proper judicial neutrality.

Nondiscriminatory neutrality is the most inclusive of the views analyzed here, but in seeking to provide a media via the position finally reveals the unresolvable ambiguity inherent in the very notion of neutrality. By seeking to embrace both the *no aid to religion* and the *equal aid to religion* policies, this view displays the irreducible tension between the concepts of "noninvolvement" and "impartiality."[61]

The basic ambiguity of the concept "neutrality" becomes clearer if we adopt an analogy from wartime behavior. A nation can be "neutral" toward two disputants either by refusing to aid any of the contending nations or by assisting all nations equally. For example, Switzerland has maintained a consistent policy of neutrality by refusing both to enter into military alliances with other nations and to send combatants into warfare during hostilities (*no aid*). It has, however, been willing to provide medical supplies and other humanitarian assistance to all parties engaged in hostilities without violating its official policy of neutrality (*equal aid*). Thus Switzerland has exemplified both the "no aid" and the "equal aid" policies associated with neutrality, but it could do so because it is a sovereign and independent nation with no antecedent ties to the nations involved in warfare.

Advocates of nondiscriminatory neutrality apparently assume that the relation between a government and its own citizens is analogous to the relations among sovereign nations. Consequently a government can *seriatim* adopt a policy of no aid or equal aid, depending upon the particular circumstance involved, without losing its claim to neutrality. But clearly a government does not possess the same degree of sovereignty and independence from its own citizens that it possesses in relation to other sovereign nations. Inevitably a government will have a complex pattern of antecedent ties with its own citizens that it need not have in relation to other nations. For this very reason, the no aid policy associated with the *strict neutrality* position simply cannot work in practice, particularly in a highly regulated society like our own. At the same time, the equal aid or impartiality policy appears unworkable because of the Court's limited theological expertise and the inherent dangers of "excessive entanglement" in the affairs of religious institutions. Nondiscriminatory neutrality thus appears to combine the worst features of the noninvolvement and impartiality policies.

Noninvolvement implies governmental isolation from matters of religion, while impartiality implies governmental engagement with religion for the purpose of treating religious groups and individuals fairly and equitably. The two policies thus stand in essential tension with one another, the former supporting the ideal of separation and the latter abetting a policy of accommodation. While the two notions might be brought into coherent relation in practice, the inability of the Court to adopt a consistent standard for adjudication of the religion clauses has made the reconciliation of these two notions of neutrality virtually impossible. The question arises whether neutrality itself is a workable judicial concept for the interpretation of the first amendment. If every attempt to construe neutrality in a consistent fashion is unsuccessful, perhaps the time has come to jettison the concept altogether.

### SUMMARY AND CONCLUSION: THE ESSENTIAL TENSION.

This extended, and somewhat agonizing, tour of judicial reasoning has, I hope, raised serious questions concerning the adequacy of the entire conceptual framework within which the Court seeks to interpret the religion clauses of the first amendment. The conceptual contradictions inherent in the notions of separation, accommodation, and neutrality render them incapable of providing guidance for a reconsideration of the role of religion in American public life. Our investigation of the justices' arguments has not been entirely negative, however, because we have identified the essential tension that bedevils every attempt to provide a coherent interpretation of the two religion clauses.

Two independent but related patterns of reasoning have emerged in the Court's post-*Everson* adjudication. The first pattern, strict separation, begins from the assumption that the independent and autonomous institutions of church and state should be kept rigorously separated. The state, an essentially secular institution, preserves the freedom and equality of all citizens by maintaining *strict neutrality* in its relations with religious and nonreligious groups. Strict neutrality requires a governmental policy of *noninvolvement* in the affairs of religious institutions. Only in those exceptional cases involving the *free exercise* of religion should any *accommodation* of this policy be considered.

The second pattern, mutual cooperation, begins from the assumption that church and state, though independently governed, share a common history and tradition. The state should acknowledge and respect the cultural and religious heritage of its citizens by developing a policy of *benevolent neutrality* toward religious groups. Given the pervasive religious character of the American people, a stance of strict neutrality between religion and nonreligion would lead to practices that are hostile to the beliefs and practices of the majority of the nation's citizens. Therefore neutrality simply requires a policy of *impartiality* in the government's treatment of various religious groups. While the government should never coerce or proselytize, it should seek to encourage widespread *public sphere accommodation* of religious symbols and behavior.

The essential tension reflected in the Court's adjudication of the Constitution's religion clauses is a manifestation of America's basic dilemma regarding the role of religion in public life. The two patterns of reasoning identified above mirror the larger cultural tension, described in chapter 2, between Christianity's legal disestablishment and its cultural and symbolic dominance. The strict separation position seeks to preserve the legacy of legal disestablishment, while often ignoring the patterns of cooperation between church and state created by our history of civic piety and by the expanding regulatory role of the welfare state. The mutual cooperation position seeks to acknowledge and encourage the traditional relation between Christianity and the state, but it does so in a way that ignores the growing religious pluralism of the nation. Consequently, its effort to expand the sphere of public accommodation often appears discriminatory toward those who do not share the religious beliefs of the majority.

The inherent tension between these two patterns of reasoning has yielded such confusion in the Court's decision making because advocates of both positions use the standard constitutional concepts of separation, accommodation, and neutrality. While they employ the same words, they use these concepts for diverse and even contradictory purposes. The Court's tendency to encourage independent standards for adjudicating nonestablishment and free exercise cases has so exacerbated the tension between the two patterns, that the confusion begins to look like sheer chaos. Whatever commonalty may still exist between the two patterns has been masked by the Court's inability to develop a consistent framework for the adjudication of all cases dealing with religion in public life.

I believe that the time has come to reject the entire framework within which the Court has operated since *Everson*. The principle, "the separation of church and state," and the associated concepts, accommodation and neutrality, have been subjected to such diverse and contradictory interpretations that they have been rendered virtually useless for the task of reconstructing a proper concept of the role of religion in public life. The knot of judicial reasoning has become so entangled that even the most dexterous attempts at clarification appear futile. Justice Kennedy's suggestion that "a substantial revision of our Establishment Clause doctrine" is needed surely seems correct, and yet that revision cannot be fruitful if the current categories are allowed to structure the Court's reconsideration of the religion clauses.

The challenge is to develop a new conceptual framework, one that seeks to integrate the concerns of both patterns of reasoning. In subsequent chapters, I will propose a principled way of thinking about religion in public life that will allow the courts, constitutional scholars, and legal practitioners to identify the situations that require separation and those in which cooperation is to be encouraged. Instead of assuming that the two religion clauses make absolute and contradictory claims, the legal profession should seek to determine the common values that both clauses are meant to serve. But to accomplish that task we must recover those values inscribed in the text of the first amendment by the framers of the Constitution. We need to discover the judicial concepts that will provide continuity between the original context in which the Bill of Rights was formulated and the changing historical situation in which the Constitution must be interpreted. But to find that new interpretive ground it will be necessary to move beyond the limitations inherent in the simplistic notion of the "separation of church and state." We need to devise a framework for interpreting the religion clauses that will honor the founders' desire to establish a republic based on liberty, equality, and mutual respect. That interpretive breakthrough might then provide the first essential step toward a basic reconsideration of the place of religion in American society.

# NOTES

**1.** Robert L. Cord, *Separation of Church and State: Historical Fact and Current Fiction* (New York: Lambeth Press, 1982), p. 3.

**2.** "When they opened a gap in the hedge or wall of separation between the garden of the church and the wilderness of the world, God hath ever broke down the wall itself, removed the candlestick, and made his garden a wilderness as at this day." Roger Williams, "Mr. Cotton's Letter," *The Complete Writings of Roger Williams*, vol. 1, edited by Perry Miller (New York: Russell & Russell, 1963), p. 392.

**3.** "I contemplate with sovereign reverence that act of the whole American people which declared that their legislature should 'make no law respecting an establishment of religion or prohibiting the free exercise thereof,' thus building a wall of separation between church and State." Thomas Jefferson, "Letter to the Baptist Association of Danbury, Connecticut," *The Complete Jefferson*, edited by Saul K. Padover (New York: Duell, Sloan, and Pearce, 1943), p. 519.

**4.** "In the words of Jefferson, the clause against establishment of religion by law was intended to erect 'a wall of separation between church and state.'" Hugo Black, *Everson* v. *Board of Education of the Township of Ewing et. al.*, U.S. 330, 15, 16.

**5.** Similar sentiments about the limitations of the rubric "church and state" are expressed by John T. Noonan, Jr., in his casebook *The Believers and the Powers that Are* (New York: MacMillan Publishing Company, 1987), p. xvi.

**6.** One of the sharpest critics of contemporary judicial interpretation of the religion clauses, Robert Cord, still believes that the phrase "separation of Church and State" should be maintained as a helpful summary of the intentions of the republic's founders. "I consider the term 'separation of Church and State' to be a useful one in the extensive dialogue concerning what the Establishment of Religion Clause constitutionally precludes government from doing. Consequently, I have no apprehension about the term itself; however, I do have a very decided quarrel with the way the term has been used." *Separation of Church and State*, p. 114. In contrast to Cord I believe that the term has outlived its usefulness and should be discarded.

**7.** *Everson* v. *Board of Education*, 330 U.S. 1, 16 (February 10, 1947).

**8.** Edwin Meese, Address to the American Bar Association, July 1985, reprinted in *The Great Debate: Interpreting Our Written Constitution* (Federalist Society, 1986).

**9.** Leonard Levy, *The Establishment Clause: Religion and the First Amendment* (New York: MacMillan, 1986), p. 84.

**10.** Philip B. Kurland, "The Religion Clauses and the Burger Court," *Catholic University Law Review*, 34, 1 (Fall 1984): 10.

**11.** Jesse Choper, "The Religion Clauses of the First Amendment: Reconciling the Conflict," *University of Pittsburgh Law Review* 41 (1980): 680.

**12.** Note, "Developments in the Law: Religion and the State," *Harvard Law Review*, 100 (1987):1677

**13.** Howard Ball, "The Separation of Church and State: A Debate," *Utah Law Review,* 4 (1987), p. 919.

**14.** See note 1.

**15.** See Howard Ball's comments in "The Separation of Church and State: A Debate," p. 911.

**16.** The menorah was owned by a Jewish religious organization, but was stored, erected, and removed by the city.

**17.** 403 U.S. 602 (1972).

**18.** 105 S. Ct. 2479 (1985).

**19.** *Allegheny County v. Greater Pittsburgh ACLU,* 109 S. Ct. 493 (1988).

**20.** *Epperson v. Arkansas,* 89 S. Ct. 266 (1968).

**21.** *Accord, Texas Monthly, Inc. v. Bullock,* 109 S. Ct. 890.

**22.** *Marsh v. Chambers,* 103 S. Ct. 3330 (1983).

**23.** 465 U.S. 668 (1984).

**24.** *Allegheny,* 535. This charge was first introduced by former Chief Justice Burger in his dissenting opinion in *Wallace v. Jaffree* 105 S. Ct. 2479 (1985) at 86.

**25.** In his dissenting opinion Justice Kennedy expressed similar worries. "This Court is ill-equipped to sit as a national theology board, and I question both the wisdom and the constitutionality of its doing so." *Allegheny,* 550.

**26.** "Memorial and Remonstrance Against Religious Assessments, 1785."

**27.** For a much more sophisticated account of how particular religious practices might be rightly encouraged by a genuinely neutral government, see Donald A. Giannella, "Religious Liberty, Nonestablishment, and Doctrinal Development. Part II: The Nonestablishment Principle," *Harvard Law Review,* 81,3 (January 1968): 513-90.

**28.** For an excellent study of such homogenized civil religion, see John M. Cuddihy, *No Offense: Civil Religion and Protestant Taste* (New York: Seabury Press, 1978).

**29.** Quoting Justice Goldberg in *Schempp v. Abingdon.*

**30.** See chapter 2.

**31.** In one of his many insightful comments, Justice Brennan notes that the holiday display outside the city/county building is hardly as "pluralistic" as Justice O'Connor had suggested. "Winter is '*the* holiday season' to Christians, not to Jews, and the implicit message that it, rather than autumn, is the time for pluralism sends an impermissible signal that only holidays stemming from Christianity, not those arising from other religions, favorably disposed the government towards 'pluralism'" (525, note). Justice Kennedy's practice of equating religion with Christianity would a fortiori be subject to similar criticisms.

**32.** In his dissenting opinion, Justice Kennedy accuses the majority of lending "its assistance to an Orwellian rewriting of history." *Allegheny,* 550. In response Justice Blackmun accuses Kennedy of slipping "into a form of Orwellian newspeak when he equates the constitutional command of secular government with a prescribed orthodoxy." *Allegheny,* 506.

**33.** *Everson v. Board of Education,* 330 U.S. 1, 15, 16 (1947).

**34.** Ibid., p. 18.

**35.** *Abingdon* v. *Schempp*, 374 U.S. at 203, 225.

**36.** *McCollum* v. *Board of Education*, 333 U.S. at 203, 212.

**37.** *Abingdon*, at 225 (1963).

**38.** *Epperson* v. *Arkansas*, 393 U.S. 97 (1968).

**39.** *Wallace* v. *Jaffree*, 105 S. Ct. 2479, 2491 (1985).

**40.** Among the many discussions of this issue see, especially Jesse Choper, "The Religion Clauses of the First Amendment: Reconciling the Conflict," *University of Pittsburgh Law Review* 41, 4 (Summer 1980): 673-701; Michael A. Paulsen, "Religion, Equality, and the Constitution: An Equal Protection Approach to Establishment Clause Adjudication," *Notre Dame Law Review* 61,3 (1986): 311-371; and Note, "Developments in the Law: Religion and the State," *Harvard Law Review* 100:7 (1987), esp. pp. 1631-75.

**41.** *Walz* v. *Tax Commission of the City of New York* 397 U.S. 664 (1970), at 668-669.

**42.** As *Allegheny* illustrates, the justices face their most difficult challenges when free exercise considerations impinge on establishment cases. On its face *Allegheny* presents a simple question, namely, does the display of Christian and Jewish religious symbols on or near government property constitute a violation of the no-establishment clause of the first amendment? In order to answer that question, however, the justices were forced to consider the situation of those citizens who are not adherents of the religious traditions under examination. As Madison clearly saw, establishment cases inevitably raise the question of the relation between majority and minority faiths in a religiously plural democracy. To ask whether a governmental action discriminates against nonadherents is to inquire concerning the nonadherents' right to free exercise. Justice O'Connor's strained attempt to develop an "objective observer" theory to adjudicate claims of discrimination would have been unnecessary if the Court had adopted a unified approach to religion clause interpretation.

**43.** In her concurring opinion in *Wallace* v. *Jaffree*, 472 U.S. 38, 67-68, Justice O'Connor noted that "a distinct jurisprudence has enveloped each of these Clauses." Justice Stewart in his concurring opinion in *Sherbert* v. *Verner*, 374 U.S. 398, 416 (1963) noted the conflict between establishment and free exercise standards and urged the Court to abandon "the resounding but fallacious fundamentalist rhetoric of . . . Establishment Clause opinions." In a similar vein, Justice Rehnquist issued a call for consistent religion clause jurisprudence in his dissent in *Thomas* v. *Review Board*, 450 U.S. 707, 726 (1981). Thus far, the Court has not taken up this challenge.

**44.** 374 U.S. 398 (1963).

**45.** *Wisconsin* v. *Yoder*, 406 U.S. 205.

**46.** Ibid. at 215.

**47.** Especially *McDaniel* v. *Paty*, 435 U.S. 618 (1978), *Marsh* v. *Chambers* (1983) and *Lynch* v. *Donnelly* (1984).

**48.** See Note, "Developments in the Law: Religion and the State," 1641-1659.

**49.** Justice Brennan in a concurring opinion in *McDaniel*.

**50.** Writing for the majority in *Lynch*, Chief Justice Burger offered the following comments. "There are countless . . . illustrations of the Government's acknowledgment of our religious heritage and governmental sponsorship of graphic manifestations of that heritage. . . . Equally pervasive is the evidence of accommodation of all faiths and all forms of religious expression and hostility toward none. Through this accommodation . . . governmental action has follow[ed] the best of our traditions and 'respected[ed] the religious nature of our people.'" *Lynch*, at 677-678.

**51.** In her concurring opinion in *Lynch*, Justice O'Connor offered the following observations: "The creche is a traditional symbol of the holiday that is very commonly displayed along with purely secular symbols. . . . These features combine to make the government's display of the creche in this particular physical setting no more an endorsement of religion than such governmental 'acknowledgments' of religion as legislative prayers . . . government declaration of Thanksgiving as a public holiday, printing of "In God We Trust" on coins, and opening court sessions with 'God save the United States and this honorable court.' These governmental acknowledgments of religion serve, in the only ways reasonably possible in our culture, the legitimate secular purposes of solemnizing public occasions, expressing confidence in the future, and encouraging the recognition of what is worthy of appreciation in society." *Lynch* at 692-693.

**52.** *Lemon* v. *Kurtzman*, 403 U.S., 612-613 (1971).

**53.** Cf. Jesse Choper, "The Religion Clauses of the First Amendment: Reconciling the Conflict," p. 685.

**54.** "Religion clause doctrine since the 1940's has exaggerated the difference between the two clauses, creating a bifurcated jurisprudence of the clauses whose operation obscures the principal values underlying them." Note, "Developments in the Law: Religion and the State," *Harvard Law Review*, p. 1639.

**55.** Laurence Tribe has identified four distinct aspects inherent in the principle of neutrality: strict neutrality, political neutrality, denominational neutrality, and free exercise neutrality. Although I do not employ his categories in my analysis, I have found his discussion very useful. Laurence Tribe, *American Constitutional Law,* 2d edition, (Mineola, New York: The Foundation Press, Inc, 1988), pp. 1188-1201.

**56.** Tribe argues that "the Court has never adopted the so-called 'strict neutrality theory,' which would prohibit government from using religious classifications either to confer benefits or impose burdens." Ibid., p. 1167. While the Court may never have "adopted" the theory, it is clear that some of the justices regularly employ the theory's logic in arguing for or against a particular accommodation.

**57.** Philip Kurland, "Of Church and State and the Supreme Court," 20 *University of Chicago Law Review*, 20:6.

**58.** Chief Justice Burger in *Walz* v. *Tax Commission of the City of New York* 397 U.S. 664 (1970).

**59.** The classic discussion of this issue is Donald A. Giannella, "Religious Liberty, Nonestablishment, and Doctrinal Development." Giannella seeks to separate the strict neutrality doctrine from the no-aid to religion strategy, but I find his attempt unpersuasive. For the purposes of my argument I am assuming that "strict neutrality," in the sense I am using it here, logically implies "no aid to religion."

**60.** "The neutrality principle produces hostility to religion by flatly prohibiting all solely religious exemptions from general regulations no matter how greatly they burden religious exercise and no matter how insubstantial the competing state interest may be. In advancing the admirable goals of government neutrality and impartiality, it downgrades the positive value that both Religious Clauses assign to religious liberty." Jesse Choper, "The Religion Clauses of the First Amendment: Reconciling the Conflict," p. 688.

**61.** I have been assisted in my thinking about this problem by John T. Valauri's fine article "The Concept of Neutrality in Establishment Clause Doctrine," *University of Pittsburgh Law Review* 48,1 (Fall 1986): 83-151. Valauri argues that the concept of neutrality, as developed by the Court, is internally inconsistent. The two principle aspects of the concept, noninvolvement and impartiality, cannot be consistently combined; therefore, the Court is doomed to a pattern of contradictory and arbitrary adjudication. Valauri shows how this problem first surfaced in Justice Black's puzzling decision in *Everson* in which he both enunciated the principle of judicial neutrality and ruled that the New Jersey statute allowing state funds to be used for busing children to parochial schools did not violate the establishment clause. In asserting the principle of judicial neutrality Justice Black employed a "noninvolvement" or "no aid to religion" interpretation of neutrality. In deciding the particular case, however, he invoked the "impartiality" or "equal aid to religion" sense of neutrality. Despite having asserted the basic principle of church/state separation, Justice Black was unwilling to apply it rigorously to the case at hand. If he had, he would have denied to these particular schoolchildren the general benefit available to other citizens of the state, thereby discriminating against them on the basis of their religion. While the principle of church/state separation appeared clear, its application became immediately problematic.

# 4

# *Political Liberalism and Public Religion*

## THE UNDERLYING VALUES: LIBERTY, EQUALITY, AND TOLERATION

In the previous chapter I have shown that the metaphor "the separation of church and state" and its attendant concepts "neutrality and accommodation" fail to provide a coherent framework for the interpretation of the first amendment religion clauses. Neither of the two predominant patterns of judicial reasoning, strict separation or mutual cooperation, captures the subtlety and insight of the rationale the founders devised for the free exercise and nonestablishment clauses.

In seeking to construct a new and broader conceptual framework, we must inquire not only about the founders' intent but also about the values they sought to inscribe in the text of the first amendment. We need to identify those values and determine their degree of applicability in the changed historical conditions under which we live.[1] To begin that task we must return to the reflections of the first amendment's chief framer, James Madison.

REPRISE: MADISON'S "REMONSTRANCE." The basic concern that animated Madison's reflection on the role of religion in the new republic was to protect the right of freedom of conscience. The principle that guided his thinking was derived from the Virginia Declaration of Rights, article 16, which asserted that all persons retain an "equal right to the free exercise of Religion according to the dictates of conscience." Madison extended the rationale of the Declaration, however, by providing an explicitly *theological* basis for his assertion of the fundamental right of the free exercise of religion. That religion "must be left to the conviction and conscience of every man" is a notion ultimately grounded in "a duty towards the Creator. It is the duty of every man to render to the Creator such homage, and such only, as he believes to be acceptable to him." Since "this duty is precedent both in order of time and degree of obligation to the claims of Civil Society," religion remains "wholly exempt from its cognizance." Moreover, since the "unalienable right" of freedom of conscience is granted to "every man" by the Creator, the *"equal* right of free exercise of Religion" follows ineluctably. Finally, if all are free and equal, then no expression of religious sentiment can be abridged or restricted; all religious expressions of the dictates of conscience are to be tolerated.

The basic philosophical structure of Madison's argument is as follows: Liberty or freedom is the fundamental human characteristic, the trait that defines essential human nature. A right is that which a human being is owed in virtue of his or her freedom; rights flow ineluctably from liberty. Conscience is that organ of judgment through which an individual determines those dictates that will guide his or her beliefs and actions. Conscience is genuinely free when an individual makes such judgments without undue interference or coercion from others. The free exercise of religion is, Madison argues, "an unalienable right . . . because what is here a right towards men, is a duty toward the Creator." Human beings have a duty to render "homage" to the Creator, but the nature and content of that homage can only be such as they "believe acceptable to God" and in accord with the "evidence contemplated by their own minds." The free conscience thus has a duty or obligation to God, but that duty cannot be forced or coerced; the homage due to the Creator must be freely given.[2] The free exercise of religion, therefore, is the uncoerced fulfillment of a human obligation to the Creator.

The basic political values that Madison sought to have inscribed in the First Amendment are those of *liberty, equality, and toleration.* Both the free exercise and the no-establishment clauses reflect these three basic values. The free exercise of religion is an essential expression of fundamental human liberty, granted equally to all persons by virtue of their equal status before the Creator, to be exercised in whatever fashion the individual's conscience deems appropriate. All expressions of religion genuinely grounded in conscience are to be tolerated, and no expression is to be proscribed or coerced by any external agency. In particular, since religious exercise is grounded in divine obligation, the claims of civil society on the believer's conscience must always be limited. An established religion will inevitably violate all three values identified above, for the religion of the majority if joined to the power of government will constitute a threat to the religions of minority populations. If citizens are to be free and equal in the exercise of religion, then it follows that no particular faith or creed can be the preferred religion of the republic. An established religion denies the freedom of some, the equality of all, and threatens minority faiths with intolerance. For all these reasons the no-establishment clause flows directly from the values of freedom, equality, and toleration.

Two important issues emerge from this analysis of the basic values underlying the two religion clauses of the first amendment. First, since the same three values provide the basis for both religion clauses, the Supreme Court's practice of adopting independent traditions of adjudication for those clauses is simply indefensible. The Court must recapture the principles that will provide a unified and consistent tradition of first amendment interpretation. Second, those who believe that the principle of the separation of church and state mandates the removal of religion from the public sphere must deal with the fact that Madison's argument securing those basic first amendment rights is overtly theological. Any contemporary secular defense of constitutional democracy that seeks to secure the status of first amendment rights by eliminating this theological rationale must contain an argument that provides (1) a philosophical or political basis sufficiently strong to secure the inalienable character of those rights, and (2) a plausible explanation for the removal of religious justifications from public argumentation. This case against public religion or theology must confront the strong historical tradition that legitimizes the use of theological arguments in defense of the constitutional values of freedom, equality, and toleration.

## POLITICAL LIBERALISM AND THE "MYTH OF NEUTRALITY"

The most prominent contemporary defenses of the constitutional values of freedom, equality, and toleration have been developed by advocates of a position most accurately called "political liberalism." Philosophers like John Rawls, Ronald Dworkin, Bruce Ackerman, Amy Gutmann, and William Galston have sought to restate the basic principles of liberal political thought for a secular pluralistic society. The major assumptions of this political position have been nicely summarized by the Catholic moral theologian, David Hollenbach. Contemporary interpreters of liberalism:

1. . . . take as the fundamental norm of social morality the right of every person to equal concern and respect.
2. . . . are committed to organizing the basic political, economic, and social structure of society in a way that will insure that society is a fair system of cooperation between free and equal persons.
3. . . . are specially sensitive to the pluralism of modern moral and political life. Because free and equal persons hold different and sometimes conflicting philosophical, moral, and religious convictions about the full human good, an effort to implement a comprehensive vision of the good society through law or state power is excluded. Such an effort would violate some persons' right to equal concern and respect. This perspective is summarized by affirming that the right is prior to the good.
4. Because persons cannot be said to deserve the circumstances of their birth, such as special talents or economic advantages, the tendency of these circumstances to lead to disproportionate outcomes must be counteracted by appropriate societal intervention.[3]

It is important to note that these interpreters of liberalism believe that the fundamental values of freedom, equality, and toleration are best preserved if religion is removed from public affairs. The defenders of political liberalism are virtually unanimous in their staunch advocacy of the "wall of separation between church and state."[4] They believe that both religious practice and pluralistic democracy are best preserved by a constitutional system that precludes religious argumentation within the public realm. According to Rawls, "religious, philosophical, and moral convictions . . . are part of what we call [persons'] 'nonpublic identity,'" matters that citizens may deal with in their 'personal affairs.'"[5] If religion enters the public arena, it inevitably precipitates the kind of irresolvable conflict that is the bane of a democratic political order. If religion is confined to the private realm, its beliefs and convictions can continue to shape personal behavior without, however, disturbing the public peace.

Why are the contemporary apologists for political liberalism so adamant in their conviction that religion must be consigned solely to the private realm? This question is particularly important, since contemporary political liberals think of themselves as the proper heirs to the political and philosophical traditions of the framers of the Constitution. Yet many of these liberals' intellectual forebears explicitly used theological arguments in devising their rationale for a democratic regime of free and equal citizens. Why then do those who defend the framers' democratic legacy argue that such public theological arguments are inimical to democratic constitutional governments?[6]

Most liberal theorists base their opposition to public religion on a larger rationale concerning the place of "conceptions of the good" within contemporary political life. Religions are ways of believing and acting that entail the pursuit of a particular understanding of the conditions necessary for genuine human flourishing. Religions, like other substantive moral and philosophical views, presuppose that the form of life they recommend provides the ultimate path to human fulfillment and happiness. In modern societies, such views are irreducibly manifold and diverse, and since they recommend unique avenues of access to the final end or ultimate good, they will inevitably be contentious and conflictual. If then governments are to treat citizens in a fair and equitable manner, they cannot show preference for any of these diverse conceptions of the good. Consequently, a liberal government will adopt a posture of "neutrality" toward all substantive religious, moral, and philosophical views.[7] According to Ronald Dworkin, "government must be neutral on what might be called questions of the good life. . . . Political decisions must be independent of any conception of the good life or what gives value to life."[8] Adding further specification to this claim, Dworkin argues that government "must be neutral in one particular way: among conceptions of the good life. Whatever we may think privately, it cannot count as a justification for some rule of law or some political institution, that a life that includes reading pornography or homosexual relationships is either better or worse than the life of someone with more orthodox tastes in reading or sex. Or that a life suffused with religion is better or worse than a wholly secular life."[9] The separation of church and state follows ineluctably from this principle of neutrality. While persons should be wholly free in their personal private lives to espouse or reject religion, religious premises should play no role in the public deliberations of a just liberal government.

In chapter 3, I argued that the concept of neutrality cannot be given coherent self-consistent formulation within the Supreme Court's deliberations regarding first amendment issues. Not surprisingly, the notion of neutrality fares little better in the hands of its liberal philosophical defenders. As I have already shown, the concept of neutrality applies only to those situations in which government either refuses to adjudicate an issue between contending parties (noninvolvement) or adjudicates that issue in a manner that transcends the particular moral concepts employed by those parties (impartiality). The first sense of neutrality is both conceptually coherent and practicable when applied to a limited range of cases. When the Court, for example, refuses to intervene in a doctrinal dispute within a religious organization, it declares its neutrality by defining doctrinal issues as beyond its sphere of competence. This limited notion of neutrality seems both philosophically and politically unproblematic.[10] When liberal theorists employ the term neutrality, however, they are referring primarily to the second sense, the requirement that political decisions be "independent of any conception of the good life or of that which gives values to life."

But how can government adjudicate controversial moral or political issues while prescinding entirely from all notions of "good" or "value"? What might it mean for the Court to be "neutral" or "impartial" on matters like abortion or pornography? The contending parties in such situations often propose conflicting public policies that emerge from their particular conceptions of the good. Opponents of abortion, for example, believe that the induced termination of pregnancy is, in most cases, the taking of innocent life. Since they hold a notion of the good in which the life of the innocent is to be especially protected, they support highly restrictive abortion laws. Supporters of permissive abortion laws, on the contrary, might hold a conception of the good in which the human freedom to determine one's own destiny, and particularly a woman's freedom to determine the use of her own body, is most highly valued. It is inconceivable that the courts could intervene in such a moral dispute while remaining neutral regarding these conflicting notions of the good.

To adjudicate such cases of moral conflict, the Court must evaluate which notion of the good possesses greater value for a pluralistic democratic society. Equitable adjudication requires the Court not to prescind from moral deliberation but to engage in careful persuasive moral argumentation. Claims to neutrality serve to obscure rather than clarify these important public issues. The bitter and divisive political debates that have ensued in the aftermath of *Roe* v. *Wade* show that the Court did, indeed, favor one of these competing conceptions of the good in reaching its decision. An assertion that the Court remained neutral in this case is an affront to the moral seriousness of all the contending parties.

Similar issues arise in public policies dealing with pornography. Those who support laws sharply limiting the sale and distribution of pornographic materials hold to a conception of the good that proscribes manipulative, abusive, and humiliating behavior in human relationships. Believing that exposure to pornography encourages the proscribed forms of behavior, they seek to restrict access to these materials. Those who oppose such restrictive laws argue from a conception of the good that values freedom to choose so highly that they find any restriction on reading material to be an unacceptable act of censorship. While they may find the activities depicted in pornographic materials morally repugnant, they believe that the social costs of censorship outweigh those of permitting the sale of pornographic materials.[11] A court or legislature faced with the question of whether to restrict the sale and distribution of pornographic materials cannot conceivably remain neutral between these two conceptions of the good. Public officials must enter the moral fray and offer arguments concerning the goods to be most highly valued in a pluralistic society.

The notion that governmental agencies must remain morally neutral has had a dual consequence within American politics. First, by fostering a view of the courts as institutions "beyond good and evil," the liberal conception of neutrality has encouraged the judiciary to be more concerned about procedures and process than about moral substance. Consequently, the justices have become reluctant to engage in serious moral deliberation. As our analysis of the Court's decision in *Bowers* v. *Hardwick* has indicated, when a case with an inescapable ethical issue does arise, the justices' moral reasoning is often flawed and even tendentious.

Second, the notion of governmental neutrality also contributes to the social strife that is so regularly occasioned by controversial moral issues. When, under the guise of neutrality, government actually prefers one conception of the good over another, it misleads the public concerning government's roles in the adjudication of volatile moral and political matters. When, as in *Roe* v. *Wade* or *Bowers* v. *Hardwick*, the Court does in fact favor a particular notion of the good, the "myth of neutrality" undermines the Court's ability to serve as a model for careful moral reasoning within a pluralistic democracy. The gap between the appearance of neutrality and the reality of moral preference inevitably contributes to the growing public suspicion about deception in government. When such suspicions are directed toward the nation's supreme judicatory institution, then the overall health of the body politic may well be in jeopardy.[12]

Defenders of contemporary liberalism would dispute the analysis I have just offered, claiming that in the situations I have cited (abortion and pornography), the courts are not choosing between two notions of the good. Rather, they would argue, the courts are acting in proper liberal fashion by giving "priority of the right over the good." In the case of pornography, government should protect the "right of free speech" even though the distribution of pornography may have deleterious social consequences. Stated more accurately: "the priority of the right over the good" is really an assertion about the priority of liberty within a pluralistic democracy. According to liberal political theory individual liberty should never be constrained by a particular conception of the good unless there is a clear and overriding danger to the public welfare.

This assertion of the priority of liberty within a pluralistic democracy may indeed be a defensible claim, but it in no way implies the notion of governmental "neutrality." In addition, the primacy of liberty does not imply that the concept of "right" is conceptually independent of all concepts of "good." Indeed, as our analysis of Madison's position has indicated, the notion of "inalienable rights" as developed by the framers clearly depended on a particular theological understanding of the good, namely, that all human beings have an obligation to return "homage" to the Creator. So also the "right to self-determination" and the "right of free speech" rely on basic concepts of the conditions necessary for genuine human flourishing. As I argued at the outset of this chapter, rights are those constitutional guarantees that protect the defining trait of human nature, freedom or self-determination. Liberty is thus a "good" (and, when linked to equality, the primary good) inherent in liberal democratic polity.

But to pretend that the defense of liberty is an exercise in "neutrality" seems an act of folly. Surely the case for liberty is not enhanced by the assertion that governmental "decisions must be . . . independent of any conception of the good life, or of what gives value to life." Rather, the case for the primacy of liberty depends on a particular conception of "what gives value to life," a conception that liberals believe essential for the well-being of a pluralistic democracy. But that case needs to be restated for each generation through the development of persuasive moral arguments. By fostering the view that political decision making transcends moral deliberation, the "myth of neutrality" actually undermines the liberal goal of creating a pluralistic democracy comprising free and equal citizens.

## POLITICAL LIBERALISM: BEYOND THE MYTH OF NEUTRALITY

Is it possible for liberal political theory to be developed independently of the "myth of neutrality?" Can contemporary liberalism develop a framework for democratic politics in a pluralistic culture that provides a coherent restatement of the values of freedom, equality, and toleration? And what will be the fate of religion in this contemporary version of political liberalism?

Among the major representatives of liberal political theory, John Rawls has developed the most carefully nuanced answers to these questions. Rawls's position is particularly significant because he has developed a rigorous but modest understanding of political justice that seeks simply to identify "certain fundamental intuitive ideas viewed as latent" within "the basic structure of a constitutional democratic regime."[13] Rawls distinguishes his "political" liberalism from the "philosophical" or "comprehensive" liberalism associated with Immanuel Kant or John Stuart Mill. Political liberalism, unlike the latter, makes no "claims to universal truth or claims about the essential nature and identity of persons."[14] Political liberalism merely attempts to make explicit the basic structure of a democratic constitutional government understood as a fair system of cooperation between free and equal citizens. Rawls's conception of liberalism should not be viewed as a metaphysical system or comprehensive world view in competition with religious or theological schemes. Rather, as a descriptive inquiry into the basic structure of constitutional democracy, political liberalism should harbor no implicit philosophical bias against religion or theology.[15]

Nonetheless, Rawls argues against the introduction of overt theological and religious arguments into political debate within a democratic society, because he believes that such arguments can undermine the attempt to achieve consensus in a pluralistic democracy. "Religious . . . conceptions tend to be general and fully comprehensive. . . . A doctrine is fully comprehensive when it covers all recognized values and virtues within one rather precisely articulated scheme of thought."[16] If democratic government is indeed a fair system of cooperation between free and equal citizens, then inevitably a diversity of beliefs and forms of behavior will emerge within democratic culture.

Free citizens will adopt various moral doctrines, life plans, and conceptions of the good and seek to pursue their own happiness in diverse and even conflicting ways. This "fact of pluralism" is, Rawls argues, a "permanent feature of the public culture of modern democracies."[17] Consequently, no moral doctrine or conception of the good pursued by particular groups of citizens could conceivably serve as the unifying scheme for democratic society as a whole. Indeed, "a public and workable agreement on a single general and comprehensive conception could be maintained only by the oppressive use of state power."[18] No comprehensive scheme—whether philosophical, moral, or religious—can gain the agreement needed to establish a fair cooperative society comprising so many diverse beliefs. Thus, such comprehensive schemes should be removed from *the realm of the political*, though they may be allowed to flourish within the personal and associational lives of citizens.

We need to look more carefully at this important argument against public religion and theology. Rawls develops his view of a just, liberal, and democratic polity in two stages. First he seeks to discern and describe "certain fundamental intuitive ideas . . . implicit in the political culture of a democratic society."[19] Among these intuitive ideas, two are of particular importance: "the idea of society as a fair system of social cooperation. . . and the idea of citizens as free and equal persons."[20] Such ideas, he claims, do not presuppose any of the particular comprehensive schemes that might be held by citizens; rather, these ideas inhere in the *"basic structure* of a constitutional democratic regime."[21] Rawls describes this first stage as the working out of "a free-standing political (but of course moral) conception for the basic structure of society."[22] In using the term "free-standing," Rawls is claiming that the ideas inherent in the basic structure of democratic society are conceptually independent from any substantive metaphysical, moral, or religious scheme.[23] Thus the "fundamental intuitive ideas" of constitutional democratic politics ought to be presented without any reference to religious notions.

After the basic structure of constitutional government has been described, the political philosopher must then address a perennial problem of diverse democratic societies. The "fact of pluralism" not only renders any particular comprehensive scheme incapable of providing the fundamental basis for democratic politics; the multiplicity of competing moral, philosophical, and religious schemes also produces an inherent instability within democratic regimes. How can any single account of the liberal democratic state gain the allegiance of those free and equal citizens whose lives are shaped by different and often conflicting conceptions of the good? How can citizens who genuinely disagree on fundamental moral and religious principles reach some degree of rational agreement regarding issues of public policy?

As we have seen, most philosophers of political liberalism have argued that democratic government gains the support of a diverse citizenry by remaining "neutral" with regard to all particular conceptions of the good. Most commonly, these philosophers suggest that governmental neutrality is preserved by a "purely procedural" conception of justice, that is, a view of justice in which government provides fair procedures by which individual and group interests can vie with one another in the free marketplace. But government must prescind from making any judgments concerning the validity or truth of those contending claims if it is to remain genuinely neutral and thereby just.

In contrast to other liberal theorists, Rawls does not employ the term "neutrality," because "some of its connotations are highly misleading, while others suggest altogether impracticable principles."[24] Rather, Rawls argues that the problem of political instability is best addressed through the notion of "an overlapping consensus, that is, a consensus in which [a regulative political conception of justice] is affirmed by the opposing religious, philosophical, and moral doctrines."[25] If a genuine political consensus is to be built, democratic governments cannot occupy an imagined place of neutral transcendence above the fray of contending substantive points of view; rather, such governments must discover the "common ground" present among those who hold diverse and conflicting comprehensive schemes.[26] For such a consensus to form, the conception of justice must be *distinguished from* all comprehensive schemes and *be accepted by* persons who hold those schemes. Thus, the notion of justice developed within political liberalism must both *separate* religion (understood as a comprehensive scheme) from politics and *relate* religion to politics, if an overlapping consensus is to be built.

The perennial question regarding religion's role in American public life reemerges in the context of Rawls's theory of justice as fairness. If religious belief and practice are wholly separated from public and political life, how can our political ideas, values, and institutions gain the allegiance of a religiously committed and motivated citizenry? If a substantial number of citizens in a constitutional democracy are motivated by religious convictions, then those beliefs will influence the character and degree of their commitment to democratic ideals. Even if their comprehensive religious beliefs cannot serve as the fundamental principles for democratic politics, those beliefs must bear some positive relation to a political conception of justice if a genuine "overlapping consensus" is to be formed within a diverse, but religiously committed, populace.

Religion, according to Rawls, is part of the broad "background culture" of civil society. Institutions like churches, universities, clubs, and learned societies contribute to the social and cultural tradition within which an overlapping consensus must be formed. The types of reasoning and discourse developed within these institutions is properly termed social not political discourse, since "the political" refers only to the free-standing basic structure of a constitutional democracy.[27] If a pluralistic society is to achieve a stable consensus, it will be necessary for citizens to "endorse" the fundamental structure of the democratic regime. Inevitably, citizens will draw upon their comprehensive schemes in devising justifications for their support of the fundamental principles of democracy, but once they have given their endorsement, they come to recognize that those principles are, nonetheless, free-standing.[28] "The political conception may be simply a part of, or an adjunct to, a partially comprehensive view; or it may be endorsed because it can be derived within a fully articulated comprehensive doctrine. It is left to citizens individually to decide for themselves in what way their shared political conception is related to their wider and comprehensive views."[29] Still, *within* the realm of the political, the fundamental principles of democracy must take precedence over the convictions of comprehensive schemes.

> A society is well-ordered by a political conception of justice so long as, first, citizens who affirm reasonable but opposing comprehensive doctrines belong to an overlapping consensus: that is, they generally endorse that conception of justice as giving the content of their political judgments; and second, unreasonable comprehensive doctrines (these, we assume, always exist) do not gain enough currency to compromise the essential justice.[30]

When the values of political justice and those of a particular comprehensive scheme conflict, the former "have sufficient weight to override *all other values* that may come into conflict with them."[31]

The distinction Rawls draws between reasonable and unreasonable comprehensive schemes is particularly important. A liberal democracy is patient of a wide range of reasonable comprehensive schemes that "are not simply the upshot of self- and class interests, or of a peoples' understandable tendency to view the political world from a limited standpoint."[32] People who espouse reasonable schemes are open to the persuasive discourse essential to democratic politics. Reasonableness is a high moral value in democracies, since the exercise of political power always involves coercion. The legitimacy of a democratic regime depends on the appropriate exercise of power— "in accordance with a constitution the essentials of which all citizens as free and equal may reasonably be expected to endorse in the light of principles and ideals acceptable to their common human reason."[33] As an example of an *unreasonable* political view, Rawls points to the religious doctrine *extra ecclesia nullum salus*. "If it is said that outside the church there is no salvation, and therefore a constitutional regime cannot be accepted unless it is unavoidable . . . we say that such a doctrine is unreasonable; it proposes to use the public's political power . . . to enforce a view bearing on constitutional essentials about which citizens as reasonable persons are bound to differ uncompromisingly."[34]

Rawls buttresses this distinction between reasonable and unreasonable schemes by defining the "conditions of publicity" essential for civil debate within a liberal democracy.[35] The principle of legitimacy quoted above entails a commitment to use only "public reason" when debating fundamental matters of constitutional democracy.

As we have said, on matters of constitutional essentials and basic justice, the basic structure and its public policies are to be justifiable to all citizens, as the principle of political legitimacy requires. We add to this that in making these justifications we are to appeal only to presently accepted general beliefs and forms of reasoning found in common sense, and the methods and conclusions of science when these are not controversial. . . . As far as possible, the knowledge and ways of reasoning that ground our affirming the principles of justice and their application to constitutional essentials and basic justice are to rest on the plain truths now widely accepted, or available, to citizens generally. Otherwise, the political conception would not provide a public basis of justification.[36]

While the use of public reason is mandated of governmental offi-cials—especially of judges and justices ("public reason is the sole rea-son the court exercises"), the idea extends as well to "citizens when they engage in political advocacy in the public forum. . . . Thus, the ideal of public reason not only governs the public discourse of elec-tions insofar as the issues involve those fundamental questions, but also how citizens are to cast their vote on these questions."[37]

How does religion fare against this criterion of public reason? Can religious arguments pass muster before Rawls's conditions of publicity, or must these arguments remain "nonpublic," relegated to their proper sphere of civil society? Rawls's position on the place of re-ligion in public life has changed considerably over the course of his writings. In *A Theory of Justice*, Rawls's treatment of religion was al-most always negative. Religion was most often invoked to exemplify an "unreasonable comprehensive scheme." In *Theory* Rawls argued that religious beliefs, when granted public status, almost always un-dermine the third basic value of a constitutional government: *tolerance*. He pointed, for example, to Aquinas's argument that the state ought to impose "the death penalty for heretics on the grounds that it is a far graver matter to corrupt the faith, which is the life of the soul, than to counterfeit money which sustains life. So if it is just to put to death forgers and other criminals, heretics may a fortiori be similarly dealt with."[38] Rawls also referred to the Reformers' "theory of persecution" and concluded that "with Aquinas and the Protestant Reformers the grounds of intolerance are themselves a matter of faith. . . . Where the suppression of liberty is based upon theological principles or matters of faith, no argument is possible."[39] Those who reason on the basis of theology or faith rely on "premises . . . [that] cannot be established by modes of reasoning commonly recognized."[40]

In his more recent *Political Liberalism*, however, Rawls provides a positive and more nuanced view of the role religious arguments (as well as arguments drawn from other comprehensive schemes) might play in public life. In a well-ordered society in which fundamental rights are secured and no injustices are perpetrated, the standard for all political discourse ought to be public reason. But in a situation in which the application of fundamental principles to specific cases is in doubt, or in which "there is a profound division about constitutional essen-tials," then an appeal to "comprehensive reasons" may be justified as long as such an appeal is necessary to "strengthen the ideal of public reason itself."[41] Thus, the abolitionists or the leaders of the civil rights movement did not violate the standard of public reason, because their use of religious arguments was "required to give sufficient strength to the political conception to be subsequently realized."[42]

Rawls's position marks an important advance beyond those liberal theorists who propose a simple and rigorous "separation of church and state," one that prohibits all religious discourse within public affairs.[43] In a well-ordered society all arguments would ideally be posed in language derived from the society's "common knowledge" and "shared practices of inquiry," because such arguments maximize the probability that reasonable agreement can be achieved within a diverse citizenry. This appeal to "common knowledge" and "shared practices of inquiry," that is, to "common, human reason,"[44] is essential because it provides a basis upon which people who hold differing conceptions of the good may still agree on the basic principles of liberal democracy. Just as important, by appealing to publicly accessible reasons, persons committed to "full publicity" also come to understand how "reasonable *disagreement*" is possible."[45] Citizens who are committed to the conditions of full publicity can acknowledge their reasonable disagreements without severing the bonds of mutual respect essential to a democratic polity, because they recognize that reasonable persons, arguing from publicly accessible premises, can still reach opposing conclusions.[46]

But when society is not well ordered, particularly when constitutional essentials are themselves being contested, then it is appropriate for religious arguments to enter public life—as long as the goal of those arguments is to restore or strengthen the idea of public reason itself. This notion is a small, but welcomed, opportunity for religious convictions to enter public debate; however, the opening created by this argument may be far wider than Rawls supposes. Religious faith often functions to provide its adherents an alternative world of meaning, one that creates a basis for more radical critique of the status quo than Rawls's overlapping consensus acknowledges.[47]

People of faith will often hold public leaders to a higher standard of justice than mere fairness. Ethical principles like the "preferential option for the poor," for example, elevate Rawls's "difference principle" to primary status in matters of economic justice.[48] Seen from the vantage point of religious conviction, the distinction Rawls draws between constitutional essentials and basic questions of justice on the one hand and ordinary political matters on the other will not hold. For example, Rawls argues that Abraham Lincoln's Second Inaugural Ad-

dress in which Lincoln provides an explicit theological interpretation
of the Civil War "does not violate public reason . . . since what he says
has no implications bearing on constitutional essentials or matters of
basic justice."[49] But surely this cannot be a correct historical interpretation of this address, particularly when it is taken in the larger context
of Lincoln's public discussion of slavery throughout his presidency.

This eloquent address stands as a summation of the arguments
Lincoln developed throughout his first term on the fundamental evil
of slavery. Drawing on the legacy of Israel's prophets, Lincoln demonstrated that slavery was fundamentally unjust before God and *therefore*
could not be acceptable in this republic. In so doing, he offered a fundamental reinterpretation of the constitutional tradition, expanding
that document's notions of freedom and equality to include those
whom the Constitution had denied citizenship.[50] Seen in this historical
trajectory, Lincoln's Second Inaugural Address is clearly directed toward constitutional essentials and basic questions of justice. But if that
is the case, does its explicit theological content violate the standard of
public reason? Or does the standard of public reason need to be enlarged in order to account for arguments set forth by Lincoln, Martin
Luther King, Jr., and others?

This line of inquiry reveals a basic flaw in Rawls's otherwise ele-
gant position. Many of the conceptual distinctions Rawls so clearly
draws depend on the existence of a "well-ordered society." As he himself admits, his theory of justice rests largely on the assumption of the
ideal conditions in such a well-ordered society. The ideal character of
his theory created few problems when his work was understood primarily as an exercise in Kantian transcendental deduction. But beginning with his famous essay "Justice as Fairness: Political not
Metaphysical," and continuing throughout his later writings, Rawls
has offered an interpretation of his work that identifies his theory as
the description of ideas latent within actual democratic societies. But
real democratic societies are not ideal realms; they are "historically extended, socially embodied" entities in which the meaning, significance, and application of even the most fundamental political notions
are constantly being contested.[51]

Precisely as citizens accept the validity of ideas like freedom,
equality, and tolerance, they seek to specify the meaning and application of those terms within particular social and historical situations.
And at times—such as during the Civil War and the civil rights movement—the fundamental significance of these ideas is recast, in partial

continuity with the past but also in fundamental discontinuity with the past. Insofar as democratic societies are historical, they will remain fallible in their grasp and exemplification of democratic ideals. From time to time these societies need to be called to account by reference to a higher standard of justice than that to which they ordinarily give allegiance. Religious traditions are often the source for those standards, and religious discourse will often be the vehicle for both critique and renewal. And when religious traditions are employed in that fashion, they become part of the proper public discourse of democratic societies.

If democratic ideals are constantly being socially and historically contested, then Rawls's attempt to establish the "free-standing" character of democratic principles cannot be sustained. The relation between democratic ideals and the comprehensive schemes of civil society is much more fluid and dialectical than Rawls's analysis implies. Surely the language of constitutional essentials and basic justice has taken on a degree of independence during the more than two hundred years of this republic's existence. And yet the specification of the meaning, significance, and application of that tradition has developed in constant interplay with the background culture of civil society—and continues to develop so today. Without that dynamic interplay, the constitutional tradition can easily become static and unresponsive to changing historical conditions. While the stability of pluralistic democratic regimes is very important, that stability cannot be gained at the cost of the elimination of the primary languages of civil society from the public realm. Rawls's own concessions to the abolitionists and Martin Luther King, Jr., open a far greater opportunity for public religious discourse than he acknowledges, but that opportunity also brings with it—as Rawls clearly understands—significant dangers.

John Rawls's restatement of the basic constitutional values of freedom, equality, and toleration marks an important advance in contemporary liberal political theory. By eliminating from his position the most problematic themes of philosophical liberalism—the neutrality and moral transcendence of democratic government—he has fashioned a view of liberalism that might lead to a revitalization of moral deliberation within the basic institutions of American constitutional democracy. By acknowledging that particular notions of the good are necessary ingredients in any overlapping consensus concerning justice, he has laid the groundwork for the development of a liberal conception of politics that seeks to embrace rather than transcend the pluralism of American public life.[52]

Rawls stops short of proposing such a pluralist view of liberal politics, in part because he clings to the notion that the fundamental ideas of constitutional democracy are conceptually independent of notions inherent in comprehensive moral schemes. But it is not clear that once he has eliminated the notions of neutrality and moral transcendence, he can still support the idea of the conceptual independence of the political realm. If it is the case that a "political conception [of justice] must draw upon various ideas of the good," then the claim concerning the conceptual independence of the political seems unjustified.[53]

While the political realm must remain a distinct sphere, not fully reducible to the sum of comprehensive schemes upon which it draws, that distinctiveness does not imply conceptual independence. If that is true, then politics becomes not the transcendent realm beyond moral pluralism but the immanent realm within which an overlapping consensus among competing moral schemes must be built. Governmental institutions within such a political realm must then play the important role of developing a persuasive moral case for the fundamental values of constitutional democracy.

While Rawls's most recent work opens the possibility for a revitalization of moral discourse within liberal democracy, it does not fully address the proper place of religion in American public life. Still his reflections point the way toward a fresh assessment of that question. Despite the influence Rawls has exercised in contemporary political philosophy, few proponents of liberalism have followed his lead, even on the matter of moral discourse in constitutional democracy. Even fewer have adopted his nuanced and subtle stance on religion. Most defenders of political liberalism continue to assert that religious and theological arguments cannot meet the conditions of publicity; that is, they are forms of discourse that cannot appeal to "shared premises" and "publicly accessible reasons" for their justification.[54] Consequently, these political philosophers remain committed to a rather naive understanding of the "separation of church and state." These liberal theorists grant virtual axiomatic status to the belief that religious convictions must be limited solely to the realm of the private.[55]

In the following chapter I will argue that this fundamental assumption of liberal political theory cannot be sustained. Religious convictions can be developed into public theological arguments that fully meet the appropriate "conditions for publicity." Consequently, the common liberal strictures against public religion are not justified; public theological arguments can and should play a role in seeking to build an overlapping consensus within a pluralistic political society. Indeed, I will argue that a proper "public theology" can make an essential contribution to the reconstruction of a public philosophy that reaffirms the central constitutional values of liberty, equality, and toleration. Thus it becomes possible to develop a revised liberal conception of constitutional democracy, one that welcomes the voices of those religious individuals and institutions committed to the fundamental values of democratic politics. This revised liberal view can then provide a more appropriate context for the adjudication of First Amendment issues—a revision that can lead us beyond the conceptual confusions and imaginative constraints of the "separation of church and state."

## NOTES

**1.** In stressing the importance of the values inscribed in the Constitution and the changed historical circumstances under which we interpret that text, my position is a version of what Michael J. Perry has called "non-originalist" constitutional interpretation. "What the constitutional text means to us, what it signifies to us (in addition to the original meaning) are certain basic, constitutive aspirations or principles or ideals of the American political community and tradition." *Morality, Politics, and the Law* (New York: Oxford University Press, 1988), p. 133.

**2.** The theme of obedience freely rendered to God is a classical theme of Christian theology. The best modern rendering of this argument is found in the work of the Swiss theologian Karl Barth. For a contemporary defense of the compatibility of the notions of freedom and obligation, see William Werpehowski. "Command and History in the Ethics of Karl Barth," *Journal of Religious Ethics* 9/2 (Fall 1981) pp. 298-321.

**3.** David Hollenbach, "Liberalism, Communitarianism, and the Bishops' Pastoral Letter on the Economy, *The Annual of the Society of Christian Ethics*, 1987, p. 21.

**4.** Even Michael Walzer, a liberal theorist whose work has been significantly influenced by the Jewish prophetic tradition, states his support for a strict separation of church and state in unequivocal terms: "The argument embedded in the United States Constitution is that the saints are free to maintain their monopoly and to rule any society (church or sect) that they themselves establish. . . . The monopoly of the saints is harmless enough so long as it doesn't reach to political power. They have no claim to rule the state, which they did not establish, and for whose necessary work divine assurance is no qualification. The purpose of the constitutional wall is the containment . . . of grace." *Spheres of Justice* (New York: Basic Books, 1983), p. 247.

5. John Rawls, "Justice as Fairness" Political not Metaphysical," *Philosophy and Public Affairs* 14,3 (Summer 1985): p. 241.

6. It is surprising how few political philosophers take up this question explicitly. They tend either to sidestep the issue altogether or to dismiss religion's public significance with sarcastic rhetorical asides. See, for example, Bruce Ackerman's characterization of public appeal to religious conviction as "some conversation with the spirit world." *Social Justice in the Liberal State* (New Haven: Yale University Press, 1980), p. 103.

7. For an excellent critique of the notion of neutrality among liberal theorists, see Michael J. Perry, *Morality, Politics, & Law*, pp. 57-76, and *Love and Power: The Proper Role of Religion and Morality in American Politics* (New York: Oxford University Press, 1991), pp. 8-28.

8. Ronald Dworkin, "Liberalism," *A Matter of Principle* (Cambridge: Harvard University Press, 1985), p. 191.

9. Dworkin, "What Liberalism Isn't," *New York Review of Books* (January 20, 1983), p. 47.

10. Neutrality, understood as noninvolvement, is possible in those situations which the Court defines as beyond its proper sphere of expertise. In such limited cases, noninvolvement is a coherent and warranted policy. This concession to neutrality does not conflict with my argument in chapter 3, namely, that as a general principle guiding the Court's overall relation to religion strict neutrality is neither conceptually coherent nor practicable.

11. For an excellent example of such nonneutral moral reasoning, see Ronald Dworkin, "Liberty and Pornography," *New York Review of Books* 38,14 (August 15, 1991): pp. 12-15.

12. Alasdair MacIntyre has made this point even more sharply (and, I believe, somewhat tendentiously) when he asserts that all liberal moral theories are versions of "emotivism." When the language of moral obligation reduces to expressions of "personal preference," then rational persuasion is no longer possible. If I want to convince you to follow the path of behavior I prefer, but cannot rely on persuasive argument, I must resort to power, deception, and manipulation. You, in return, will view all my ethical discourse with suspicion, seeking at every turn to unmask my moral pretensions to reveal the manipulative power lurking beneath the surface. Thus does politics become "civil war waged by other means." *After Virtue* (Notre Dame: University of Notre Dame, 1981), especially pp. 235-236.

13. "The Priority of the Right and Ideas of the Good," *Philosophy and Public Affairs* 17:3 (Summer 1988): 252.

14. "Justice as Fairness," p. 223.

15. "It is important to observe that [political liberalism] does not imply either skepticism or indifference about religious, philosophical, or moral doctrines." "Kantian Constructivism in Moral Theory: The Dewey Lectures 1980," *The Journal of Philosophy* 77,9 (September 1980): 542.

**16.** "The Domain of the Political and Overlapping Consensus," *New York University Law Review* 64,2 (May 1989): 240.

**17.** "The Idea of an Overlapping Consensus," *Oxford Journal of Legal Studies* 7,1 (Spring 1987): 4.

**18.** Ibid.

**19.** "The Domain of the Political," p. 240.

**20.** Ibid.

**21.** "[A] political conception . . . is neither presented as, nor as derived from, such a [comprehensive] doctrine applied to the basic structure of society." Ibid., p. 12 (italics added).

**22.** Ibid.

**23.** "The conception of justice should be, as far as possible, independent of the opposing and conflicting philosophical and religious doctrines that citizens affirm. . . . Political liberalism, then, aims for a political conception of justice as a free-standing view." *Political Liberalism*, pp. 9-10.

**24.** Ibid., p. 191.

**25.** "Overlapping Consensus," p. 1.

**26.** *Political Liberalism*, p. 191.

**27.** "Comprehensive doctrines of all kinds—religious, philosophical, and moral—belong to what we may call the 'background culture' of civil society. This is the culture of the social, not of the political." Ibid., p. 14.

**28.** "We now assume citizens hold two distinct views; or perhaps better, we assume their overall view has two parts. One part can be seen to be, or to coincide with, a political conception of justice; the other part is a (fully or partially) comprehensive doctrine to which the political conception is in some manner related." Ibid., p. 38.

**29.** Ibid.

**30.** Ibid., pp. 38-39.

**31.** "Domain of the Political," p. 243 (italics added). Rawls wants to stress that the priority of the political to the religious (or any other comprehensive scheme) is limited to the political arena alone. He does not mean to imply that political ideas have *absolute* priority over moral or religious values. "Political good, no matter how important, can never in general outweigh the transcendent values—certain religious, philosophical and moral values—that may possibly come into conflict with it." "The Priority of the Right," p. 275. If Rawls holds consistently to the view articulated here, then he must allow some significant role for religious and moral *dissent* within the political realm.

**32.** *Political Liberalism*, p. 37.

**33.** Ibid., p. 137.

**34.** Ibid., p. 138.

**35.** Rawls initially developed these conditions of publicity in "Kantian Constructivism," pp. 535-543. Cf. "The Idea of an Overlapping Consensus," pp. 5-12; and "The Domain of the Political," pp. 244-249. His most recent statement on the matter is "The Idea of Public Reason," *Political Liberalism*, pp. 212-254.

**36.** *Political Liberalism*, pp. 224-225.

**37.** Ibid., p. 235 and 215. Rawls goes on to say, "The justices cannot, of course, invoke their own personal morality, nor the ideals and virtues of morality generally. Those they must view as irrelevant. Equally, they cannot invoke their or other people's religious or philosophical views. Nor can they cite political views without restriction. Rather, they must appeal to the political values they think belong to the most reasonable understanding of the public conception and its political values of justice and public reason. These are values that they believe in good faith, as the duty of civility requires, that all citizens as reasonable and rational might reasonably be expected to endorse," (p. 236). This point of view, of course, conflicts with the position I argued in the previous chapter.

**38.** *A Theory of Justice,* p. 215.

**39.** *Theory,* p. 216.

**40.** Ibid., p. 215.

**41.** *Political Liberalism,* p. 247.

**42.** Ibid., p. 251.

**43.** The most unrelenting argument in this regard is Robert Audi, "The Separation of Church and State and the Obligations of Citizenship," *Philosophy and Public Affairs* 18,3 (Summer 1989): 259-296.

**44.** "The Domain of the Political," p. 244.

**45.** "The ideal also expresses a willingness to listen to what others have to say and being ready to accept reasonable accommodations or alterations in one's own view . . . [Or failing this, the disagreement] can be seen as at least not unreasonable in this sense: that those who oppose it can nevertheless understand how reasonable persons can affirm it". *Political Liberalism,* p. 253.

**46.** Alasdair MacIntyre has argued that liberalism's inability to acknowledge the depth and pervasiveness of moral disagreement has created a social situation in which rational persuasion has been reduced to political manipulation. Liberalism grounds moral arguments in the primacy of reason but it cannot appeal to reason to adjudicate arguments based upon "rival and incommensurable premises." Consequently, one party in a moral debate must show that the other party is unreasonable or irrational for refusing to accept the inevitable conclusion of a rational argument. If the other party adopts a similar strategy, then moral argumentation is reduced to an unseemly struggle for the moral high ground. See Alasdair MacIntyre, *After Virtue* (Notre Dame: University of Notre Dame Press, 1981), pp. 1-34, and *Whose Justice? Which Rationality?* (Notre Dame: University of Notre Dame Press, 1988), pp. 1-11, and 349-403.

**47.** Stephen Carter, *The Culture of Disbelief: How American Law and Politics Trivialize Religious Devotion* (New York: Basic Books, 1993).

**48.** While this principle was developed in the context of Latin American liberation theology, it has received its most sophisticated statement in the American Catholic bishops' Pastoral Letter on Catholic Social Teaching and the U.S. Economy "Economic Justice for All" (Washington, D.C.: National Conference of Catholic Bishops, 1986).

**49.** *Political Liberalism,* p. 254.

**50.** See Garry Wills, *Lincoln at Gettysburg.*

**51.** The phrase is Alasdair MacIntyre's, in *After Virtue,* p. 207.

**52.** Other political theorists have pursued this issue with greater vigor than Rawls. See especially William Galston, "Pluralism and Social Unity," *Ethics* 99,4 (July 1989): 711-726; "Liberalism and Public Morality," *Liberals on Liberalism* edited by Alfonso J. Damico (Totowa, New Jersey: Rowman & Littlefield, 1986), pp. 129-150; "Moral Personality and Liberal Theory: John Rawls' *Dewey Lectures*," *Political Theory* 10,4 (November 1982): 492-519; "Defending Liberalism," *American Political Science Review* 76 (1982): pp. 621-629; and Michael J. Perry, *Morality, Politics, & Law* and *Love and Power*.

**53.** "The Priority of Right," p. 17.

**54.** The language of "shared premises" and "publicly accessible reasons" has been developed by Kent Greenawalt in his helpful study *Religious Convictions and Political Choice* (New York: Oxford University Press, 1988).

**55.** David Tracy's wry remarks on this matter are instructive. "Religion is . . . the single subject about which many intellectuals can feel free to be ignorant. Often abetted by the churches, they need not study religion, for 'everybody' already knows what religion is: It is a private consumer product that some people seem to need. Its former social role was poisonous. Its present privatization is harmless enough to wish it well from a civilized distance. Religion seems to be the sort of thing one likes 'if that's the sort of thing one likes.'" *Analogical Imagination* (New York: Crossroads, 1981), p. 13.

# 5

# *Political Liberalism Revisioned*

The analysis in the first four chapters has identified the strengths and weaknesses of the American tradition of political liberalism. As devised by the framers of the Constitution, and inscribed in the Bill of Rights, the liberal tradition has defined three values as central to American public life: liberty, equality, and toleration. As we have seen, the arguments in defense of these values were often overtly theological, and the framers and ratifiers of the Constitution looked to religion to provide the moral context within which public virtue could flourish. Although eighteenth-century society was considerably more homogeneous than our diverse contemporary culture, the framers were remarkably prescient in their concern for the rights of minorities. Recognizing the inherent danger of majoritarian tyranny within a democratic polity, they gave particular emphasis to freedom of conscience, free exercise of religion, and toleration of minority beliefs in devising the Bill of Rights.

As I have shown, however, the framers were finally ambivalent regarding pluralism within American public life. While recognizing that free citizens will inevitably embrace diverse and even conflicting patterns of belief, they also feared that religious convictions joined to group self-interest would create a deeply factionalized society. The system of checks and balances built into the Constitution was designed to curb the potential excesses of a citizenry motivated by passionate self-interest, but the framers stopped short of developing a theory of virtue that would specify the proper relation between government and those public but nongovernmental associations (e.g., churches, synagogues, unions, and civic associations) within which character is often decisively shaped. Consequently, they bequeathed to their heirs the essential dilemma of American public life. If democratic government cannot serve as a "school of virtue" for a pluralistic society, where will those virtues essential for a responsible public life be nurtured? How should government relate to those public associations within which such virtues are developed? Should government actively seek to encourage those public associations that contribute positively to a pluralistic democratic culture? If religious communities are among those public-spirited associations, can government encourage their civic involvement without violating the letter and spirit of the first amendment? If religious communities are encouraged to participate actively in public life will they enflame those passions and interests that contribute to divisive factionalized politics?

The failure of the eighteenth-century founders to provide an adequate solution to the problem of pluralism is understandable, given the relative homogeneity of Colonial society. For contemporary liberal theorists, however, pluralism has become the central challenge for political theory. As we have seen, the doctrine of governmental neutrality represents one standard liberal response to the moral diversity of contemporary American society. If government is to treat competing notions of the good equitably, then it cannot show preference to any particular moral or religious belief. Therefore, so the standard liberal argument runs, government must be neutral toward all such beliefs, thereby transcending the untidy realm of moral discord. Particular moral doctrines, and perforce religious doctrines, cannot serve as the basis for public policy because they are incapable of providing common ground for a diverse democratic public. If moral and religious beliefs are not properly introduced into the public or governmental realm, in what sphere are such beliefs appropriate? According to most liberal theorists, moral, philosophical, and religious beliefs belong to the constitutionally protected sphere of privacy, the realm that must remain immune from government interference. In return for such protected privacy, however, citizens must agree to forgo reliance on these personal beliefs when they enter the public or governmental sphere. Only a neutral and secular public realm can preserve the freedoms of a diverse democratic society.[1]

This separation of the public and private introduces yet another conceptual problem into liberal theory. Liberal theorists define the public sphere as the realm of governmental action, a sphere in which the diverse and conflicting private interests of groups and individuals are mediated through various neutral means of adjudication. This public/private distinction has a dual consequence: (1) by identifying the public solely with government it decisively limits the number of actors allowed to play on the public stage, and (2) by characterizing the activities of various nongovernmental communities and associations as expressions of private or individual interests, it obscures the intentions of such groups to serve the public welfare and common good. Contemporary liberal theorists have taken the most questionable aspect of eighteenth-century constitutional thought, the theory of factions, and enshrined it at the center of its political philosophy, thereby concealing the public, though nongovernmental, character of voluntary associations. Far from providing the theory of virtue needed to shore up the otherwise stable edifice of constitutional theory, contemporary liberals tend to remove moral considerations entirely from political deliberation. The doctrine of governmental neutrality elevates the public realm to a place "beyond good and evil," and the theory of factions reduces the private realm to a battleground of conflicting desires and interests.

The notion of the separation of church and state thus rests on the three most questionable principles of standard liberal theory: governmental neutrality, governmental secularity, and the separation of the public and private realms. In an attempt to provide a justification of democratic polity under the conditions of contemporary pluralism, liberal theorists have proceeded from the least defensible of the framers' constitutional principles—the theory of factions—to devise a conceptually incoherent account of public life. The interaction of these three suspect principles seriously constrains attempts to engage in careful moral reasoning about the fundamental values of democracy. By asserting the moral transcendence of government and characterizing the moral intentions of voluntary associations as collections of self-interested passions, contemporary liberal theory has made itself vulnerable to a potentially debilitating critique. The moral universe projected by this form of liberalism appears to be a place in which self-interested individuals and groups engage in a continuous struggle for political power, while government, standing above the battlefield, applies morally neutral procedural rules to adjudicate the conflicts. Questions of mutual interest, common good, and public welfare seem almost irrelevant within this world of conflicting desires and contending interests.

## TOWARD A MORE VIRTUOUS LIBERALISM

*Is liberalism a salvageable political theory? Can liberalism, despite its evident defects, be reconstituted to provide a morally viable polity for contemporary America? Is it possible to devise a liberal theory of virtue, one that genuinely honors the cultural and moral pluralism of American society? Can liberalism provide an appropriate political context within which the religious convictions and practices of the American people can be given public expression?*

Contemporary commentators are sharply divided on the question of whether liberalism is a salvageable political theory. The harshest critics of liberalism—commonly called "communitarians"—have argued that virtuous character and religious conviction cannot be nurtured within the self-interested polity of liberal society. Liberalism is, for these critics, a morally and religiously vacuous theory that can no longer provide a hospitable context for those who seek to nurture virtuous character. This communitarian critique has generated an equally vigorous defense of modern classical liberalism. These writers, the "modern liberals," some of whose work has been analyzed and criticized in the early chapters of this book, defend the distinctive liberal notions of governmental neutrality and secularity and argue that liberalism's focus on individual freedom is essential for a modern pluralistic society.[2] A third group of authors, let us call them "revisionists," are seeking a middle way between the sharply sectarian vision of the communitarians and the unreconstructed individualism of the modern liberals.

My argument in the previous chapter suggests that John Rawls's later work goes beyond the classical modern liberal position and begins to sketch the outlines of a revisionist position. The revisionist project has been taken up by an eclectic group of philosophers and political theorists, all of whom seek to save liberalism from its worst excesses by reintroducing notions of community, solidarity, and the common good. Staunch defenders of liberal pluralism, they nonetheless believe that a defense of pluralism need not involve the troubling concepts of governmental neutrality and secularity. This revisionist position, I will argue in the final chapter, provides the basis for a reconception of the place of religion in American public life.

Questions concerning the future of liberalism have been central to the "liberal-communitarian debate" of the past decade. The "communitarians"—a diverse group of philosophers, political theorists, and theologians—have faulted liberalism for its deficient view of the person and for its underdeveloped view of political community. They decry the cultural and social fragmentation created by liberal polity, and they seek to foster communities within which virtuous lives can be nurtured. Wary of the individualism inherent in liberalism's commitment to personal freedom, these thinkers have urged a reappropriation of the traditions, narratives, and practices of coherent intact communities.

While the label "communitarian" has been useful in identifying a common interest shared by these critics of liberalism, it has also obscured some fundamental differences among them. Concern with virtue, communal practice, and narrative capacity can be offered either as a program of reform within liberalism or as proposal for the replacement of liberal polity. These critics differ decisively on the question of whether liberalism is patient of communitarian reform. For some, those I would call "sectarian communitarians," liberalism is a spent moral and political force, a polity that can no longer nurture the virtues so desperately needed within American culture. For others, those I have called "revisionists," liberalism is a flawed but corrigible political theory capable of significant revision and reform. For the purposes of my analysis, I will use the term "communitarian" solely to denote the sectarian position I describe below. I will use the term "liberal" for defenders of the classical modern position and the term "revisionist" for those who seek a middle way between these two disjunctive alternatives.

SECTARIAN COMMUNITARIANS. Representatives of this group offer philosophical or theological arguments to show the incompatibility of liberalism with fundamental theories of virtue, thereby exposing the moral vacuity of the liberal tradition.[3] Theologian Stanley Hauerwas has stated the charges against liberalism with characteristic bluntness.

> The genius of liberalism was to make what had always been considered a vice, namely unlimited desire, a virtue. . . . Liberalism is a political philosophy committed to the proposition that a social order and corresponding mode of government can be formed on self-interest and consent. . . . Liberalism thus becomes a self-fulfilling prophecy; a social order that is designed to work on the presumption that people are self-interested tends to produce that kind of people.[4]

According to Michael Sandel, liberalism's failings stem from its problematic view of the person, "a choosing self, independent of the desires and ends it may have at any moment. . . . Freed from the sanctions of custom and tradition and inherited status, unbound by moral ties antecedent to choice, the liberal self is installed as sovereign, cast as the author of the only obligations that constrain."[5] The central moral category of liberal theory is *choice*; autonomous agents acknowledge only those values, ends, and obligations that they freely choose to accept. But choice, Alasdair MacIntyre has argued, is a flimsy moral category upon which to base obligation, for when persons with conflicting moral positions appeal to autonomous choice as the basis for their beliefs and behavior there is no evident means available to adjudicate their conflict. If opponents contending for conflicting policies on abortion or pornography must finally justify their fundamental moral premises by an appeal to choice, then their disagreement becomes little more than a contest of self-assertion.

> If we possess no unassailable criteria, no set of compelling reasons by means of which we may convince our opponents, it follows that in the process of making up our own minds we can have made no appeal to such criteria or such reasons. If I lack any good reasons to invoke against you, it must seem that I lack any good reasons. Hence it seems that underlying my own position there must be some non-rational decision to adopt that position.[6]

If our moral convictions are ultimately the product of our nonrational autonomous choosing, then we cannot appeal to rational impersonal criteria to justify those convictions. But without such criteria how can we persuade others of the rightness of the course of action we recommend? Rational persuasion is essential to the formation of just policies in a pluralistic democracy, and yet liberalism, by enshrining choice at the center of its moral program, seems to rob us of the resources we need to engage in serious moral argument. If moral arguments are ultimately grounded in autonomous choice, then moral reasoning appears to be reducible to the expression of personal preference. If liberalism's view of the self is correct, then a sentence like "You ought oppose abortion because it is the taking of innocent life" is fully translatable to "I disapprove of abortion, you should as well." But why should I feel obliged to act under the constraint of another person's preferences, particularly if my preferences differ?

If moral persuasion cannot be achieved, then opponents must employ other means by which to obtain their policy goals, particularly the use of manipulative political power. Those who hold such power will seek to conceal the fact that their moral language is simply the expression of their own personal preferences, and those who seek such power will endeavor to unmask the moral pretensions of their opponents. Political debate thus becomes an interminable process of assertion and counterassertion, of manipulation and protest, of deception and unmasking. Consequently modern politics becomes "civil war carried on by other means."[7] The ironic but inescapable conclusion is that the liberal view of the self fails to provide the moral resources so desperately needed to achieve consensus within a contentious pluralistic democratic culture. Individual choice proves a far too fragile basis on which to rest a solution to the vexing problem of conflict within public life. By enshrining the unencumbered self at the center of its political philosophy, contemporary liberal theory turns the founders' worry about factions into a self-fulfilling prophecy.

A related concern of the communitarians is that liberal theory has an underdeveloped view of political community. The highest view of human association to which liberals can aspire is what Sandel has called "community in the cooperative sense. . . . Uencumbered selves . . . are free to join in voluntary association with others, whether to advance our private ends, or to enjoy the communal sentiments that such associations often inspire."[8] But citizens bound to a liberal view of politics cannot aspire to "community in the constitutive sense."[9]

> What is denied to the unencumbered self is the possibility of membership in any community bound by moral ties antecedent to choice: he cannot belong to any community where the self itself could be at stake. Such a community would engage the identity as well as the interests of participants, and so implicate its members in a citizenship more thoroughgoing than the unencumbered self can know. More than a cooperative arrangement, community in this second, stronger sense describes a mode of self-understanding, a shared way of life that partly defines the identity of the participants.[10]

It is this longing for a greater sense of political community that defines the nascent alternative emerging from the communitarian critique. Representatives of this movement urge a more coherent understanding of political community, one that allows for the affirmation of common values, the appropriation of tradition, and the nurturance of those virtues essential to the common good. They decry the fragmentation of contemporary life, and they accuse liberalism of fostering a form of individualism that is destructive of human well-being. If the individual is the sole source of authority, then, these communitarians argue, there is no need to remember one's history, no need to retell the stories that define one's identity. "Ironically, the most coercive aspect of the liberal account of the world is that we are free to make up our own story. The story that liberalism teaches us is that we have no story, and as a result we fail to notice how deeply that story determines our lives."[11]

If, however, we believe that human beings can create communities that are more than collectives of mere strangers; if we believe that human well-being requires stronger and deeper bonds of fellowship, then we must be about the task of recovering our traditions and retelling our stories. Communitarians seek to rekindle the narrative capacity that will enable people to discover a common heritage and to chronicle their shared history. Then they might be capable of building communities within which a sense of common purpose and value might be nurtured. Then they might once again discover that "we can know a good in common that we cannot know alone."[12]

That common good, however, cannot be known or nurtured in the civil society created by liberal polity. Liberalism, the sectarian communitarians argue, is fundamentally flawed and cannot be sufficiently reformed to provide the resources needed to nurture character-shaping communities. Consequently, they do not look to the polis for the resources essential to the recovery of virtue-forming tradition. Sectarians are not seeking to reconstitute citizenship or civic virtue in the modern liberal state; rather, they seek to provide resources to help smaller associations and intact communities recover their own traditions so that they might provide alternative modes of socialization and identity formation to counter the destructive impulses of liberalism.

> What matters at this stage is the construction of local forms of community within which civility and the intellectual and moral life can be sustained through the new dark ages which are already upon us. And if the tradition of the virtues was able to survive the horrors of the last dark ages, we are not entirely without grounds for hope.[13]

Sectarians do not share the interest of the liberal revisionists in introducing moral, philosophical, and religious conceptions of the good into civil society. Far from seeking to contribute to the common good of society or to the construction of an overlapping consensus, sectarian communitarians are convinced "that modern politics cannot be a matter of genuine moral consensus."[14]

> Since liberalism is one of the polities that know not God. . . the challenge is always for the church to be a "contrast model.". . . For the church to adopt social strategies in the name of securing justice in . . . a [liberal] social order is only to compound the problem. Rather the church must recognize that her first social task in any society is to be herself. . . . The first task of the church is not to supply theories of governmental legitimacy or even to suggest strategies for social betterment. The first task of the church is to exhibit in our common life the kind of community that is possible when trust, not fear, rules our lives.[15]

Sectarian communitarians would not support the effort to eliminate the notion of the separation of church and state from the lexicon of public life.[16] If anything, they seek a strengthening of that concept, not on the grounds set forward by Thomas Jefferson or by contemporary liberals, but on the grounds first enunciated by Roger Williams. The wall of separation is designed by God to preserve the integrity of the church's life; efforts to breech that wall can only lead to the invasion of "the garden of the church" by "the wilderness of the world." In seeking to be a "contrast model," the church gives witness to the fact that its primary allegiance and loyalty is to God, not to the state. Therefore, the community that becomes the object of reform is not civil society but the church itself.

> The problem in liberal societies is that there seems to be no way to encourage the development of public virtue without accepting a totalitarian strategy from the left or an elitist strategy from the right. By standing as an alternative to both, the church may well help free our social imagination from those destructive choices. For finally social and political theory depends on people having the experience of trust rather than the idea of trust. But we must admit the church has not been a society of trust and virtue. . . . Therefore any radical critique of our secular polity requires an equally radical critique of the church.[17]

Sectarian communitarians have been successful in opening an important critical conversation about the future of liberalism, but their position lacks both precision and persuasiveness. The sectarian's critique of liberalism, while illuminating some of the weaknesses of liberal theory, is clearly one-sided and even tendentious. By viewing liberalism solely through the prism of individual self-interest and personal preference, the sectarians ignore many strengths of the tradition, especially its salutary emphasis on liberty, equality, and toleration. By urging local communities to withdraw from liberal society, they fail to provide a genuine program of reform, thereby abandoning democratic polity to its own worst tendencies. The danger inherent in the sectarian critique is that its advocates will deconstruct and dismantle the liberal tradition without offering anything enduring in its place. That strategy could create a sense of alienation from liberal political structures that might precipitate the very moral nihilism that the communitarians so vigorously warn us against. It would be ironic indeed if the communitarian critique served to foster the cultural and moral despair that its advocates argue is inherent in classical liberalism.

Many analysts have observed that the communitarians have not developed a genuine alternative to liberal polity.[18] Their critique gains its evocative power from operating at a high level of generality, thereby ignoring the most vexing problems that face any theory of modern political society. Chief among these problems is the challenge of pluralism. In chapter 2 I noted that the framers of the Constitution were wary of classical republicanism because of the exclusionary and bellicose tendencies of that ancient communitarian tradition. Contemporary communitarians have, for the most part, failed to reckon with the fact that the tradition they extol has engendered solidarity among citizens in two fundamental ways: (1) by limiting citizenship to an elite homogenous group, thereby disenfranchising heterogeneous elements of society,[19] and (2) by identifying an external enemy whose threat demands the sacrifice of individual self-interest for the sake of the public welfare.[20] As long as contemporary communitarians fail to address the exclusionary and bellicose qualities of the republican tradition, their position will appear unacceptable for a pluralist society such as ours. If communitarian solidarity requires an elitist society divided against itself and armed against an external aggressor, then liberalism, for all its flaws, appears a far preferable alternative.

Communitarianism is clearly more effective as a philosophical or theological critique of liberal theory than as a genuine political alternative to liberal practice. I am in agreement with Michael Walzer's assessment that communitarianism is not a viable independent philosophical or political position but "a consistently intermittent feature of liberal politics and social organization. . . . No communitarian critique, however penetrating, will ever be anything more than an inconstant feature of liberalism."[21] If communitarians cannot devise an enduring alternative to liberal polity, the question becomes whether liberalism can be reformed so as to respond to the more trenchant aspects of the communitarian critique. Is liberalism compatible with a socially constituted self, a community-based notion of virtue, and a conception of the good adequate to a pluralist society? These are the questions taken up in various revisionist proposals regarding liberalism.

LIBERAL REVISIONISTS.  In this section, I want to present a revised conception of political liberalism, relying on the work of those philosophers and political theorists who are seeking to find a middle way between classical modern liberalism and sectarian communitarianism.[22] While these thinkers are not in total agreement on all aspects of a revised liberalism, I believe that the shape of a coherent revisionist position is beginning to emerge.

In contrast to the sectarians, liberal revisionists do hope to reform current political society by encouraging a more robust sense of civic obligation and virtuous citizenship. While acknowledging that earlier American traditions of virtue, particularly those of civic republicanism and biblical religion, lie fragmented within contemporary American culture, they believe that this heritage can be recovered and applied to our current pluralistic society. Liberal revisionists are often sharply critical of liberal theory and practice, but they are confident that appropriate reforms can be instituted to create some sense of genuine political community within American public life.

For the revisionists, liberalism is not a comprehensive philosophical doctrine with a particular metaphysical view of the self but a conceptual description, endorsement, and justification of a complex set of democratic political practices. Revisionists view liberalism as a coherent but revisable descriptive account of those political practices that are best suited for a free, mobile, and pluralistic society. At bottom, liberalism is the descriptive justification of a free, equal, and tolerant society. Liberal societies prize liberty, equality, and diversity and seek noncoercive ways in which to encourage citizens to act responsibly for the good of the commonwealth.

As communitarians have rightly noted, the individual freedom fostered by liberal democracies creates a mobile, and to some extent, unsettled society. Liberty, as Michael Walzer has argued, inevitably abets movement: geographical, social, marital, and political mobility. "Liberalism is, most simply, the theoretical endorsement and justification of this movement. In the liberal view, then, the Four Mobilities represent the enactment of liberty, and the pursuit of (private or personal) happiness. . . . Any effort to curtail mobility in the four areas described here would require a massive and harsh application of state power."[23]

Walzer acknowledges that liberal mobility "has an underside of sadness and discontent. . . . All in all, we liberals probably know one another less well, and with less assurance, than people once did. . . . We are more often alone than people once were, being without neighbors we can count on, relatives who live nearby or with whom we are close, or comrades at work in the movement."[24] Communitarians have given effective expression and philosophical shape to these feelings of loss, but they have exaggerated the degree to which we have become separated from one another.

> The ties of place, class or status, family, and even politics survive the Four Mobilities to a remarkable extent. . . . Whatever the extent of the Four Mobilities, they do not seem to move us so far apart that we can no longer talk to one another. We often disagree, of course, but we disagree in mutually comprehensible ways. . . . Even political conflict in liberal societies rarely takes forms so extreme as to set its protagonists beyond negotiation and compromise, procedural justice, and the very possibility of speech.[25]

Liberal revisionists disagree decisively with communitarians concerning the nature of political disagreement within liberal democracies. The sectarian position gathers its plausibility from the argument that contemporary moral disagreements stem from incommensurable premises and are therefore irresolvable in principle.[26] Ironically, this communitarian argument restates the modern *liberal* position most clearly enunciated by Isaiah Berlin in his classic essay, "Two Concepts of Liberty."[27] Berlin argues for the primacy of "negative freedom," that is, individual freedom from interference by others, because he is convinced that "ultimate values are irreconcilable," and therefore "the clash of values [is] at once absolute and incommensurable."[28] Liberal democracies must be based on the protection of the rights of individuals that are grounded in the fundamental inviolability of "negative freedom." Should a government ever favor a particular understanding of "positive freedom"—the freedom that impels persons to seek some *telos* of happiness or fulfillment—it would inevitably violate the freedom of those citizens who seek other conflicting *teloi*. Consequently, democratic governments must limit themselves to the protection of those rights necessary to guarantee the inviolability of the sphere of privacy that is "negative freedom."

Ironically, then, both sectarian communitarianism and classical modern liberalism are grounded in the conviction that moral disagreements in a pluralistic society are inadjudicable because competing moral arguments emerge from incommensurable premises and values. Revisionists, on the other hand, part company with both positions on this decisive issue.[29] Moral disagreements, revisionists argue, are often vigorous and occasionally irresolvable in practice, but such disagreements take place against a broad background of fundamental consensus concerning the goods that ought to be pursued in a liberal democracy.[30] That consensus is itself revisable and open to critical questioning, but the elements comprised by it are never simultaneously and universally called into question. Indeed, genuine disagreement requires *some* common premises or else the contending positions would simply "talk past one another" rather than engage in true conflict.

There is a philosophical and a political point to be made here, and both are essential to the revisionist position.[31] The claim that moral premises are "conceptually incommensurable" is an exceedingly strong philosophical assertion. Incommensurability implies that competing moral premises rest within conceptual frameworks that differ utterly one from another. But what would be the meaning of such wholly disparate conceptual schemes? And if there were such divergent frameworks, how could genuine disagreement take place between them? As Donald Davidson has shown, true disagreement requires a background of more basic agreement if we are even to define the terms of our dispute.[32] If we disagreed about *everything*, that is, if our premises were truly *incommensurable*, then we would be unable to disagree; we would simply "talk past one another." Jeffrey Stout gives a homely example to illustrate Davidson's point.

If you and I disagree about some proposition, moral or nonmoral, we will at least have enough in common to make sense of that proposition. We couldn't disagree about it if we couldn't make sense of it. If you push the disagreement down too far, it tends to disappear by becoming merely verbal. Suppose you and I disagree about clocks. I say that clocks are vehicles one drives to work, that nearly all new clocks nowadays cost many thousands of dollars, and that one needs a license to operate them legally. You hold the more orthodox opinions about clocks. Here is a case where apparent disagreement goes so deep that it becomes merely verbal. We begin by assuming that we're disagreeing about clocks, but it soon becomes clear that we don't share enough beliefs about what we're each calling clocks to identify a common subject matter to disagree over.[33]

The philosophical conclusion to be drawn, then, is that genuine moral disagreement requires a substantial background of agreement in order for the dispute to be coherent. That does not mean, however, that we will always be able to identify the moral principles to which we can appeal to resolve such disputes. Moral disagreement may remain practically intractable, even if the premises are not conceptually incommensurable.

The political consequences of this philosophical point are particularly important for the revisionist position. If moral disagreement in our pluralist society is not irresolvable *in principle*, then a basic presupposition shared by classical modern liberalism and sectarian communitarianism can be overturned. Thus, we need not choose between the unhappy alternatives of a neutral secular government "beyond good and evil" or separated local communities nurturing virtue in isolation from civil society. Even if liberal societies cannot agree on the ultimate *telos* for all human beings, it does not follow that they are unable to generate a limited but still real consensus concerning the common goods such societies should pursue. *Despite* the pluralism of contemporary life, it remains possible that liberal society can define a range of virtues appropriate for cultivation within our shared civic life. Yet *because* of the pluralism of contemporary life, it is necessary to limit the scope of that overlapping consensus. "In other words, certain features of our society can be seen as justified by a self-limiting consensus on the good—an agreement consisting partly in the realization that it would be a bad thing, that it would make life worse for all of us, to press too hard for agreement on all details in a given vision of the good."[34]

If progress is to be made toward this vision of a limited consensus, revisionists recognize that they must find a more appropriate balance between personal freedom and political solidarity than that characteristic of classic modern liberal theory.[35] Liberal revisionists differ from classical liberals in that they seek a dialectical balance between individual freedom and communal solidarity within a pluralistic society. While endorsing the fundamental liberal values of liberty, equality, and toleration, they also attempt to find a place for the theory of virtue that has for so long been lacking in American liberal polity. While revisionists affirm the centrality of individual liberty, they are nonetheless convinced that a free democratic society can endure only if its citizens share some sense of public good and common destiny. The freedom so prized by the liberal tradition can only be preserved as long as the diverse elements of society are held together by some common bonds. A free and diverse society cannot survive as a political union unless citizens share some common goals and values. Democratic governments, however, cannot coerce actions that serve the common good from a free citizenry; rather, they must be able to appeal to shared underlying beliefs and convictions that will animate activity freely offered for the sake of the nation's common enterprise. Democratic governments must inspire sufficient love of country to motivate citizens to act not simply in support of their own self-interest but also for the common good.

The central challenge of revisionist liberal politics is to develop a polity that honors personal freedom and yet appeals to a sense of common obligation freely offered by the citizenry. Liberal polity requires a notion of civic responsibility that is not coercive, exclusionary or bellicose.[36] Revisionists differ on the precise relation that ought to be achieved between freedom and solidarity, but they agree that liberalism must welcome more robust notions of civic virtue and the common good.

Among the revisionists, Charles Taylor has offered the strongest argument concerning the priority of communal solidarity to individual freedom. Like the communitarians with whom he is often linked, Taylor appeals to republican political traditions, but he does so in an effort to reform the worst excesses of liberal individualism. According to Taylor, all genuine republics

> are animated by a sense of a shared immediate common good. . . . The bond of solidarity with my compatriots in a functioning

republic is based on a sense of shared fate, where the sharing itself is of value. This is what gives this bond its special importance, what makes my ties with these people peculiarly binding,
what animates my 'virtu' or patriotism. . . . The essential condi-
tion of a free (nondespotic) regime is that citizens have this kind
of patriotic identification.[37]

Common actions on behalf of the common good "that would be ex-
ternally imposed by fear under a despotism have to be self-imposed
in its absence, and only patriotic identification can provide the motivation. . . . Republican solidarity underpins freedom, because it provides the motivation for self-imposed discipline."[38]

The liberal emphasis on individual freedom can be supported as
long as that freedom is anchored in a prior sense of republican solidarity. While liberalism's notion of freedom as "immunity from interference by others" is important, it is incomplete without the
correlative conception of civic freedom, "the freedom we enjoy together to the extent that we govern ourselves as a society and do not
live under tutelage to despotism."[39] These two senses of freedom will
always exist in tension with one another. Liberal freedom encourages
individuals to pursue their life goals by attending primarily to their
own self-interest, while civic freedom encourages individuals to
shape their actions with reference to values and practices they share
in common with other citizens. Liberal freedom encourages the cen-
trifugal movement characteristic of pluralistic democracies, while
civic freedom provides the centripetal counterbalance needed to hold
a diverse populace together.

Taylor argues that republican solidarity and civic freedom provide the fundamental and prior basis for the notions of liberty, equality, and toleration that are so highly valued by the liberal tradition.
Thus Taylor, unlike his sectarian counterparts, does not reject the liberal tradition in its entirety. Rather, he hopes to ground liberalism's
characteristic emphases in a prior sense of communal commitment.
Without some "socially endorsed conception of the good democratic
regimes simply cannot survive the fragmenting consequences of unre-
strained liberal freedom.[40] If liberalism's fundamental commitment to
freedom, equality, and toleration is to be preserved, then some notion
of the goods and virtues shared in common within liberal society must
be identified.

The question that has always bedeviled classical liberalism is how to identify such goods and virtues while still honoring the pluralism of liberal society. One of the classical mistakes of modern liberal theory, however, has been to equate the pluralism of American society simply with its individualism.[41] As Taylor's analysis makes clear, freedom in a liberal democracy must be conceived as both individual and corporate. As individuals, we are free to pursue those *personal* life plans and goals that we believe will assist us in living happy and fulfilled lives. As citizens, we are free to determine together the *public* goals, plans, and policies that will best serve the welfare of the commonwealth.

Both senses of freedom imply forms of pluralism. Personal freedom encourages persons to pursue individual happiness, thereby creating a pluralism of self-interested individuals. Civic freedom encourages persons to pursue corporate plans and policies, thereby creating a pluralism of associations. Classical liberalism has always tacitly recognized both senses of freedom, but from the time of the founders onward, the liberal tradition has valued personal freedom more highly than civic freedom. Since civic freedom has historically been linked to the founders' theory of factions, the pluralism of associations has not played a significant role in the shaping of the American liberal tradition. Classical modern theorists have only rarely attended to the fact that "liberalism expresses strong associative tendencies."[42] Consequently the view of the person that has emerged from classical modern liberalism is precisely the "unencumbered self" that has become such an easy target for communitarian critics.

If liberal theory and practice are to be reformed, then a proper balance must be achieved between personal and civic freedom, between individual and associative pluralism. As Michael Walzer has argued, "it is a mistake, and a characteristically liberal mistake, to think that the existing patterns of association are entirely or even largely voluntary and contractual, that is, the product of will alone."[43] Many of the associations that are decisive for shaping personal values, virtues, and character are those which people do not choose: the corporate identities bequeathed by family, race, gender, class, and religious community. The decisions people make concerning which voluntary associations to enter will often be deeply influenced—both positively and negatively—by the fact that their personal identities have been fundamentally shaped by earlier nonvoluntary associations. The personal freedom so prized by modern classical liberalism *presupposes* a social network of corporate life. Individual freedom in liberal societies functions primarily to allow people to forsake those groups and associations that no longer contribute to their happiness or personal well-being. Individual freedom is primarily a dissociative force. Voluntariness in liberal society is essentially an exit privilege.

Revisionist liberalism recognizes both the associative and dissociative tendencies of pluralist societies and seeks to devise means whereby these countervailing forces can remain in balance. Since personal freedom both presupposes and destabilizes associational life, the key question facing liberal theory is whether government can properly play a role in supporting and encouraging the communal aspects of citizens' lives.

> It is a critical question for liberal theory and practice whether the associative passions and energies of ordinary people are likely over the long haul to survive the Four Mobilities and prove themselves sufficient to the requirements of pluralism. There is at least some evidence that they will not prove sufficient.[44]

As long as liberalism remains committed to the doctrine of governmental neutrality, it will lack the resources needed to respond to the most telling points of the communitarian critique. But as I have argued throughout this book, the doctrine of neutrality is conceptually confused and need not be a defining idea of liberal theory. The essential commitments of liberal political theory—liberty, equality, and toleration—in no way depend on the notion of governmental neutrality.

In the view of the revisionists, democratic governments must be "deliberately nonneutral."[45] They must seek to define those goods, purposes, and virtues that support a liberal society's fundamental commitment to liberty, equality, and toleration. While those commitments must always be subject to critical scrutiny, and while provision must be made for individual dissent, liberal governments can and ought to support associations that contribute to a democratic society's "self-limiting conception of the good." Since associations are always at risk in a liberal society, it becomes especially important that the state "endorse and sponsor . . . those [communities] that seem most likely to provide shapes and purposes congenial to the shared values of a liberal society."[46] Among the virtues essential to a vital pluralistic liberal society are independence, fidelity, tolerance, courage, loyalty, and responsibility.[47]

Perhaps most important of all, a revised liberal polity would provide support and encouragement for those communities that foster the skills of pluralist citizenship: the ability to function virtuously and effectively within a diverse society. Modern human identity is inevitably shaped within a variety of communal settings, and conflicts of values and purposes are commonplace within contemporary life. The modern pluralist citizen must learn to value diversity while still forging a coherent, though revisable, sense of self. This self is neither the "unencumbered self" of classical modern liberalism nor the "constitutive self" shaped within a single intact community. Rather, the self of the pluralist citizen is—to use a religious metaphor—the "pilgrim self," a person shaped within inherited communities of character but free to enjoy the mobility of liberal society. Inevitably the sense of self changes as communal influences vary over a lifetime and as personal freedom functions to create a distinctive individual. The pilgrim self is always "in progress," but as the pluralist citizen develops it must be equipped to evaluate critically the many alternatives that a mobile society will present. In order to survive, much less to flourish, in such a world, the pluralist citizen must nurture those virtues and values distinctive to a liberal society committed to liberty, equality, and toleration. And a liberal society is fully justified in encouraging those communities and associations that properly contribute to the formation of the pluralist citizen.[48]

According to the revisionists, liberal society is best understood, in John Rawls's helpful phrase, as a "social union of social unions."[49] Democracies seek both to foster the diversity of associational life and to forge a critical "overlapping consensus" concerning the fundamental values and virtues of liberal society. Government neither stands "beyond good and evil" neutrally arbitrating conflicts between warring factions nor simply defines a *summum bonum* or common good for the whole culture. Rather, public life—including government and other public but nongovernmental associations—provides the forum within which the ongoing discussion concerning the goods and purposes of liberal society takes place. The goal of the democratic political process is not to define for all time the essence of liberal society but to engage in the continuing critical conversation about the many aims and goals we share in common.[50] Ironically, the best definition of a revised liberal polity has been provided by that archcommunitarian Alasdair MacIntyre. His definition of a "living tradition" applies equally well to the revisionist view of liberal polity. Liberal society is "an historically extended, socially embodied argument, and an argument precisely in part about the goods which constitute that [society] . . . [Liberal societies] when vital, embody continuities of conflict."[51]

If a liberal society does indeed embody ongoing arguments about the goods and purposes of that society, the question still remains: what role can religious communities play in that pluralistic argument? Does the revised view of liberalism sketched in this chapter make possible a renewed public voice for communities of faith? Can religious communities take their place among other associations that seek to define the values of the liberal "social union of social unions?"[52] How should we reinterpret the religion clauses of the first amendment in light of this revised view of liberal theory and practice? These are questions I will address in the final two chapters of this work.

## NOTES

1. For one of the strongest statements concerning the essential secularity of liberal government, see Robert Audi, "The Separation of Church and State and the Obligations of Citizenship," *Philosophy & Public Affairs* 18,3 (Summer 1989): 259-296. See also the subsequent discussion: Paul Weithman, "The Separation of Church and State: Some Questions for Professor Audi," *Philosophy & Public Affairs* 20,1 (Winter 1991): 52-65; and Robert Audi, "Religious Commitment and Secular Reason: A Reply to Professor Weithman," ibid., pp. 66-76.

2. I include in this category writers such as Bruce Ackerman, Ronald Dworkin, Amy Gutmann, Stephen Macedo, and Judith Shklar.

3. I include in this category thinkers such as Stanley Hauerwas, Alasdair MacIntyre, and Michael Sandel. Sandel's position is the least fully developed, and thus his identification as a "sectarian communitarian" may be problematic. Sandel's early philosophical critique of liberalism, and particularly of John Rawls, suggested that liberalism and communitarianism were incompatible philosophical positions. But in recent essays Sandel may be developing a more "revisionist" point of view (cf. footnote 16).

4. Stanley Hauerwas, *A Community of Character* (Notre Dame: University of Notre Dame Press, 1981), pp. 82, 78-79.

5. Michael Sandel, "Freedom of Conscience or Freedom of Choice?" *Articles of Faith, Articles of Peace*, edited by James Davison Hunter and Os Guinness (Washington, D.C.: The Brookings Institution, 1990). Sandel's thorough and influential analysis of the liberal tradition is found in *Liberalism and the Limits of Justice* (Cambridge: Cambridge University Press, 1982).

6. Alasdair MacIntyre, *After Virtue* (Notre Dame: University of Notre Dame Press, 1981), p. 8.

**7.** Ibid., p. 236.

**8.** Sandel, "Freedom of Conscience or Freedom of Choice?" p. 76.

**9.** Ibid.

**10.** Ibid. For related comments see *Liberalism and the Limits of Justice*, pp. 175-183.

**11.** Hauerwas, *A Community of Character*, p. 84.

**12.** Sandel, *Liberalism and the Limits of Justice*, p. 183.

**13.** MacIntyre, *After Virtue*, p. 245.

**14.** Ibid., p. 236.

**15.** Hauerwas, *A Community of Character*, pp. 83 - 85.

**16.** While this is certainly true of Hauerwas and MacIntyre, Sandel's position on the separation of church and state is less clear. Indeed, in Sandel's most recent reflections on the question of religion's role in public life he appears to be developing a position that brings him closer to the "liberal revisionists." "Is religion among the forms of identity likely to generate a fuller citizenship and a more vital public life? Or does it depend on the religion; might some religious convictions erode rather than enhance the civic virtues required of citizens in a pluralistic society? . . . Perhaps an attempt to address [these questions] would itself enrich the discourse of American public life." Sandel, "Freedom of Conscience or Freedom of Choice?" p. 92.

**17.** Hauerwas, 86.

**18.** For a thorough-going treatment of the structural weaknesses of communitarian thought, see Stephen Holmes, "The Permanent Structure of Antiliberal Thought," *Liberalism and the Moral Life*, edited by Nancy L. Rosenblum (Cambridge: Harvard University Press, 1989), pp. 227-254.

**19.** The most thorough treatment of the exclusionary character of the communitarian position is Susan Moller Okin, *Justice, Gender, and the Family* (New York: Basic Books, 1989). Note, for example, her discussion of MacIntyre's argument: "MacIntyre does not confront the pivotal fact that 'the good life' not only excludes but *depends* upon the exclusion of the great majority of people, including all women. . . . MacIntyre points out that Aristotle's meritocratic theory of political justice 'unfortunately' depends on his belief that farmers, artisans, merchants, and women cannot exercise the virtues 'necessary for participation in the active life of the polis.' But he does not explain how a modern Aristotelian might overcome this rather large problem. In fact, although the Aristotelian tradition, as presented by MacIntyre, is supposedly aimed at the human good, only those whose productive, reproductive, and daily service needs are fully taken care of by others, and who are therefore free to engage in the highest goods—political activity and intellectual life—are regarded as fully human. This would seem to be a philosophy in need of some considerable adaptation, if it is to be relevant in the late twentieth century!" pp. 52, 54.

**20.** The role of "armed civic virtue" in creating solidarity within republican regimes has been traced by Jean Bethge Elshtain, *Women and War* (New York: Basic Books, 1987). Throughout the republican tradition, she argues, "Machiavelli's emphasis on war as vital social force as well as dire necessity, as creator of social solidarity as well as destructive tragedy, comes through loud and clear. As the penultimate form of collective struggle, war symbolizes what solidarity, one for all and all for one, is about. Civic virtue is armed and willful, the source of legitimacy, stability, the basis of the *res publica*. Machiavellian themes echo through the subsequent history of political discourse in the West" (p. 59). The recent outpouring of patriotic fervor in our otherwise fragmented nation during the Gulf War supports Elshtain's thesis that republican solidarity requires periodic outbreaks of hostilities. The relatively short life of that fervor may indicate, however, that Americans are ready for a kind of solidarity that does not require the presence of an external enemy.

**21.** Michael Walzer, "The Communitarian Critique of Liberalism," *Political Theory* 18, 1, (February, 1990), p. 6.

**22.** I include in this category such thinkers as Jean Bethge Elshtain, William Galston, Michael Perry, Nancy Rosenblum, Jeffrey Stout, Charles Taylor, and Michael Walzer. On the basis of the interpretation I offered in chapter 4, John Rawls would also be considered a liberal revisionist.

**23.** Walzer, "The Communitarian Critique of Liberalism," p. 12.

**24.** Ibid., pp. 12-13.

**25.** Ibid., pp. 13-14. A similar argument has been made—at greater length and with more philosophical precision—by Jeffrey Stout in *Ethics after Babel* (Boston: Beacon Press, 1988), pp. 191-242: "Moral discourse in our society can itself be understood as held together by a relatively limited but nonetheless real and significant agreement on the good. . . . Our disagreements about moral issues have proved especially difficult to resolve, but our disagreement about what human beings are like and what is good for us does not go all the way. . . . Complete disagreement about something leaves us unable to identify a common matter to disagree over. It therefore makes sense to speak of disagreement, in morals as much as elsewhere, only if we are prepared to recognize a background of agreement. . . . Most of us do agree on the essentials of what might be called the provisional telos of our society" (pp. 211-212).

**26.** The classical statement of this position is in MacIntyre's *After Virtue*, pp. 6-21. He addresses the consequences of this problem in *Whose Justice? Which Rationality?* (Notre Dame: University of Notre Dame Press, 1988), pp. 1-11 and 349-403. While MacIntyre's position in the latter book is developed with enormous philosophical sophistication, it does not depart decisively from the sectarian position he had developed earlier.

**27.** Isaiah Berlin, "Two Concepts of Liberty," *Four Essays on Liberty* (Oxford: Oxford University Press, 1979), pp. 118-172. For a contemporary defense and restatement of Berlin's position in the classical liberal tradition see, Stephen Macedo, *Liberal Virtues: Citizenship, Virtue, and Community in Liberal Constitutionalism* (Oxford: Clarendon Press, 1990), pp. 203-253.

**28.** Berlin, pp. 169-170. In his more recent work Berlin has developed his position in such a way as to soften the claim of mere incommensurability. "Some among the Great Goods cannot live together. That is a conceptual truth. We are doomed to choose, and every choice may entail an irreparable loss." "The Pursuit of the Ideal," *The Crooked Timber of Humanity* (New York: Knopf, 1991), p. 13.

**29.** At precisely this point, a fundamental tension arises in John Rawls' position. Rawls, like the revisionists, wants to assert the political possibility of an "overlapping consensus," but, like the classical liberals, he fears that the introduction of fundamental values into the political discussion will provoke the kind of moral and political disagreement that democratic governments cannot resolve. Because Rawls does not follow either Berlin or MacIntyre on the issue of incommensurability, however, his position remains open to revisionist correction. It is important to note that Rawls also argues that liberalism does encourage the development of a range of civic goods and virtues essential to democratic citizenship. See *Political Liberalism*, pp. 173-211.

**30.** The fundamental values inscribed within the American Constitution continue to provide the common framework for political discussion and disagreement within the United States. Contending parties regularly appeal to the Constitution to show that their positions are in keeping with the fundamental principles of liberal democracy. Given the generality of constitutional values and the changing historical contexts within which they must be interpreted, these shared principles are often underdeterminate for resolving conflicts regarding public policy. But underdeterminacy is not the same as incommensurability, because the former assumes a context of common beliefs and principles while the latter denies that such a context exists. While underdeterminacy can create the vexing problem of intractable moral debate, that is considerably less threatening than the problem of disputes that are irresolvable in principle. The former problem is patient of practical and political resolution; the latter is not. For a helpful discussion of underdeterminacy in moral disputes, see Michael J. Perry, *Love and Power: The Proper Role of Religion and Morality in American Politics* pp. 91-112.

**31.** The best discussion of the nature of moral disagreement in liberal society is Jeffrey Stout, *Ethics After Babel* (Boston: Beacon Press, 1988), pp. 13-59 and 191-242.

**32.** Donald Davidson, "On the Very Idea of a Conceptual Scheme," *Inquiries into Truth and Interpretation* (Oxford: Oxford University Press, 1984), pp.

**33.** Stout, *Ethics After Babel*, pp. 19-20.

**34.** Stout, p. 212. If the revisionist position is correct, as I believe it to be, then the analysis offered by commentators such as Alasdair MacIntyre and, more recently, James Davison Hunter presents an exaggerated view of moral conflict within contemporary public life. Hunter seeks to describe *sociologically* the problem of incommensurable moral debate that MacIntyre has defined *philosophically*. He claims that American culture is caught in the grip of a "culture war" between two groups, the progressives and the orthodox, who hold fundamentally "differing worldviews" (42) and operate from "different and opposing bases of moral authority" (43). Hunter's statement of the incommensurability of progressive and orthodox disagreement clearly echoes MacIntyre's earlier work. For example, Davison writes: "The central dynamic of the cultural realignment is not merely that different public philosophies create diverse public opinion. These alliances, rather, reflect the *institutionalization and politicization of two fundamentally different cultural systems*. Each side operates from within its own constellation of values, interests, and assumptions. At the center of each are two distinct conceptions of moral authority—two different ways of apprehending reality, of ordering experience, of making moral judgments. Each side of the cultural divide, then speaks with a different moral vocabulary. Each side operates out of a different mode of debate and persuasion. Each side represents the tendencies of a separate and competing moral galaxy. They are, indeed, 'worlds apart'" (128). Nevertheless, Hunter's description of contemporary moral debate depicts vivid and genuine disagreements about the nature and limits of personal freedom, the definition and values associated with the family, the character of human sexuality, and the goals and functions of public education. While these debates are vigorous, and occasionally even fierce, they are surely genuine disagreements about the definition of the fundamental values of American democracy. Precisely because they are genuine disagreements they *cannot* be incommensurable positions "representing separate and competing moral galax(ies)." While Hunter's descriptions of moral conflict are useful and compelling, his analysis is flawed, in large part because of the faulty sociological theory he employs. For further treatment of Hunter's position, and particularly his view of the "sacred," see chapter 6.

**35.** "From our site in the present, appeals to either old notions of a robust, coherent community or a robust, coherent individualism fall short of mapping the terms of a civic ethos that can continue to sustain us and form both personal and civic identities." Elshtain, *Women and War*, p. 250.

**36.** These values, of course, have limits. Criminals who violate the law must be coerced; persons who commit treason or threaten the overthrow of government can be excluded; and governments can arm themselves for the purposes of defense. But these are precisely limiting cases that define the centrality of noncoercion, inclusivity, and peaceful means of conflict resolution for liberal democracies.

**37.** Charles Taylor, "Cross-Purposes: The Liberal-Communitarian Debate," *Liberalism and the Moral Life*, edited by Nancy L. Rosenblum (Cambridge: Harvard University Press, 1989). pp. 169-70.

**38.** Ibid., p. 171.

**39.** Charles Taylor, "Religion in a Free Society," *Articles of Faith, Articles of Peace* (Washington, D.C.: The Brookings Institution, 1990), p. 94. These notions of liberal and civic freedom are derived from Isaiah Berlin's classic discussion of "negative" and "positive" freedom in *Two Concepts of Liberty* (Oxford: Oxford University Press, 1979), pp. 118-172. It is important to note that both notions of freedom that Taylor describes represent the fundamental liberal value of non-coercion.

**40.** Taylor, "Cross-Purposes: The Liberal-Communitarian Debate," p. 172.

**41.** The critique of the individualism of liberal society has, of course, been the major theme of two important projects of the sociological team headed by Robert Bellah. *Habits of the Heart: Individualism and Commitment in American Life* (Berkeley: University of California Press, 1985), and *The Good Society* (Berkeley: University of California Press, 1991).

**42.** Walzer, "The Communitarian Critique of Liberalism," p. 15.

**43.** Ibid.

**44.** Ibid., p. 16.

**45.** Ibid. This argument is made at great length and in much greater detail by William Galston, *Liberal Purposes: Goods, Virtues, and Diversity in the Liberal State* (Cambridge: Cambridge University Press, 1991), pp. 70-237, and Michael Perry, *Love and Power: The Proper Role of Religion and Morality in American Politics* (New York: Oxford University Press, 1990), pp. 8-28.

**46.** Walzer, "The Communitarian Critique of Liberalism," p. 17.

**47.** Galston, *Liberal Purposes*, pp. 213-237.

**48.** It is essential that this argument *not* be understood as disadvantaging either relatively homogenous social groups or associations that define themselves primarily as "communities of dissent." Under the revisionist understanding of pluralist citizenship, government must seek to protect those communities which, because they differ from the majority, contribute to the fabric of pluralist culture. Such communities deserve the same support and encouragement as other, more obviously pluralist associations as long as they do not seek to undermine the fundamental democratic commitment to liberty, equality, and toleration.

**49.** John Rawls, *A Theory of Justice* (Cambridge: Harvard University Press, 1971), p. 527.

**50.** Jeffrey Stout has articulated a congenial notion of liberal politics in *Ethics After Babel:* "The languages of morals in our discourse are many, and they have remarkably diverse historical origins. They are embedded in specific social practices and institutions—religious, political, artistic, scientific, athletic, economic, and so on. We need many different moral concepts because there are many different linguistic threads woven into any fabric of practices and institutions as rich as ours. It is a motley; not a building in need of new foundations but a coat of many colors, one constantly in need of mending and patching, sometimes even recutting and restyling. We can make good use of Aristotelian and civic republican talk about the virtue and politics as a social practice directed toward the common good without supposing that this sort of moral language requires us to jettison talk of rights and tolerance. We can use this talk by thinking of liberal political institutions as oriented toward a provisional *telos*—a widely shared but self-limiting consensus on the highest good achievable under circumstances like ours. But this *telos* justifies a kind of tolerance foreign to the classical teleological tradition. And it rightly directs our moral attention to something our ancestors often neglected, namely, the injustice of excluding people from social practices because of their race, gender, religion, or place of birth" (pp. 291-292).

**51.** MacIntyre, *After Virtue*, pp. 207, 206.

**52.** Charles Taylor discusses this issue in his article "Religion in a Free Society," but he is content merely to describe the dilemma regarding religion's place in American public life. His insightful comments are, nonetheless, worth quoting at length. "For some, America is founded on certain religious visions, and one departs from the common purpose in wanting to exclude God from the public realm. For others, there is an obvious liberal solution based on respecting different private choices in this matter, and those who resist this are illiberal and go against the American way. The very nature of a Kulturkampf resides in this certainty that only one solution is defensible . . . Liberal American intellectuals tend to be extraordinarily blind to the force of religion even in their own lives, let alone in those of their compatriots. On the other side, proponents of the Christian right are often ready to indulge in crude conspiracy theories that utterly caricature the deeply felt convictions of their more secular-minded neighbors. If one could get beyond this . . . the conflict might be transformed. A struggle in which each could understand something of the force of the other's response to a common dilemma would virtually by definition be proof against degenerating into a Kulturkampf" (p. 112).

# 6

# *Public Religion in a Pluralistic Democracy: A Proposal*

The argument of the previous chapter has shown that liberal democracy, appropriately revisioned, is capable of including within its purview diverse conceptions of the good derived from a variety of public communities and associations. If a liberal democracy is a "social union of social unions," then, as John Rawls has acknowledged, government "must draw upon various ideas of the good" in devising just policies for a pluralistic society.[1] Politics ought to provide the realm within which contending parties seek to *persuade* one another that a particular course of action best serves the common good of the citizenry, that is, helps forge an "overlapping consensus" concerning issues of public importance. But for that process to be effective, representatives of governmental institutions must articulate the fundamental liberal values (liberty, equality, and toleration, among others) that undergird the entire process of policy development. Far from being neutral with regard to these goods and purposes, representatives of a liberal democracy must strive both to state the basic moral principles of democratic government and to show how they apply to particular policy choices. Without such thoughtful moral reasoning, the political process will certainly degenerate into a contentious, manipulative, even ruthless exercise of sheer power. While the exercise of power will inevitably be an enduring aspect of democratic politics, it must be balanced and modified by the noncoercive process of rational moral persuasion. If we despair of our ability to *persuade* one another, even in the most pluralistic of cultures, then we abandon a fundamental principle of democratic government—the commitment always to prefer noncoercive, nonviolent means of conflict resolution.

The question remains, however, whether specifically *religious* conceptions of the good may contribute to the formation of the overlapping consensus essential to the development of policies within a pluralistic democracy. Can religious beliefs contribute to the democratic process of moral persuasion? Do religious beliefs meet the basic criteria of accessibility and publicity or do such beliefs inherently rest on hidden and private sources of conviction? It may be the case that even a revisioned liberalism, one that rejects notions of governmental neutrality, might still properly demand that rational justification within a pluralistic democracy be purely *secular*.

Indeed, many liberal revisionists remain skeptical about assigning a public role to arguments grounded in religious premises. Kent Greenawalt, for example, argues that individuals are justified in relying on religious convictions in their political decision making whenever "shared premises of justice and criteria for determining truth cannot resolve critical questions of fact [or] fundamental questions of value."[2] When shared premises and criteria are available, however, a liberal democracy rightly requires of its citizens that they justify their political choices in purely secular terms. Moreover, while citizens are justified in *holding* political positions based on their personal religious convictions, they should not employ those beliefs in the process of *persuading* others to accept their positions. Thus, religious convictions can play a personal or private but not a public justificatory role.

> The government of a liberal society knows no religious truth and a crucial premise about a liberal society is that citizens of extremely diverse religious views can build principles of political order and social justice that do not depend on particular religious beliefs. The common currency of political discourse is nonreligious argument about human welfare. Public discourse about political issues with those who do not share religious premises should be cast in other than religious terms. . . . Fully public discourse advocating political positions should not rely on explicitly religious arguments.[3]

Liberals, including those committed to revisionist principles, are understandably skittish about the public role of religion. Even as sympathetic an interpreter of religion as Jeffrey Stout expresses reservations about the role of public religion and theology in a pluralistic democracy. Any discussion of moral reasoning within contemporary public life, Stout writes, dare not neglect the role that theological ideas and religious conflict played in bringing about the modern world. A more adequate treatment of these themes would, I think, make evident the risks of reshaping public discourse according to the dictates of a set of theological ideas. It would be one thing if we had already resolved our religious differences and settled rationally on a common public theology. . . . Suppose we render the polemics and warfare of the Reformation and Counter-Reformation as a contest between two (or more) fully articulated conceptions of the good, fleshed out in competing schemes of the virtues. Might it be that theology got into trouble with the intellectuals largely because it was unable to provide a vocabulary for debating and deciding matters pertaining to the common good without resort to violence? Could it be that the distinctive vocabularies of modern politics and ethics—the language of human rights, of Benthamite utility, of respect for persons, and so on—owe their existence in part to a complicated history of attempts to minimize the unhappy consequences of religious conflict?[4]

As Stout points out, liberalism first emerged as a reaction against the post-Reformation religious wars, and its advocates sought to devise a political philosophy that tolerated religious diversity while eschewing any particular religious justification for its democratic polity. Liberalism, as the late Judith Shklar so vividly taught us, was devised as a bulwark against cruelty, including the cruelty perpetrated in the name of religion. Her remarks about the genesis of liberalism are instructive for the issue of religion's public role within a liberal democracy. Liberalism's

origins are in the terrible tension within Christianity between the demands of creedal orthodoxy and those of charity, between faith and morality. The cruelties of the religious wars had the effect of turning many Christians away from the public policies of the churches to a morality that saw toleration as an expression of Christian charity. . . . Others, torn by conflicting spiritual impulses, became skeptics who put cruelty and fanaticism at the very head of the human vices. . . . In either case the individual, whether the bearer of a sacred conscience or the potential victim of cruelty, is to be protected against the incursions of public oppression. . . . Liberalism's deepest grounding is in place from the first, in the conviction of the earliest defenders of toleration, born in horror, that cruelty is an absolute evil, an offense against God or humanity. It is out of that tradition that the political liberalism of fear arose and continues amid the terror of our time to have relevance.[5]

By defining cruelty as the primary human vice, liberalism disregards "the idea of sin as it is understood by revealed religion. . . . By putting it unconditionally first, with nothing above us to excuse or to forgive acts of cruelty, one closes off any appeal to any order other than that of actuality."[6] Liberalism, Shklar argues, must remain an essentially secular polity.

The basic questions facing any proposal for the revival of public religious discourse within a pluralistic democratic polity are (1) can religious arguments be introduced into public political conversation without reviving the factionalism and contentiousness so feared by the framers of the Constitution? and (2) can religious arguments meet the criteria of publicity that must govern all rational noncoercive speech within a liberal democracy? In this chapter, I will review the arguments against public religious discourse and offer an account of public religion and theology that is appropriate for a pluralistic liberal democracy.

## PLURALISTIC DEMOCRACY AND CRITERIA OF PRECLUSION

John Rawls's recognition that a democratic consensus must draw on various notions of the good inherent in comprehensive schemes while still remaining distinct from those schemes provides a fundamental insight into the "conditions of publicity" required by democratic societies. Seen from the vantage point of democratic government, conditions of publicity should be broadly defined so that they might be maximally inclusive of the manifold voices comprised by a pluralistic culture, thereby identifying the common or shared beliefs of that culture. Seen from the vantage point of citizens whose values are shaped by comprehensive schemes, the conditions of publicity must at the same time respect the particularity of each citizen's commitments and convictions. Conditions of publicity ought, therefore, to address the criteria governing arguments that seek to form a democratic consensus and the criteria justifying proper withdrawal from such a consensus. Conditions of publicity ought properly to address issues of *dissent* as well as *consent* within democratic conversation.

Most recent discussions of this issue have focused solely on the threshold conditions that any argument must meet in order to participate in democratic discussion. Moreover, most liberal theorists have construed these threshold requirements negatively; that is, they have devised various "principles of preclusion" designed to exclude certain arguments, primarily religious ones, from entering political debate.[7] Public speech, so the standard argument goes, must appeal to "shared premises" and "publicly accessible reasons" in order to be justifiable within a democratic polity.[8] Religious and theological discourse, most liberal theorists argue, should not function in the public square because such speech cannot meet these basic criteria of publicity.

In its strongest version, the argument for preclusion states that any issue which precipitates a disagreement concerning moral truth should be removed from the democratic political agenda. Bruce Ackerman states the case this way.

> When you and I learn that we disagree about one or another dimension of the moral truth, we should not search for some common value that will trump this disagreement; nor should we try to translate it into some putatively neutral framework; nor should we seek to transcend it by talking about how some unearthly creature might resolve it. We should simply say *nothing at all* about this disagreement and put the moral ideals that divide us off the conversational agenda of the liberal state.[9]

Underlying this position is a conviction that conceptions of the good that may be valid for one's personal beliefs and conduct, namely, within the sphere of privacy, cannot serve as reasons for the justification of public policies precisely because they are not shared by all participants in a pluralistic society. When such conceptions of the good do enter the public debate, they are invariably irresolvable and resist adjudication within the framework of democratic politics. To avoid interminable fractious debate, such issues need to be excluded altogether from the democratic political agenda.

But surely this position is hopelessly restrictive. It seems odd indeed to suggest that disputants who disagree ethically about some policy issue should forgo reliance upon their deepest moral beliefs simply because these beliefs are the source of disagreement. Surely one essential aspect of the democratic political process—the process of rational justification and persuasion—is the attempt to persuade one's fellow citizens that a particular policy is preferable because it best serves the common good. Proponents of differing welfare policies, for example, regularly and rightly appeal to moral principles to justify "workfare" programs, or expansion of aid to dependent children, or strengthening of paternal support laws. If these disputants were to deny the relevance of their moral reasons for supporting such policies *at the outset of the debate*, then there would seem little reason to continue the discussion at all. Either the parties would have to resort to nonrational, that is, coercive or manipulative, means of prevailing or they would simply agree to disagree.[10] In either case, the liberal value of noncoercive rational persuasion would hardly be advanced, and such restrictive criteria would make it virtually impossible to gain consensus for policies that are fundamentally important to the republic.

In a pluralistic democracy, citizens will inevitably, and often reasonably, disagree concerning the morality of public policies. If political deliberation is not to come to a grinding halt before every moral disagreement, then some principles must be discerned that can guide our public life when we are faced with moral heterogeneity. The problem of contemporary pluralistic politics is this: We need to find some common ground on which to base policies designed to serve the public welfare, but given our cultural diversity, we are unlikely to discern universal principles upon which all will agree. If we are to forge some kind of overlapping consensus, we must identify those criteria which will allow us to seek a middle ground between universal norms agreed on by all and the conflicting and competing interests and preferences of groups and individuals. In other words, conditions of publicity must designate a public space in which acceptable arguments are justified by criteria claiming less than universality but more than mere subjectivity.

The liberal attempt to state criteria of preclusion that eliminate religious arguments *tout court* from consideration, is, I believe, doomed to failure. We have already seen that these arguments either rely on an indefensible view of religion as inherently irrational or exclude religious arguments from public discussion at the expense of eliminating important moral arguments as well. Still some liberal theorists persist in making the case against religion, in large part because they fear that if religious arguments are accepted within public debate, then any argument, no matter how irrational or fanatical, must be admitted as well. But the categories these theorists employ to make their case against religion simply do not stand up to careful scrutiny.

Thomas Nagel, for example, is concerned primarily with the problem of coercion in democratic societies. Given the diversity within most democratic cultures it is inconceivable that policies can be devised that gain universal support of the citizenry. Inevitably, some citizens who oppose a policy must be coerced to abide by it once it has attained the status of law. But how can we rationally justify such coercive action? To what moral grounds can we appeal?

> The real difficulty is to make sense of . . . the idea of something which is neither an appeal to my own beliefs nor an appeal to beliefs that we all share. It cannot be the latter because it is intended precisely to justify the forcible imposition in some cases of measures that are not universally accepted. We need a distinction between two kinds of disagreement—one whose grounds make it all right for the majority to use political power in the service of their opinion, and another whose grounds are such that it would be wrong for the majority to do so.[11]

Though he rejects the strict standard of universally shared premises, Nagel still proposes a "common ground of justification," an impartial, impersonal and objective foundation that provides a proper public basis for judgment other than a mere "appeal to our beliefs."[12] Public justification, Nagel argues, requires a commitment to "the exercise of a common critical rationality."[13] Without some common ground of justification for my moral and political beliefs, I become "guilty of appealing simply to my belief." A pluralistic democracy must have some common standards of rational justification if the chaos of mere assertion and counterassertion is to be avoided.

Nagel suggests that two essential criteria for publicity are entailed by this commitment to a common rationality, criteria which, he asserts, cannot be satisfied by religious beliefs.

> Public justification in a context of actual disagreement requires, first, preparedness to submit one's reasons to the criticism of others. . . . This means that it must be possible to present to others the basis of your own beliefs, so that once you have done so, *they have what you have,* and can arrive at a judgment on the same basis. That is not possible if part of the source of your conviction is personal faith or revelation—because to report your faith or revelation to someone else is not

to give him what you have, as you do when you show him your evidence or give him your argument. Public justification requires, second, an expectation that if others who do not share your belief are wrong, there is probably an explanation of their error which is not circular. . . . One may not always have the information necessary to give such an account, but one must believe there is one, and that the justifiability of one's own belief would survive a full examination of the reasons behind theirs. These two points may be combined in the idea that a disagreement that falls on objective common ground must be open-ended in the possibility of its investigation and pursuit, and not come down finally to a bare confrontation between incompatible personal points of view. I suggest that conflicts of religious faith fail this test, and most empirical and many moral disagreements do not.[14]

In devising these criteria of publicity, Nagel is seeking a middle ground between the unattainable ideal of universally shared premises for political decision making and the unsettling specter of a chaotic political arena in which combatants irrationally assert their conflicting personal opinions. Without some common critical rationality, all political debate would be reduced to the incommensurable disagreement characteristic of religious strife.

Nagel's dilemma is a familiar one, for it replays a classic conundrum of modern philosophy. Since the time of Descartes, modern philosophers have been obsessed with a single fundamental question: how can we be certain that our beliefs are rationally justified? Nagel has simply given a distinctive political twist to that basic query: how, given the many fundamental disagreements that arise in pluralistic societies, can we resolve our differences by peaceable and rational means? Without some firm foundation, some common ground of justification, we are left with the chaos of warring factions and conflicting personal beliefs or preferences. Either we discern a common critical rationality or we are doomed to interminable irrational bickering. Thus Nagel manifests the symptoms of the modern philosophical malady that Richard Bernstein has termed the "Cartesian anxiety," that "grand and seductive Either/Or. *Either* there is some support for our being, a fixed foundation for our knowledge, *or* we cannot escape the forces of darkness that envelop us with madness, with intellectual and moral chaos."[15] But as the philosophical discussion of the past two decades has taught us, and, as I have argued throughout this volume, these choices are false alternatives.[16] We need choose neither an objectivism that narrowly defines universal criteria of rationality nor a relativism that despairs of all rational conversation and moral consensus. It is possible, both philosophically and politically, to find a way between these two equally unhappy options.

To his credit, Nagel does not seize the standard foundationalist alternative of seeking criteria of rational justification that will ineluctably resolve all moral disagreements. He recognizes that the appeal to "common ground does not mean that people will actually reach agreement, nor does it mean that only one belief is reasonable on the evidence."[17] It is possible for disputants to disagree rationally, for rivals to find one another's public justification unpersuasive without charging each other with unreasonableness or irrationality. "We therefore have to recognize that there can be enough considerations on more than one side of a question in the public domain so that reasonable belief is partly a matter of judgment, and is not uniquely determined by the publicly available arguments."[18] Having admitted that personal judgment inevitably plays a role in rational justification and persuasion, Nagel acknowledges that his appeal to impartiality and objectivism may appear hopelessly compromised. However, to keep subjective forces at bay and religious convictions on the sideline of public debate, he struggles to distinguish personal judgment from subjective conviction or religious faith. "Judgment," he asserts, "is not the same as faith, or pure moral intuition. . . . The distinction between a disagreement in the common, public domain and a clash between irreconcilable subjective convictions" remains significant.[19]

In one final effort to maintain his notion of a "common ground of justification" while still acknowledging a role for personal judgment, Nagel draws a (fatal) distinction between "belief" and "truth." Such a distinction must be drawn, Nagel argues, if rational disagreement about matters of truth is to be possible. "Disagreements over the truth must be interpreted as resulting from differences of judgment in the exercise of a common reason. Otherwise, the appeal to truth collapses into an appeal to what I believe, and belief carries a very different kind of weight in political arguments."[20] If I seek to coerce you to act in accord with what I *believe*, you will undoubtedly resist such a subjective ground of justification. But if I seek to coerce you to act by an appeal to the *truth*, you will have less reason to quarrel or complain, for my position will bear the marks of impartiality and objectivity.[21]

But surely this distinction between belief and truth cannot be maintained, at least not as Nagel seeks to defend it. Although truth and justified belief are not conceptually equivalent, they cannot be separated in the fashion Nagel proposes. I assert *p* to be true, because I believe I am rationally justified in asserting *p*. Thus "the appeal to truth" is inevitably "an appeal to what I believe," unless I am to become a hopelessly bifurcated person. Jeffrey Stout has stated the relation between truth claiming and justified belief with particular clarity.

> My talk of moral disagreement makes sense only if I grant that there is some truth of the matter in ethics to disagree over and only if I am prepared to say of people who disagree with me over the truth of moral propositions that it is they who are wrong. . . . We need impute no dishonor to those who disagree with us. Nor need we lack humility when we conclude that our beliefs are true, and, by implication, that those who disagree with us hold false beliefs. To hold our beliefs is precisely to accept them as true. It would be inconsistent, not a sign of humility, to say that people who disagree with beliefs we hold true are not themselves holding false beliefs. . . . When I am speaking of a proposition that I, here and now, take myself to be warranted in asserting or justified in believing, it will normally be a proposition that I, here and now, will accept and assert as a truth. If not my rationality or candor will be suspect."[22]

The effort to rescue rationally justified public arguments from the corrosive acids of religious subjectivity cannot be accomplished through the separation of truth and belief.

The liberal attempt to create restrictive conditions of publicity for a pluralistic democracy appears to face insuperable difficulties. In an effort to eliminate the most contentious issues from political debate, and particularly in the attempt to ban religious discourse from the public sphere, liberal arguments fail to sustain their desired conclusions. As the analysis of Nagel's position has shown, arguments for restrictive criteria of publicity are conceptually unstable. To be sufficiently broad to encompass the diversity of beliefs within a pluralistic society, the criteria must be so general as to provide little guidance for public discourse; to be sufficiently narrow to provide analytic rigor, the criteria must rely upon a standard of rationality that eliminates the most fundamental beliefs of many of the citizens whose consent is essential for a constitutional democracy. An inevitable conclusion begins to emerge: the effort to eliminate religious discourse from the public sphere by defining restrictive conditions of publicity appears doomed to failure. If liberal democracies are to honor the diversity of their own societies, they must be open to the variety of arguments (including religious arguments) that seek to define the common goods these societies should seek. The challenge facing revisionist liberal politics has been aptly stated by Joseph Raz.

> One must find a reasonable interpretation of the intuitively appealing idea that political principles must be accessible to people as they are. It is not enough, according to this intuition, that those who are totally rational and open to rational conversion will be persuaded, and be radically changed. Politics must take people as they come and be accessible to them, capable of commanding their consent without expecting them to change in any radical way.[23]

In the next section of this chapter I offer an account of public religion that seeks to contribute to devising a form of liberal politics appropriate for a pluralistic American society. While I will argue for the inclusion of religious arguments within democratic politics, I will also sketch some appropriate limits on the kind of religious discourse acceptable within a polity committed to the fundamental values of liberty, equality, and toleration.

## PUBLIC RELIGION IN A PLURALISTIC DEMOCRACY

In order to devise conditions of publicity that are true to democratic polity and yet compatible with a range of religious beliefs, we must distinguish between proper and improper understandings of the role of "faith" in public religious argumentation. Many interpreters, both within and without religious communities, define faith as the fundamental, nonrational, incorrigible sense of the sacred that embraces all of the believer's life and determines his or her beliefs, values, and behavior. Since faith is often construed as an internal, private source of personal conviction, it is thought by many to be inaccessible to reason, immune from doubt, and beyond the reach of argument. Thus, James Davison Hunter suggests that the so-called culture wars currently gripping American society stem from fundamentally opposed notions of moral authority grounded in irreconcilable notions of the sacred.

> In the final analysis, each side of the cultural divide can only talk
> past the other. . . . This is true because what both sides bring to
> the public debate is, at least consciously, non-negotiable. . . .
> What is ultimately at issue are deeply rooted and fundamentally
> different understandings of being and purpose. . . . What is ulti-
> mately at issue are different conceptions of the sacred. . . . Com-
> munities cannot and will not tolerate the desecration of the
> sacred. The problem is this: not only does each side of the cul-
> tural divide operate with a different conception of the sacred, but
> the mere existence of the one represents a certain desecration of
> the other.[24]

If Hunter is correct in his characterization of the role of the sacred in public debate, then the liberal inclination to prohibit religious
arguments from the public realm is certainly sound. But I want to propose a different view of religious faith, one that I believe is compatible
with the beliefs and practices of a wide range of believers in American
society. The view of faith I am offering here has ancient roots, but I will
restate this view in a contemporary vocabulary that is accessible to
those who are unfamiliar with the theological tradition from which it
is drawn.[25]

If we are to understand the proper role of faith in public discourse, it must placed within its proper communal context. In the
view I am proposing, faith is not primarily an individual phenomenon; it is, rather, an aspect of the life, practice, and world view of
a religious community.[26] Religions are best understood as "comprehensive interpretive schemes, usually embodied in myths or narratives and heavily ritualized, which structure human experience and
understanding of self and world."[27] As comprehensive schemes, religions seek to interpret the whole of reality with reference to the fundamental core of convictions, narratives, myths, and rituals that establish
the identity of a community. Properly understood, faith is the set of
convictions that defines the identity of a community and its members.
Those convictions do not dwell in some private inaccessible realm;
they are present "in, with and under" the myths, narratives, rituals,
and doctrines of the community.[28] If you seek to understand the faith
of a religious community, you must inquire into its literature, lore, and
liturgy.

Take, for example, one of the most peculiar beliefs of Christianity, the faith that Jesus Christ is risen and present within the contem-

porary Christian community. This apparently arcane belief is manifest in a variety of ways: in creedal formulation, in a body of sophisticated philosophical and theological reflection, in the ritual practice of the eucharist, and in biblical narratives. While some may find the belief odd, implausible, or even patently false, it is surely not private, inaccessible, or hidden from public scrutiny. While few people outside the Christian community have undertaken the study necessary to understand this belief, that is not because the belief itself is private or inaccessible. Even though it is not a widely shared belief (perhaps not even within the Christian community), it is still a genuinely *public* belief, namely, a belief available for public analysis. Many other beliefs to which religious folk might appeal will, in this same sense, be publicly accessible.[29]

A liberal skeptic may accept for the sake of argument that religious beliefs are, in the sense specified, public, but the skeptic may still assert that such beliefs ought not be admitted into political debate because they are not open to the reasoned exchange essential to a democratic polity. Religious beliefs, the skeptic may argue, are incorrigible, and thus proponents of such beliefs cannot possess the openness requisite for democratic deliberation. This objection is particularly important, since many believers seem to share the skeptic's notion that religious beliefs are incapable of correction.

Certainly within the Christian community (the religious community of which I am a member and thus know best), there is much disagreement regarding the corrigibility of religious belief. As recent sociological research has shown, most religious communities are divided within themselves on this question.[30] Those who represent the orthodox or conservative wing will accept considerably less correction of traditional belief than those who represent the progressive or liberal wing. Nonetheless, every confessional or denominational tradition has a view of the historical development of the community's faith, and must then allow for some degree of change or correction of those beliefs. Even fundamentalist Christians who accept a strict view of biblical authority must offer reasons why, for example, the entirety of the Levitical Code is no longer binding upon the Christian community. Thus, not even the most conservative of religious traditions accepts the utter incorrigibility of religious belief.

Yet certain beliefs and practices are so definitive of the identity of a community and its members that these beliefs cannot be given up without decisive change in communal self-understanding. These beliefs serve as basic convictions or background beliefs. Every coherent system of beliefs rests on certain convictions that are assumed to be true and thus provide stability for the whole framework. These beliefs are *basic* because the coherence of many other beliefs depends on the acceptance of these beliefs as true, and they are *background* because their axiomatic status makes their explicit justification unnecessary. While these background beliefs are not immune to revision, they must remain relatively fixed for the framework to remain stable. Revision or suspension of a background belief or basic conviction requires a rearrangement of all dependent beliefs and the possible rejection of some. These defining convictions are resistant to change, because they provide the community's essential identity.

Two important consequences follow from this discussion of basic religious convictions or background beliefs. First, while these fundamental beliefs resist revision, they are not in a logically strong sense incorrigible. The history of religion is replete with examples of fundamental restructuring of communal identity that have occurred when basic convictions have been revised or jettisoned (e.g., the Gentile mission of early Christianity, the Protestant reformations, the rise of historical criticism of the Bible). While religious believers may hold these convictions tenaciously, that tenacity need not (and should not) lead to fanaticism. Second, precisely because certain communal beliefs play a decisive role in shaping religious identity, democratic citizens who are also religious believers may experience divided loyalties if the expectations of the state and those of the faith community clash. That is why people of faith insist that conditions for publicity define criteria for dissent as well as consent. But freedom of dissent, of course, is precisely what the religion clauses of the first amendment are designed to protect.

It is important to observe that every community or social organization that functions to define the identity of its members will be characterized by basic convictions or background beliefs. The tenacity with which these convictions are held will largely depend on the community's effectiveness in shaping or nurturing its members' identity. Thus churches, synagogues, temples, mosques, and ashrams do not differ in kind from labor unions, voluntary associations, political parties, or other groups that provide a basic orientation for individual belief and behavior. Indeed, some evidence suggests that nonreligious groups or associations—especially self-help groups and political associations—often play a more definitive role in shaping the convictions and values of their members than do many communities of faith in contemporary society.[31]

The preceding discussion has shown that there is nothing inherent in religious belief or in communities of faith that should preclude them from participating fully in the persuasive forum of democratic politics. Indeed, this discussion of the characteristics of religious belief should assist us in devising conditions of publicity that are more fully attuned to the many convictions, values, and notions of the good that are inevitably a part of contemporary pluralistic public life.

## THE PLURALIST CITIZEN AND CONDITIONS OF PUBLICITY

In a pluralistic democracy in which the freedom of speech is guaranteed, it is a mistake, I believe, to define any "threshold requirements" that political arguments must meet in order to enter the political debate.[32] Rather, we should seek to define those virtues of citizenship that we seek to instill in all participants in our pluralistic democracy. These virtues will then suggest conditions of publicity that should guide citizens in their efforts to sift through the many arguments they will hear and make in a pluralistic conversation. Conditions of publicity should function not as threshold requirements but as norms of plausibility, that is, as criteria that democratic citizens should employ to evaluate arguments in the public domain.

THE NORM OF PUBLIC ACCESSIBILITY.   The fundamental insight of democratic polity, namely, that policy formulation within a pluralistic society must rely upon noncoercive means of building an overlapping consensus, provides the starting point for my proposal concerning public religion. If liberal democracies are societies in flux, self-critical communities seeking to forge some sense of common aims and purposes from the diverse interests and commitments of their citizens, then they will inevitably assign high value to the broad accessibility of public arguments. Arguments whose premises are open to public examination and scrutiny contribute to the democratic goal of peaceful and reasonable resolution of conflict and disagreement. Such arguments also contribute to the mutual understanding and respect so essential to the development of the pluralist citizen. Opponents who *understand* one another's reasons may not be *persuaded* by them, but they are more likely to remain in communal solidarity with one another than opponents who believe they are being deceived or manipulated. Consequently, public accessibility should be *encouraged* in all arguments that seek to contribute to the democratic process of building an overlapping consensus. Such accessibility cannot, however, be *demanded* in a society that protects free speech as a fundamental right. Persons are free to offer public arguments that appeal to emotion, base instincts, and private sources of revelation, but democratic societies should encourage citizens to resist such appeals as incompatible with the fundamental values of liberal polity.

THE NORM OF MUTUAL RESPECT.   In a pluralistic society, moral disagreement about public issues of great significance is commonplace. Throughout this volume I have argued that moral disagreement in our culture, while deep and pervasive, is not in principle irresolvable. The challenge to pluralistic democracies, then, is to encourage those habits of mind and behavior that will allow citizens to resolve their disagreements through noncoercive deliberative means and to live peacefully together when those disagreements cannot be resolved.[33] Mutual respect goes beyond mere toleration in that it requires of citizens that they grant to those with whom they disagree the same consideration that they themselves would hope to receive.

> Like tolerance, mutual respect is a form of agreeing to disagree. But mutual respect demands more than toleration. It requires a favorable attitude toward, and constructive interaction with, the persons with whom one disagrees. It consists in a reciprocal positive regard of citizens who manifest the excellence of character that permits a democracy to flourish in the face of (at least temporarily) irresolvable moral conflict.[34]

Citizens who manifest the virtue of mutual respect acknowledge the moral agency of those with whom they disagree and thereby treat their arguments as grounded not simply in personal preference or self-interest but in genuine moral conviction.

The criterion of mutual respect encourages citizens to affirm and develop the ties of solidarity associated with "civic freedom." Since those bonds are particularly fragile in a mobile, pluralistic society, it is necessary to cultivate those civic virtues that are essential to a deliberative democracy. By acknowledging the moral force of an argument with which one disagrees, a citizen remains open to the persuasive power of an alternative point of view. The intellectual openness fostered through mutual respect encourages citizens to value the process of moral persuasion and to hold their own positions with an appropriate degree of certainty. The recognition that there are morally defensible alternatives to one's own point of view allows citizens to affirm their positions with genuine conviction without lapsing into the dangers of fanaticism.

Fanaticism requires the obliteration of the opponent's point of view, a total rejection of the other's comprehensive scheme. True conviction simply implies that with reference to this argument or that policy, one holds the morally preferable position, but such a stance is fully compatible with a genuine appreciation for many of the other moral positions and political views within the other's comprehensive scheme. Moral disagreement, even on fundamental public issues, need not imply a conflict of world views. Citizens who disagree over a particular public issue can still affirm the broader consensus they share in their commitment to a democracy dedicated to liberty, equality, and mutual respect.

THE NORM OF MORAL INTEGRITY.   Amy Gutmann and Dennis Thompson have identified the traits characteristic of persons who exemplify moral integrity in their public lives. "*Consistency of speech* . . . indicates that a person holds [a political] position because it is a moral position, not for reasons of political advantage."[35] Public officials, for example, should espouse their political positions consistently, even among various constituencies who may hold opposing points of view. A politician who opposes use of public funds for busing of children to parochial schools should uphold that position when speaking to residents of a heavily Irish ward in the city as well as when addressing the teachers' union of a suburban public school district. "*Consistency between speech and action*" is a second trait associated with public moral integrity.[36] A candidate for public office who supports the reintroduction of prayer into the public schools in a campaign, but does nothing to introduce or support such legislation once in office should be held morally culpable for failure to act in congruence with his speech. A third aspect of the criterion of moral integrity is the "*integrity of principle*." Citizens should seek in their public lives to apply their moral principles consistently across a variety of cases. Thus, "those who oppose abortion out of respect for fetal life should be equally strong advocates of policies to ensure that children are properly fed."[37] Moral integrity asks that citizens seek consistency in their speech, actions, and application of principles.

While these dimensions of moral integrity are surely important, they do not address one aspect of integrity that is essential, especially for religious believers seeking to act consistently in a pluralistic democracy. From time to time, people of faith will discover that an emerging democratic consensus conflicts with one of those basic convictions that defines the identity of a believing community. In such situations, conscience dictates that the person of faith *dissent* from this consensus.[38] Dissent can take many forms, ranging from quiescent dissatisfaction with a policy to active civil disobedience against a policy. Many religious believers are unhappy with the lack of governmental benefits available to children educated in parochial schools; while they may work to secure benefits such as transportation and textbooks for their children, they are rarely motivated to disrupt school board meetings or picket Congress about such matters. Though they may disagree with the current policies, their commitment to the principle of mutual respect keeps them from engaging in more dramatic civil disobedience. While they find such policies unfair, they do not judge them to be a violation of their basic religious convictions. But on occasion, a governmental policy may violate the defining basic convictions of a community, and religious believers may find it necessary to engage in stronger acts of dissent.

Are acts of dissent, particularly those that involve civil disobedience, congruent with the virtues appropriate to the pluralist democratic citizen? As I argued in the previous chapter, individual freedom in a pluralistic democracy is primarily a dissociative force; voluntariness in liberal society is essentially an exit privilege. Therefore, the right of dissent must be defended in any account of proper public behavior within a democratic polity. Dissent that is grounded in genuine religious conviction is not only a fundamental right deserving of governmental protection, it also meets the more stringent requirements demanded by revisionist liberalism.

Dissent grounded in genuine religious conviction (indeed, in any fundamental moral conviction) is an expression of the moral integrity pluralist citizens should seek to exemplify. For the abolitionists, the institution of slavery so violated their fundamental religious and moral convictions that they were moved to radical and sometimes violent acts of dissent. For those involved in the civil rights movement, the laws that enforced segregation in the South were an affront to conscience, and therefore acts of civil disobedience were morally and politically justified as expressions of moral integrity. For many Roman Catholics and Protestant Evangelicals, abortion is similarly a violation of conscience, and thus they have exercised their right to dissent, often in dramatic fashion. The criterion of moral integrity must acknowledge and defend this fundamental right to dissent.

The right to dissent, understood as an expression of moral integrity, operates in concert with the other two basic criteria: the criteria of public accessibility and mutual respect. Citizens engaged in acts of dissent should seek, so far as possible, to make the moral reasons for their actions available to a broad democratic public. They should also comport themselves in such a way that their dissent manifests the moral seriousness of those committed to the practice of mutual respect. While they may vigorously oppose the practices, behavior, and policies of those with whom they disagree, they should avoid behavior that denies the moral agency of their opponents. To dehumanize one's opponents in the process of dissent is to undermine the moral integrity of the very conscience that motivates these actions.

While the distinctions I am drawing regarding appropriate and inappropriate forms of dissent may seem to be extraordinarily fine, they are, I believe, distinctions of genuine significance for a pluralistic democracy. Unless we find ways to disagree civilly, even in matters of conscience, we run the risk of undermining the moral character of contemporary democracy. There is a difference between the militant civil disobedience advocated by Martin Luther King, Jr., and the violent acts of dissent committed by some abolitionists or right-to-life advocates. Dr. King's defense of nonviolent resistance, first offered in the late 1950s, remains relevant for our situation today.

> The alternative to violence is nonviolent resistance. . . . The nonviolent resister is just as strongly opposed to the evil against which he protests as is the person who uses violence. His method is passive or nonaggressive in the sense that he is not physically aggressive toward his opponent. But his mind and emotions are always active, constantly seeking to persuade the opponent that he is mistaken. . . . Nonviolent resistance does not seek to defeat or humiliate the opponent, but to win his friendship and understanding. . . . The aftermath of nonviolence is the creation of the beloved community, while the aftermath of violence is tragic bitterness.[39]

The right of dissent is fundamental to any consideration of the criteria for speech and action in contemporary public life, but dissent itself must be governed by criteria internal to its own moral rationale. Dissent should have as its ultimate goal the return of the community to its fundamental constitutive values.

Pluralist citizens who engage in the politics of dissent are, in the words of Michael Walzer, "connected critics."[40] Connected critics are those who are fully engaged in the very enterprise they criticize. Because they care so deeply about the values inherent in the democratic enterprise, their critique serves to call a community back to its better nature. Connected critics recognize the ambiguity that clings to the life of every political or social organization, and they seek to identify both the virtuous and the vicious dimensions of the common life in which they participate. Connected critics exemplify both the commitment characteristic of patriotism and the critique characteristic of loyal dissent. This dialectic between commitment and critique is the identifying feature that distinguishes acts of dissent that display genuine moral integrity from those that represent mere expediency or self-interest. The role of connected critic is, I believe, appropriate for those people of faith who want to be full participants in a pluralistic democracy.

If the arguments I have developed in this chapter are persuasive, then I have shown that there is no fundamental incompatibility between public religious arguments and the essential conditions of publicity in a pluralistic democracy. Arguments that arise from religious beliefs or religiously based moral premises can meet the criteria of plausibility that should govern all public speech and action in a liberal democracy. Indeed, religiously based arguments can serve to elevate the discourse of the republic by emphasizing the essential moral dimension inherent in most political positions. If moral arguments are to be welcomed into the political debate, then religious arguments must also be allowed. But all these arguments—political, moral, and religious—should be governed by the criteria of public accessibility, mutual respect, and moral integrity. Arguments that do not meet those criteria cannot be banned from public debate, but citizens need to be encouraged to ignore or resist arguments that appeal to inaccessible warrants, that belittle one's opponents, that appeal to prejudice or base instincts, or that seek to coerce or manipulate the public discussion.

*Some* religious arguments may manifest those vices of public speech and action, and when they do they should carry no weight in political debate. But the burden of my argument in this chapter has been to assert that religious arguments are not inherently or inevitably subject to such vicious tendencies. Religious arguments can function to advocate on behalf of the needy in our society or to encourage policies that serve the common good, just as they can function to serve private interests or fanatical ends. The attempt to prohibit religious arguments from the public sphere simply because they are religious is finally doomed to failure. Rather, we must undertake the more difficult, but far more important, task of analyzing and evaluating such arguments according to the criteria of plausibility that should govern all public activity. If we learn to recover our capacity for moral analysis, then we will learn how to identify and refute arguments that foster values inimical to the aims of our liberal pluralistic democracy. And in so doing, we will have revitalized those public virtues that the founders of the republic believed essential to the flourishing of our democratic form of government.

## NOTES

1. John Rawls, "The Priority of the Right and Ideas of the Good," *Philosophy and Public Affairs* 17,3 (Summer 1988): 17.
2. Kent Greenawalt, *Religious Convictions and Political Choice* (New York: Oxford University Press, 1988), p. 12.
3. Ibid., pp. 216-217, 220.
4. Jeffrey Stout, *Ethics After Babel: The Languages of Moral and Their Discontents* (Boston: Beacon Press, 1988), p. 222.
5. Judith Shklar, "The Liberalism of Fear," *Liberalism and the Moral Life*, edited by Nancy Rosenblum (Cambridge: Harvard University Press, 1989), p. 23.
6. Judith Shklar. *Ordinary Vices* (Cambridge: Harvard University Press, 1984), pp. 8-9.
7. This phrase is used by Amy Gutmann and Dennis Thompson in their helpful article "Moral Conflict and Political Consensus," *Liberalism and the Good*, edited by R. Bruce Douglass, Gerald M. Mara, and Henry S. Richardson (New York and London: Routledge, 1992), p. 125.
8. This argument has been set forth by a diverse set of liberal theorists including Bruce Ackerman, Kent Greenawalt, Charles Larmore, Thomas Nagel, and John Rawls, among others.
9. Bruce Ackerman, "Why Dialogue?" *Journal of Philosophy* 86:1 (January 1989): 16. Quoted by Galston, p. 103.
10. Again, we see how the classical liberal and the sectarian communitarian analyses of moral disagreement fully reinforce one another.
11. Thomas Nagel, "Moral Conflict and Political Legitimacy," *Philosophy & Public Affairs*, 16,3 (Summer 1987): 215-240.

**12.** Ibid., p. 230.

**13.** Ibid., p. 232.

**14.** Ibid.

**15.** Richard J. Bernstein, *Beyond Objectivism and Relativism: Science, Hermeneutics, and Praxis* (Philadelphia: University of Pennsylvania Press, 1983), p. 18.

**16.** I have reflected on these issues in two previous works, *Revelation and Theology: The Gospel as Narrated Promise* (Notre Dame: University of Notre Dame Press, 1985), especially pp. 9-91 and *Constructing a Public Theology: The Church in a Pluralistic Culture* (Louisville: Westminster/John Knox Press, 1991), especially pp. 15-28 and 45-62.

**17.** Nagel, "Moral Conflict," p. 234.

**18.** Ibid, p. 235.

**19.** Ibid.

**20.** Ibid., p. 236.

**21.** "There would be no inclination to accept impersonally a general right to try to use state power to limit the liberty of others in order to force them to live as I believe they should live. None of us would be willing to have our liberty limited by others on such grounds. But if I am right, the appeal to the truth of a certain religion to justify enforcement collapses into just such an appeal to belief." Ibid.

**22.** Jeffrey Stout, *Ethics After Babel* (Boston, Beacon Press, 1988), pp. 25-26.

**23.** Joseph Raz, "Facing Diversity: The Case of Epistemic Abstinence," *Philosophy & Public Affairs* 19:1 (Winter, 1990), p. 46.

**24.** James Davison Hunter, *Culture Wars: the Struggle to Define America* (New York, Basic Books, 1991), p. 131.

**25.** I have developed this understanding of faith in two previously published works, *Revelation and Theology: The Gospel as Narrated Promise* (Notre Dame: University of Notre Dame Press, 1985) and *Constructing a Public Theology: The Church in a Pluralistic Culture* (Philadelphia: Westminster/John Knox Press, 1991).

**26.** George Lindbeck, *The Nature of Doctrine* (Philadelphia: Westminster, 1984), p. 32.

**27.** The phrase "in, with and under" is derived from Lutheran sacramental theology. In its original context the phrase denotes the union of sacramental elements (bread and wine) to Christ's body and blood. See Martin Luther's letter to Paul Speratus in L. Enders. *Flugschriften* aus der Reformationszeit, Number 3 (Halle, 1902), p. 399.

**28.** It is important to distinguish two senses of "public". The sense in which I employ the term here refers to a belief's intelligibility or accessibility. The second sense of "public" refers to the assessment of the reasons for holding a belief to be true. I will address this second sense of public in Chapter 7.

**29.** See Robert Wuthnow, *The Restructuring of American Religion* (Princeton: Princeton University Press, 1988), and James Davison Hunter, *Culture Wars*.

**30.** Robert Wuthnow, *Acts of Compassion: Caring for Others and Helping Ourselves* (Princeton: Princeton University Press, 1991).

**31.** The least objectionable set of threshold requirements have been proposed by Amy Gutmann and Dennis Thompson in their important article, "Moral Conflict and Political Consensus." They set forth three requirements which any argument must meet in order "for a position to count as a moral one." They are (1) "the argument for the position must presuppose a disinterested perspective that could be adopted by any member of a society whatever his or her other particular circumstances (such as class, race, or sex)"; (2) "Any premises in the argument that depend on empirical evidence or logical inference should be in principle open to challenge by generally accepted methods of inquiry"; and (3) "premises for which empirical evidence or logical inference is not appropriate should not be radically implausible" (p. 130). These requirements, limited as they may be, are neither neutral nor benign with regard to a fairly wide range of moral arguments.

Surely it is the case that specific attention to issues of class, race, or gender is one important means for highlighting a moral issue that might otherwise be ignored in the public debate. The unique plight of single African American and Hispanic mothers living in poverty demands special attention from those responsible for economic policy, since this particular group bears a disproportionate burden within our current welfare system. An argument that presented this case to policymakers would hardly be "disinterested," but it would surely count as a moral position. Indeed, the first of the Gutmann/ Thompson criteria would appear to make inadmissible to the public debate the "preferential option for the poor," the primary moral principle invoked by the U.S. Conference of Catholic Bishops in their pastoral letter "Economic Justice for All."

The second and third threshold requirements are equally problematic. An appeal to "generally accepted methods of inquiry" is far too vague a criterion to be helpful in sorting through moral arguments. If it is too broadly defined, it will admit virtually every argument into the public debate; if it is too narrowly defined, it will inevitably eliminate forms of moral reasoning, for example, those associated with liberation theology or deconstructive philosophy, that, while not "generally accepted methods," have an important role to play in a pluralistic conversation. Finally, the "not radically implausible" requirement would seem, once more, too vaguely defined to permit it to function with any degree of precision.

Indeed, the brief case that the authors discuss, the place of arguments favoring racial discrimination in public debate, shows the ineffectiveness of their proposed criteria. They seek to show, unsuccessfully I believe, that proponents of racial discrimination are not presenting a moral position at all, and thus deserve no hearing in our democratic polity. This familiar liberal attempt to rule an argument out of debate by procedural rules is not only unsuccessful; it is also counterproductive to the moral health of public debate. The argument for racial discrimination is not *amoral*; it is *immoral*, and those who oppose such arguments must learn the skills of moral reasoning that will allow them to refute (not just ignore) such arguments in the public domain.

**32.** In discussing the next two criteria I have profited enormously from Gutmann and Thompson's treatment of the "principles of accommodation" essential to a democratic polity in "Moral Conflict and Political Consensus," pp. 134-147.

33. Ibid., pp. 134-35.

34. Ibid., p. 136 (italics added).

35. Ibid. (italics added).

36. Ibid., p. 137. This principle is reminiscent of the "consistent ethic of life" advocated by the U.S. Conference of Catholic Bishops. See also my analysis of Mario Cuomo's address to the Theology Department at the University of Notre Dame, Chapter 1.

37. For an excellent discussion of the role of faith in encouraging dissent, see Stephen L. Carter, *The Culture of Disbelief* (New York: Basic Books, 1993).

38. Martin Luther King, Jr., "Nonviolence and Racial Justice," *A Testament of Hope: the Essential Writings of Martin Luther King, Jr.*, edited by James M. Washington (San Francisco: Harper & Row, 1986), pp. 7-8.

39. Walzer develops this notion in two of his recent works *Interpretation and Social Criticism* (Cambridge: Harvard University Press, 1987), and *The Company of Critics: Social Criticism and Political Commitment in the Twentieth Century* (New York: Basic Books, 1988).

# 7

# Beyond the Wall of Separation: Reconceiving American Public Life

## AMERICA IN THE 1990s: A MATTER OF DIFFERENCE

The decade of the 1990s appears to be a time of testing for the American republic. The fabric of our common life has been stretched to the breaking point by a series of divisive social issues, for example, abortion, welfare reform, race relations, women's rights, homosexuality. The disputes over these matters have often been bitter and the adversaries unwilling to seek the compromises that might adjudicate their differences. Our ability to discern a common ground on which to resolve these disputes has been further complicated by the rapid growth in ethnic diversity that occurred during the 1980s. Most recent immigrants to the United States come from cultures other than the Anglo-European nations that decisively influenced American society for more than 300 years. This pattern of immigration has greatly enriched the cultural diversity of our country, but it has also spawned new fears and prejudices that too often erupt into ethnic and racial violence. At a time of economic stagnation, new immigrants appear to pose a threat to established but still struggling populations, and possibilities for conflict abound.[1] The American republic is experiencing an unprecedented degree of diversity, and the fragile bonds that unify us have come under great strain.

A spate of recent books has bemoaned the divisions that this new diversity has created within American public life.[2] A worry common to all these works is that the current focus on particularity—racial, ethnic, cultural, or gendered—threatens permanently to divide American society into separate contentious cultural enclaves, thereby undermining the notions of unity or commonality essential to the identity of the nation. The politics of particularity, these authors argue, will finally destroy the sense that all Americans are engaged in a common enterprise. Thus the distinguished American historian, Arthur Schlesinger, Jr., suggests that the new "cult of ethnicity" imperils the "historic idea of a unifying American identity."[3]

> *E pluribus unum.* The United States had a brilliant solution for the inherent fragility of a multiethnic society: the creation of a brand-new national identity, carried forward by individuals who, in forsaking old loyalties and joining to make new lives, melted away ethnic differences. . . . The point of America was not to preserve old cultures, but to forge a new American culture. . . . [But now] instead of a transformative nation with an identity all its own, America in this new light is seen as preservative of diverse alien identities. Instead of a nation composed of individuals making their own unhampered choices, America increasingly sees itself as composed of groups more or less ineradicable in their ethnic character. The multiethnic dogma abandons historic purposes, replacing assimilation by fragmentation, integration by separatism. It belittles *unum* and glorifies *pluribus*. [4]

Schlesinger's concern about the fragmentation of American culture is surely well placed, but his analysis does little to help us out of our current difficulty. By perpetuating the "melting pot" mythology and by characterizing the early history of the United States as one in which "individuals" were free to make "their own unhampered choices," he is simply engaging in odd history. A careful study of American immigration shows that the maintenance of cultural identity has always been essential to the successful integration of immigrant populations into the larger American society. The presence of Irish, German, Polish, and Italian subcultures in American cities clearly facilitated the transition of successive waves of immigrants to these shores during the nineteenth century. The genius of the American experience has not been that immigrant populations were required to abandon their previous identities as "alien," but that the framework of American democracy was sufficiently flexible to allow new citizens to understand themselves as both Irish and American, Polish and American, and so on. In the process of Americanization, both identities were transformed, that is, the identities of those European immigrants were decisively modified by the American experience, but at the same time, the definition of what it means to be an American was decisively modified by the phenomenon of European immigration.

The United States became a multiethnic society with a single national identity precisely because our democracy did not make ethnic identity the basis for citizenship. Thus, Schlesinger is surely wrong, and dangerously so, when he quotes with approval the remark of Hector St. John Crevecoeur "What then is the American, this new man? . . . Here individuals of all nations are melted into a new race of men."[5] The genius of America is that it did not require persons to abandon their ethnic identity as the price for citizenship. Our democracy seeks to shape neither a new uniform American culture nor a new "race of men"; it seeks rather to create a diverse nation whose citizens are dedicated to the fundamental values of democracy: liberty, equality, and mutual respect.

The question facing American democracy today is whether our national identity can embrace the new American pluralism. Can we shape a conception of the *unum* that is in continuity with the past and yet genuinely open to the new realities of the contemporary *plures*? The founders sought to create a democratic polity grounded in particular core values yet sufficiently flexible to respond to the changing social and historical conditions of a growing nation. Enlightenment notions of liberty and equality did not include slaves or women in its purview, yet the struggle to extend the full rights of citizenship to women and persons of African descent expanded those notions beyond their eighteenth-century limitations. Advocates of those rights argued successfully that the full meaning of such ideas could not be realized as long as persons were excluded from citizenship simply by virtue of their gender or race. The full meaning and application of the values of liberty and equality can only be determined as we seek to follow the historical and social trajectory of such ideas. In a similar manner I have argued that the founders' notion of toleration needs to be expanded in our own time and is better expressed through the idea of mutual respect. The core values of American democracy are historically and socially situated and are constantly being debated and reinterpreted.

In contrast to many contemporary cultural critics, I want to argue that the politics of the particular are not necessarily a threat to the historic sense of a national identity. Whenever new groups seek to find a place within the democratic polity, political debate becomes more strident and sharp-edged, because questions of power and privilege are at stake. The excluded will inevitably challenge the prerogatives of those who hold power, and the established will often develop a defensive posture against such protests. Stridency and passion may be signs of the robustness of democracy rather than indications of its decay. Our national identity is established through the tradition of democratic debate concerning the core values of our polity. If a tradition is "an historically extended, socially embodied argument" about the meaning of the values that constitute that tradition,[6] then vigorous and passionate debate should be expected. It is only when the debate undermines the core values of the democratic tradition that our national identity is genuinely threatened. Ironically, Schlesinger himself identifies the crucial challenge facing American democracy today.

> The American identity will never be fixed and final: it will always be in the making. Changes in the population have always brought changes in the national ethos and will continue to do so: but not, one must hope, at the expense of national integration. The question America confronts as a pluralistic society is how to vindicate cherished cultures and traditions without breaking the bond of cohesion—common ideals, common political institutions, common languages, common culture, common fate—that hold the republic together.[7]

Though Schlesinger has rightly characterized the challenge, his nostalgic invocation of the myth of American unity provides little help in forging a fresh national identity in face of the new American pluralism. The current fashionable bashing of efforts to introduce multicultural education, for example, does little to assist the nation in developing citizens capable of dealing with cultural, ethnic, racial, and moral diversity. Surely there are a few advocates, primarily in the universities, who use "multiculturalism" as a club to beat up on the Anglo-European traditions that have dominated American society and to forward various notions of cultural separatism. The intellectual pretensions of such ideologues have been effectively exposed by scholars who are concerned to defend a more textured and historically grounded notion of multiculturalism.[8] Robert Hughes has offered an eloquent and helpful account of the term.

> Multiculturalism asserts that people with different roots can coexist, that they can learn to read the image-banks of others, that they can and should look across the frontiers of race, language,

gender and age without prejudice or illusion, and learn to think against the background of a hybridized society. It proposes—modestly enough—that some of the most interesting things in history and culture happen at the interface between cultures. It wants to study border situations, not only because they are fascinating in themselves, but because understanding them may bring with it a little hope for the world.[9]

The fundamental question facing American democracy today is how to nurture such citizens within the context of our constitutional tradition.[10] I have argued throughout this book that the framers of the Constitution devised a democratic polity designed for a pluralistic population. They identified the core values of that polity—liberty, equality, and toleration—and they developed a political process that allowed for the continual interpretation, appropriation, and application of those values in new and unanticipated historical situations. They recognized that if those values were to be passed from generation to generation certain virtues of citizenship would have to flourish in the people. The framers had little to say, however, about how those virtues were to be fostered within the citizenry, relying instead on an aristocratic view of representative leadership. Fearing the factionalism and self-interested behavior of the masses, they devised a system of government designed to balance interests one against another, thereby precluding any one group from seizing power over the decisions of government.

The founders' theory of factions recognized the inherent instability of a diverse population, and constitutional doctrine of the balance of powers created appropriate safeguards against the dangers of pluralism. The lack of a corresponding theory of virtue acknowledging the positive nature of cultural and social pluralism has made it difficult to identify any particular constitutional doctrine affirming the good of diversity. In my analysis of Madison's reflection on the religion clauses of the first amendment, however, I have sought to show that there are resources within our constitutional tradition upon which we can build as we address the issue of the new American pluralism.

Madison's argument for the free exercise of religion provides a fundamental justification for a pluralistic society. Madison begins by asserting that human freedom is a gift of a benevolent Creator.[11] Having been created by God, human beings have an obligation to return to the Creator the "homage due Him." Yet that obligation cannot be coerced lest humans deny the very gift of freedom granted them by God. Therefore human beings must determine from "the dictates of their conscience" how and in what manner they will worship the divine. More, since the gift of freedom is divinely granted to all, all human beings stand as equals before their Maker, no matter how diverse their expressions of homage may be. Because human beings are free, the forms and patterns of their worship will inevitably differ; nonetheless, even in their differences they stand equal before God. Genuine freedom implies diversity; diversity before God entails equality; and equality demands the toleration of the various forms of human worship. For Madison, the fundamental values of democratic government are derived from his defense of the free exercise of religion; even more striking is the fact that the argument through which he discerns these core values is explicitly theological.

I do not intend to argue that the core values of democracy can only be derived from a theological argument, but the fact that Madison employs such an argument in justifying the good of a pluralistic society is an "illuminating suggestion."[12] As I argued in chapter 4, the theological character of Madison's argument raises a basic challenge to John Rawls's assertion that the core values of democracy constitute a "free standing conception," derived independently of the comprehensive schemes that might serve to confirm these values. As my analysis of Madison shows, the core values can in fact be derived from a particular comprehensive scheme and yet be inclusive of the beliefs of those who do not share that scheme. Particular moral and religious beliefs can be developed with sufficient generality to provide an overarching framework within which an overlapping consensus can be developed. If that is the case, then it surely follows that religious beliefs should not be prohibited from providing public justifications within a democratic polity, as long as those beliefs genuinely contribute to the building of an overlapping consensus. Still, as history clearly demonstrates, not all religious beliefs can or ought to function in public life, but the recognition that some religious beliefs can and do function in that manner should set aside, once and for all, the argument against religious arguments per se in the public sphere. The question is not whether religious arguments qualify as genuinely public, but what kind of religious arguments so qualify.

That question becomes particularly important as we seek to develop a clearer national identity at a time of increasing cultural pluralism. Can religious beliefs function to help us construct an understanding of the public in which we honor the genuine differences that constitute the richness of contemporary American culture and yet identify those fundamental values that constitute the national identity we all hold in common? I believe that religious beliefs can so function, but before we address that question, we must first gain new clarity regarding the definition and scope of "the public." If we gain such clarity regarding "the public," then perhaps we can begin to see beyond the "wall of separation" that has so long limited the role of religion in public life. Then we may also discover how communities of faith can play a salutary role in the renewal of a genuinely pluralistic public life. Perhaps this new understanding of religion might even help us glimpse new possibilities for constructing an understanding of our national identity in which difference and commonality can live in balance with one another. Then, at last, religion may not only pose a dilemma but also provide a source of renewal for American public life.[13]

## REDEFINING THE PUBLIC

For most Americans, and for many liberal theorists, the word "public" connotes the sphere of government. This use of the term has become commonplace since the 1930s when, in response to the Great Depression, the federal government began instituting social and economic programs that form the basis for today's welfare state. Public works, for example, are those projects instituted by government and funded by levies on taxpayers. Public works in this sense are often contrasted with economic initiatives undertaken by the so-called private sector, or private enterprise, that is, the business community. Thus in this context the public/private distinction refers primarily to the source of funding that undergirds a particular project—whether funding comes from taxpayer monies raised by government or from one of the many sources available in a free-market economy. The identification of businesses, including multinational corporations, as constituting the "private sector" is, of course, somewhat of a misnomer, since businesses are among the world's largest and most complicated social organizations. While funding for the corporate world is not derived primarily from taxpayer monies, government is directly involved in the private sector through its vast network of regulatory agencies. Moreover, corporations exercise enormous influence on governmental decision making both nationally and internationally. They are in that sense major public actors on the domestic and world stages. It is becoming increasingly clear that the terms "public" and "private" are no longer sufficient to identify the roles played by the welfare state, on the one hand, and multinational corporations on the other.

The other sphere within which the public/private distinction has played an essential role is that of liberal political theory. That distinction has come under withering assault by a wide range of contemporary critics,[14] and in previous chapters of this book I have offered my own criticisms of this commonplace liberal distinction. In this chapter I want to focus on one particular shortcoming of this distinction, namely, the contribution it makes to the atrophy of citizenship in a pluralistic society. By limiting the notion of the public to policy decisions made within governmental institutions, modern liberal theory radically truncates the sphere of the *res publica*, the sphere which in classical political theory refers to civil society as a whole. Civil society includes all those forms of organizational life in which citizens engage in activities designed to affect their social or associational existence.

Associational life is political and public; it seeks to address issues of the polis broadly conceived and to engage the broad interests and concerns of citizens. Participation in a range of voluntary associations, for example, unions, civic clubs (e.g., Rotary), homeless shelters, citizen action groups (e.g. Common Cause), neighborhood associations, church-related human service agencies (e.g., hospices), is essential to the well-being of a pluralistic democracy.[15] It is precisely within such public but nongovernmental associations that people learn and cultivate the virtues of citizenship. Since democratic governments function through the consent of the citizenry, it is in the best interest of democracy that associational life flourish. If the relationship between the governing and the governed is limited to the mere exercise of the vote, then the power of citizens is reduced to the election and recall of their representatives. The ability of citizens to influence governmental policy is drastically reduced if their public action is limited to the electoral process alone. Indeed, one can argue that the current "turn the rascals out" mood of the American electorate stems in large part from citizens' sense of powerlessness in relation to government.[16] If the deepest personal convictions and most important civic activities of citizens are deemed to be "merely private," then it is not surprising that we are experiencing an atrophy of citizenship today.

Despite the obvious limitations of the liberal definition of the sphere of privacy, it is important to remember that one reason for the liberal tradition's concern about privacy was to define an area that would be free of governmental influence. The private sphere was to be that area of thought and behavior in which individuals would be free from government's scrutiny, intervention, or domination. While such a notion is conceptually defensible, it is not clear that it is socially achievable under the conditions of contemporary society. Alan Wolfe has recently argued that the combined growth of governmental bureaucracies and global economic markets threaten the very social conditions that make individual freedom possible.[17] The dominance of these two forces in all aspects of human life makes it increasingly difficult for individuals to find independent spheres of meaning in which to develop alternative and genuinely free life choices.[18] If we are concerned about individual freedom in the contemporary world, then we must be concerned about the health and well-being of associational life. "We need civil society—families, communities, friendship networks, solidaristic workplace ties, voluntarism, spontaneous groups and movements—not to reject, but to complete the project of modernity."[19] Civic associations—including communities of faith—provide the essential public spaces within which individuals can explore alternative worlds of meaning. Without these alternative public spaces, citizens cannot develop modes of thought and behavior independent of those encouraged within the governmental and economic sectors.[20] Those who are concerned about individual freedom today, should focus not on the realm of privacy but on the viability of civil society and on the defense of the public function of voluntary associations.

Communities of faith can be among the most important associations within which the virtues of citizenship are fostered. As David Hollenbach has recently shown, the role of churches in the 1989 revolutions in Eastern and Central Europe was crucial in overthrowing authoritarian communist regimes. "In East Germany, Czechoslovakia, Hungary, as well as in Poland, the recovery of freedom, the revival of civil society, and the public presence of the churches (Catholic, Orthodox, and Protestant) were closely connected phenomena."[21] By providing a context within which citizens could engage in ways of thinking and acting not sanctioned by the governments, communities of faith provided cells of resistance to the totalitarian intent of these regimes. While we as citizens of democratic governments are not threatened with totalitarian control, we are experiencing a serious decline in the vitality of civil society. As the Jewish intellectual and Solidarity activist Adam Michnik has argued, the absence of civil society in Poland undermined the very pluralism that would have served as a counterforce to the totalitarian claims of the State.[22] The fact that the communist government was unable fully to suppress the Church made it possible for some independent sources of free thinking to exist. Thus, Michnik argues a position strikingly similar to that of James Madison, namely, that freedom of religion is essential for a flourishing civil society, and civil society provides the public context within which a pluralistic culture can develop. "An active, public role for religion, therefore, would seem to be one of the preconditions of a vibrant democratic life."[23]

A public role for religion is not, however, always a force for good. The classical liberal concern that religion can have a factionalizing and repressive role in society is not entirely misplaced. As the drama of Eastern and Central Europe has continued to unfold we have seen Christian churches contribute substantially to the rise of anti-Judaic and anti-Islamic sentiments among the emerging ethnic republics. As we seek to define a role for communities of faith in our democratic polity, we must examine more closely the ways in which religious beliefs might properly contribute to American public life.

## DEBUNKING THE MYTHS ABOUT RELIGION

Efforts to define a proper role for public religion in America have been impeded by the widespread acceptance of certain fundamental misunderstandings about the nature and function of religious belief and practice. These "myths" about religion often distort the thinking of even the most sophisticated contemporary analysts. The debate concerning religion's proper role in society cannot proceed with clarity until these misleading myths are debunked.

*Myth: "Religious belief is inherently irrational or nonrational; therefore religious warrants can never meet appropriate standards of publicity."*
The assumption that religious belief is irrational or nonrational is widely held among adherents and critics of religion alike. The commonplace distinction between faith and reason often leads both parties in the debate to develop this distinction into an absolute dichotomy. Too often religious apologists seek to defend their beliefs by defining faith as an independent or autonomous sphere wholly insulated from external scrutiny or critique. In so doing, they hope to provide a protected space within which religious belief and practice can develop and flourish without outside interference. To some extent, the notion of the "wall of separation between church and state," par-

ticularly as it was conceived by Roger Williams, relies on this familiar but misguided attempt to separate religion from those "alien" forces that might dilute or defile it. Critics of religion often seize upon this religious self-definition as evidence that such beliefs and practices can never meet standard criteria of publicity. Accepting the believers' claim to "privacy" at face value, they develop arguments designed to exclude all matters of faith from public discussion.[24]

No matter how widespread this strategy of separation may be, it is finally doomed to failure. As I argued in chapter 6, it is a mistake on religious grounds to construe faith as an invisible inaccessible spiritual enclave residing within the human soul, [25] what Gilbert Ryle called "the ghost in the machine." While faith is certainly profoundly personal, it is not properly identified as private. "Faith" identifies the fundamental convictions that guide and direct the beliefs and practices of religious believers. Such convictions are religious in that they orient the life of the believer toward a supreme reality that calls forth the deepest and most pervasive commitment of one's life, a reality which many religious traditions name "God." The convictions of faith may, therefore, call forth from the religious person a distinctive level of commitment and devotion, but the fact and function of such basic orienting convictions is common to every human life. Thus, religious convictions, though they are directed toward a distinctive "object" or "horizon of meaning," do not differ in kind or in function from the fundamental commitments that orient the lives of nonreligious persons.

It is a mistake for believers or nonbelievers to treat faith as a private enclave immune from inquiry or critique. To inquire concerning the faith of an individual or community, it is necessary to explore the set of practices within which the convictions of faith are displayed. To understand Christian notions of "love," for example, it would be helpful to read biblical texts (e.g. the parable of the Good Samaritan, the teachings on love in the Gospel and Epistles of John), to study theological treatises on the topic, and to learn about the benevolent practices of Christian communities across the centuries. Such a process is no more unusual or difficult than that which is required to understand a notion like "freedom" in the American constitutional tradition.

To inquire into the meaning of "freedom" one should read the Declaration of Independence and the Constitution, study important interpretive documents like *The Federalist* and *A Letter from a Birmingham Jail*, and learn something of the struggles and practices by which the scope of freedom slowly expanded across centuries of American history. Fundamental, orienting convictions are accessible to public inquiry and critique, but they require careful attention to the texts, practices, and traditions of the communal life within which they are embedded. Contemporary cultural analysts would not dream of commenting on political notions of freedom without having read the Constitution or Declaration of Independence, but they are often ready to pronounce on the nature of religious beliefs without having read the Pentateuch or the Gospels.

As long as criteria of publicity are not explicitly designed to exclude religion from public discussion, religious beliefs are capable of meeting primary public standards of accessibility. It does not follow, however, that all religious warrants should be accorded the same welcome in public debate. The important issue is not whether an argument appeals to a religious warrant; the issue is whether the warrant, religious or not, is compatible with the basic values of our constitutional democracy. Arguments that appeal to racist ideologies or to doctrines of religious persecution are incompatible with basic democratic values. We should not seek to preclude these arguments from the public sphere; that strategy could easily lead to a violation of free speech. Instead, we should seek to educate the citizenry regarding the fundamental values of democracy, so that when they encounter such arguments they will reject them. The point is that we cannot by philosophical or political fiat decide in advance which arguments we will accept in the public sphere. Rather, we must learn to understand and evaluate all arguments that seek a public hearing.

The foregoing analysis does not imply that the values of constitutional democracy must be the final arbiter of the validity of all beliefs, including religious ones. Rather, the argument proposes that within the public realm the values of liberty, equality, and mutual respect function as the ideals toward which our political actions should strive. Precisely because these notions are general principles, they function heuristically to orient our society to a set of common goals. Because these principles are historically situated and socially embodied, their meaning is constantly being contested in the public realm. Nonetheless, they provide a common framework within which genuine debate can be carried on. These values are exemplified in various democratic practices and institutions (courts, legislatures, political parties, special purpose groups, voluntary associations) within which their meaning, function, and application are constantly being tested.

In the process, religious beliefs may function to confirm and support the reigning interpretations of these values, or they may challenge and criticize established definitions. Thus religious beliefs, like other non-political convictions, contribute to the ongoing discussion concerning the meaning and scope of fundamental democratic values.

An example may illustrate the role of religious beliefs in supporting and criticizing policy proposals. After taking office, the Clinton administration developed an ambitious proposal concerning health care reform. In presenting this proposal the administration asserted that the one nonnegotiable principle was the universality of health care coverage. The current health care system in the United States falls far short of this goal, and it is not self-evident that universality should be a major goal of health care coverage. What sort of argument might justify this major principle of the administration's proposal? While a variety of moral arguments could be brought to bear on this topic, one of the most effective is surely derived from an aspect of the Christian tradition, namely, the parable of the Good Samaritan.[26] This parable begins with agreement between Jesus and his questioner concerning the basic moral principle: "love your neighbor as yourself." The issue at question is the principle's scope of application, "Who is my neighbor?" By depicting the Samaritan (in contrast to the priest and the levite) as the one who provides aid to the Jew "fallen among thieves," the parable makes the bold assertion that the neighbor is the stranger who is in need of care. Thus social solidarity is established not primarily by ties of kinship, tribe, or religion, but by need or vulnerability. Neighbor-love is to be extended to all those in need of care.

This parable has its primary obligatory force within a particular religious tradition. It is embedded within a rich and complex pattern of beliefs, practices, and social relations that constitute the life of Christian discipleship. The obligation to extend neighbor-love to the stranger in need emerges from the commitment of the Christian disciple to follow the one who fully embodied this love in word and deed, Jesus Christ. Indeed, the pattern of Jesus' ministry, teaching, death, and resurrection provides the primary exemplification and enablement of the self-giving love to which his followers are now called. To understand this moral principle fully, one must view it as part of a larger pattern of religious life and devotion.

But can such a religious conviction properly provide the rationale for health care policy in a pluralistic democracy? Many would argue that the mere fact that a conviction has a religious root disqualifies it from serving as a public rationale. The argument presented by Peter Singer and Helga Kuhse in the first chapter of this book is representative of a larger class of arguments that would exclude a religiously based moral conviction from public debate. As I have argued throughout this book, however, such a position is hopelessly narrow and finally self-defeating. At the same time, it is not at all clear why a moral conviction with such a particular social and conceptual home should be given more general applicability in a society that includes a sizable minority of non-Christians.

The commitment to neighbor-love cannot simply be lifted from its Christian context and applied in the same fashion to a pluralistic society. While it may be the case that for some Americans the obligations of Christian discipleship demand care for the neighbor in need, it is not the case for all or even most Americans. The challenge for those who are committed to this conviction is to seek a way of stating it that is not only true to its original context but also applicable to the contemporary setting of pluralistic America. Can this particular conviction be developed into a principle of justice with sufficient scope as to be persuasive to a broad and diverse populace? Does the Christian obligation to provide care for the neighbor in need resonate with a fundamental democratic value familiar to all citizens?

Inherent in the democratic values of equality and mutual respect are two notions that intersect with the Christian conviction concerning neighbor-love: fairness and concern for the vulnerable. Our democratic commitment to equality suggests that whenever possible citizens should be treated equitably or fairly. While we may not be able to agree on a full theory of equality, we do often reach consensus concerning actions that seem in clear violation of fair play.[27] The fact that millions of American children do not have access to proper health care and that the infant mortality rate in this country is among the highest in the industrial world seems genuinely wrong to most Americans. That those who are most vulnerable, namely children, are most at risk under the current health care system seems clearly unjust. This recognition of a deficiency or injustice can serve to mobilize a broad consensus to seek broader coverage for those who are most vulnerable.[27]

As citizens seek to develop arguments in support of broad or universal health care, they will reach into their particular communities of commitment to provide the positive warrants to justify such a policy. For Christians the warrant may be the obligation of neighbor-love;

for secular political liberals the warrant may be a rights-based argument for universal health care; for others a prudential self-interested argument that recognizes the potential vulnerability of all citizens in an uncertain economy may be decisive. The disagreements at this level of justification are not important because each of these particular warrants is compatible with a fundamental value of our common democratic polity. In addition, all of these warrants can be developed into arguments that justify universal health care.

This example shows that warrants grounded in the convictions of particular communities, including religious communities, can be used to support policy proposals applicable to a diverse pluralistic population.[28] It is also important to see, however, that these same particular convictions can also be used to develop a moral critique of policy proposals. The Clinton health care plan proposed universal coverage for all American citizens; it did not extend coverage to illegal or unregistered immigrants.[29] Christians committed to an ethic in which the stranger in need is the neighbor to be loved may find the limitations of the Clinton plan unacceptable. Therefore the same conviction that justified support for the principle of universal care can also justify criticism of limits placed upon "universality." Religious convictions, indeed the particular convictions of any community of belief and practice, can foster both consent for and dissent from policy proposals. But most important, religious convictions can properly be employed to address fundamental issues of democratic polity without violating the integrity of the community of faith or the pluralistic society.

*Myth: "Religious beliefs, particularly those that make claims to truth, are not compatible with democracy's fundamental value of tolerance or mutual respect and should therefore be prohibited from the public realm."*

This criticism has considerable historical evidence to support it. As we saw earlier, liberal political theory arose in part as a response to the terror unleashed in Europe by the post-Reformation religious wars. The founders of the American republic feared the link between religion and self-interest and sought to defend the new nation against the threat of religious factionalism. Historically religion's role in exacerbating tensions in the quarrelsome debates over slavery and prohibition is clearly evident. Contemporary examples abound—one thinks especially of the issues of abortion and homosexuality—to document the deeply divisive role religion can play in public life. On the face of it, then, this criticism seems less like a myth than a well-established historical conclusion.

My point is not to dispute the historical evidence establishing religion's divisive role in public life but to dispute the theological contention that religion must play such a role because its claims to truth are inevitably absolute. The mythology of religious absolutism has often dominated the self-understanding of communities of faith and has thereby contributed to religion's bellicose place in political history.[30] My theoretical defense of public religion will be of little effect unless religious communities reform their views of faith's contribution to a pluralistic society.

Sociologists of religion have documented the deep divisions within contemporary communities of faith on matters of public importance.[31] A growing rift between conservative and liberal or orthodox and progressive wings of every Christian denomination has become evident. Conservative/orthodox movements have sought to defend traditional religious doctrines and moral values, often in alliance with political neoconservatives. Representatives of these movements often see themselves as having lost influence within their own denominational institutions and thus wage a battle on two fronts: against the liberal elements of their own communities and against the secularizing forces within the larger society.[32]

Liberal/progressive forces have sought to reform, restate, and in some cases, jettison traditional doctrines in response to critiques of religion's negative or oppressive role in society. Liberals gained control of many national ecumenical bodies in the 1960s and 1970s and have also exercised significant influence through denominational departments of church and society. During the past fifteen years, however, liberals have come under continued attack from more conservative forces, and their power now seems to be waning.[33] This denominational internecine warfare continues unabated, and consequently the churches seem poorly prepared to develop innovative strategies for engaging the range of problems facing contemporary society. Moreover, the divisions within denominations appear to mirror the conservative/liberal divide within political society and, as such, bear little intrinsic interest for outside observers.

Of course, some important exceptions relieve this otherwise dreary picture. Roman Catholicism in the United States exemplifies the pattern described above, but also offers some important alternatives to it. On issues of sexuality and the role of women in the church,

Roman Catholicism has reflected the primary trends in Christian engagement with society. On issues like nuclear warfare and the economy, however, Catholics have provided genuine theological leadership for the society as a whole. The pastoral letters of the U.S. Conference of Catholic Bishops on these latter topics are models of careful, innovative, and accessible public theological reflection on matters of concern to the whole society.[34] Grounded firmly in traditional Catholic moral theology, these documents provide fresh ways of appropriating and communicating that tradition in light of new challenges. Recognizing that tradition is a dynamic developing reality, the authors of the letters develop thoughtful and creative proposals to both church and society. Widely influential within the ecumenical church, the pastoral letters have also received a welcome reading in the broad pluralistic and secular society.

Despite the importance of these letters, they remain striking exceptions to the norm in American Christianity today. For the most part, churches have provided little leadership on issues of public concern because they are uncertain of their own identity in our pluralistic culture. Consequently most communities of faith wobble back and forth between *sectarian* strategies designed to separate the faithful from the surrounding alien environment and *accommodationist* strategies by which believers simply reflect positions already fully developed in the secular society. But these strategies allow neither a critical appropriation of religious tradition nor a faithful engagement in public debate. Neither strategy positions churches or other communities of faith to be full and active contributors to discussions of important issues in contemporary public life.

As long as the "myth of absoluteness" dominates the self-understanding of religious communities, they cannot be confident participants in a pluralistic society. Communities of faith must come to recognize the compatibility between deep and abiding commitment to the truth claims of one's tradition and an openness to and respect for the claims of another tradition. Truth claiming and an acceptance of religious pluralism are not inconsistent. Nicholas Rescher has stated the issue well:

> Pluralism holds that it is rationally intelligible and acceptable that others can hold positions at variance with one's own. But it does not maintain that a given individual need endorse a plurality of positions—that the fact that others hold a certain position

somehow constitutes a reason for doing so oneself. . . . Pluralism is a feature of the collective group; it turns on the fact that different experiences engender different views. But from the standpoint of the individual this cuts no ice. We have no alternative to proceeding as best we can on the basis of what is available to us. That others agree with us is not proof of correctness; that they disagree, no sign of error.[35]

Fundamental to the philosophical acceptance of pluralism is the conviction that we have no self-evident, incorrigible means of establishing the truth of our assertions.[36] This is not to say that we have no means available; however, the means at our disposal will not necessarily convince those with whom we disagree. Consequently, we must hold open the possibility that those who disagree with us do so rationally. This position implies neither relativism nor indifferentism to truth. It simply suggests that we cannot coerce others into believing as we do. We can offer our reasons for so believing, but these reasons, even if sufficient to support our claims, will not compel others to accept our beliefs.[37]

The nonfoundational position I am defending here has gained widespread acceptance in both philosophical and theological circles. Yet many religious people find the position difficult to adopt, because it seems to undermine the certainty of faith. As I have acknowledged, religious faith calls forth a distinctive level of commitment and devotion from believers; ideally, faith is the most deeply felt and most broadly encompassing conviction a person can have. And yet it would be a profound theological mistake to equate the confidence of faith with apodictic or absolute certainty. Within the Christian tradition, faith is defined as "the assurance of things hoped for, the conviction of things not seen" (Hebrews 11:1).

Other religious traditions have analogous ways of defining faith as a spiritual reality, a mystery not fully comprehensible to finite and fallible human beings. Whether notions of the ineffable are developed in terms of emptiness, transcendence, or eschatology virtually every religious tradition resists the temptation to identify spiritual confidence with rational certainty. For my Christian tradition, Lutheranism, faith is our finite, sinful grasping of the saving grace of God, offered as a gift through the person and work of Jesus Christ. God's grace reorients the believer's life and inaugurates a lifelong journey of discipleship. Since faith is always embedded in the texts, traditions, rituals, and practices of the community, the meaning of faith only emerges as one identifies more fully with that community. The life of discipleship is a process of "faith seeking understanding."

Central to that process are the biblical narratives through which the identity of God in Jesus Christ is displayed to the reader. At the heart of the gospel narratives is a remarkable sequence whereby Jesus undergoes death at the hands of the Romans and yet "on the third day" is raised to life by God. At that very point in the narrative the reader is invited to share in this "strange new world of the Bible,"[38] and to join with those in this narrative who are followers of Jesus. There is no inevitability that those who read this text will decide to enter upon a life of faith and discipleship, but those who do accept this invitation commit themselves to the belief that Jesus, the crucified, now lives. That commitment entails an act of faith that contradicts ordinary experience concerning the finality of death.

I have argued at length in other contexts that such a commitment is warranted and intelligible, but it is by no means inevitable.[39] The ultimate explanation of the mysterious movement from unbelief to faith lies beyond the competence of theology. Whether God's promise is reliable, whether the path of discipleship leads to its promised end, we cannot know with certainty now, for "we see through a glass darkly." Still believers follow on in hope, awaiting that day when we may "see face to face." For now we have only faith, the demands of discipleship, and the beckoning presence of one who bids us come and follow. And for some, that is enough.[40]

I have engaged in this extended piece of theological analysis in order to show that the warrants for my position on the nonabsoluteness of Christianity are derived not from a strategy of liberal accommodation to the world but from the foundational sources of Christianity itself. It is precisely my commitment to a set of traditional theological beliefs, including belief in the resurrection, that grounds both the confidence of my own faith and my recognition that it could be otherwise, that others situated differently from myself might reasonably hold other, even contradictory, convictions. Moreover, since I recognize that my own faith is the gift of a gracious God, I cannot limit God's graciousness to others simply because I have come to believe in God through the person of Jesus Christ. I do not claim to *know* with certainty that there are many equally true paths to God; therefore, I do not propose a theological *theory* of pluralism. But I cannot consistently, given my Christian convictions, deny that possibility. Therefore I must affirm theologically both the reality and the gift of religious diversity.

My analysis is not a universal theological defense of pluralism. It is the attempt of one theologian, working within a particular tradition, to display the theological reasons for the compatibility between the truth claims of my religion and a commitment to democratic pluralism. I am confident that similar strategies are available to other traditions within Christianity and to other communities of faith. Believers do not need to assert the absoluteness of their own tradition to hold to the truth claims of their faith. A commitment to pluralism is fully compatible with a robust assertion of the truth of one's own beliefs.

## BEYOND THE WALL OF SEPARATION: THE ROLE OF THE COURTS

The time has now come to indicate the significance of my discussion of public religion and democratic values for the decision-making process in the nation's courts. Though I have sought to be an informed critic of the judiciary, I am acutely aware that I write as a theologian, not as a constitutional scholar or a jurist. Nonetheless, I believe that my attempt to clarify the proper public role of religion does have consequences for the judicial branch's treatment of religion. I will highlight four issues: (1) the anachronistic categories of church and state; (2) the limited significance of the notion of "separation"; (3) the need to return to fundamental constitutional values; and (4) the necessity of developing a consistent conceptual framework within which to consider both religion clauses.

Even if the courts had not embarked upon their confusing conceptual journey in the aftermath of the *Everson* decision, the very categories of "church" and "state" would force a reconsideration of first amendment adjudication. Given the rapid increase in religious diversity within the United States, the term "church" is simply not sufficient to refer to the varieties of religious practice in our country. Moreover, by privileging the Christian term for religious community, the courts give the unfortunate impression that they define religion through the perspective of Christianity. That impression would not be so serious had the court's actions not reinforced that view. Two recent cases raise particular concern.[41]

In 1986, the Supreme Court upheld a lower court decision prohibiting Captain Simcha Goldman, an Orthodox Jew, from wearing a yarmulke while on duty in a health clinic in which he served. In writing for the majority, Justice Rehnquist stated that the standard military uniform encourages "the subordination of the desires and interests of the individual to the needs of the service."⁴² In this characterization, the wearing of the yarmulke is identified not as an aspect of required religious practice but of mere individual desire and interest. Consequently, the religious dimension of the case was simply side-stepped, and the Court rendered its opinion by supporting the need of the military for a uniform dress code. The irony is that the Court thus avoided altogether the religious question and refused to treat this case as one of free exercise.

Had they taken more seriously the wearing of the yarmulke as a matter of required Orthodox religious practice and applied the "compelling governmental interest" test, the case undoubtedly would have been decided otherwise. Had the question of religious obligation been considered, it is difficult to imagine that the Court could have sustained a judgment that the state had a compelling governmental interest. Surely the wearing of a yarmulke is a significant religious practice and deserved the protection of the first amendment guarantee of freedom of religion. The fact that minority religious practice received this discriminatory ruling is of particular concern.

An even more troubling free exercise case is *Employment Division v. Smith*, 1990. In this case, the Supreme Court upheld Oregon's denial of unemployment compensation sought when two employees were dismissed from their jobs for using a controlled substance, peyote, in a native American religious ritual. Here the majority explicitly rejected the common "compelling interest" criterion, arguing that such a standard "would be courting anarchy," because it "would open the prospect of constitutionally required religious exemptions from civic obligations of almost every conceivable kind."⁴³ What the Court failed to acknowledge is that religious exemptions are essential precisely for those minority faiths that the free exercise and nonestablishment clauses are designed primarily to protect. The "compelling interest" criterion is crucial for the protection of the rights of minority religions that are unlikely to fare well in a legislative context in which majority rule holds sway. It is important to remember that when alcohol was officially a "controlled substance" during the Prohibition era, the sacramental use of wine was specifically exempted from the ordinance. Had it not been, it is inconceivable to imagine that the Court would not have acted to exempt a practice so central to the faith of the majority religion. Why should a minority religious practice not be similarly protected?⁴⁴

Clearly, these cases are influenced by factors more complicated than the mere use of the term "church," but that word does serve as a symbolic reminder that the notions of church and state have become dangerously outmoded. The Court must engage in much more sophisticated analysis of the relation between religious belief and practice and the long regulative arm of the government. "Church" no longer suffices to describe the religious reality of America, and "state" does not capture the complexity of the government's extensive net of welfare regulations.

The notion of separation is similarly outmoded. At best the idea of separation identifies a single aspect of the relationship between religion and government, namely, that neither institution should exercise final authority over the values, beliefs, and practices of the other. But "separation" is surely an odd word to use to make that important point. Independence of authority is necessary precisely because religion and government are deeply intertwined in so many ways. The interdependence of these two complex realities requires that the issue of independent authority be stated explicitly. Given the significant confusion that the notion of separation—and its associated concepts of neutrality and accommodation—has introduced into judicial reasoning, it is surely time to jettison it.

The courts need to engage in a fundamental reconsideration of the criteria for religion clause adjudication, focusing on the basic constitutional values of freedom, equality, and equal respect. The judicial branch needs to sit again at the feet of Madison and reassert his fundamental insight that both religion clauses are designed to defend religious freedom.[45] Madison's presentation clearly shows that the free exercise and nonestablishment clauses are both grounded in an argument regarding freedom of conscience. Both clauses are designed to defend religious freedom in its individual and corporate expressions. If both clauses are concerned with religious freedom, then the attempt by the Supreme Court to develop independent traditions of adjudication for the free exercise and nonestablishment clauses is virtually doomed to failure.

More important, the Court needs to develop a conceptual framework that will take us beyond the judicial and cultural impasses created by the notion of the "separation of church and state." The religion clauses are designed to protect the freedom of religion in its individual and communal expressions and to prohibit the state from favoring any particular form of religious belief or practice. The clauses are not designed to prohibit religious individuals or communities of faith from entering into the pluralistic conversation that constitutes a liberal democracy. The Court's reasoning has been undermined by the conceptual burden imposed by the unwieldy notions of neutrality, separation, and accommodation. The Court should forgo further tinkering with the problematic "Lemon test" and should return to the fundamental values that undergird the entire Constitutional tradition and the First Amendment in particular: freedom, equality, and toleration.[46] Four principles should guide the Court's reconsideration of religion clause adjudication. First, religious freedom should be protected as a fundamental right to be constrained only if there is a compelling governmental interest at stake. Religious freedom and diversity constitute no threat in a pluralistic democracy. Second, religious traditions should be dealt with equally under the law. Government should not give preference to any one tradition, particularly the majority tradition of the nation. But this principle does not justify the "secular purpose" criterion, or prohibit government from supporting initiatives that allow for the equal flourishing of diverse religious practices. Third, if religion is to play a larger role in American public life, the courts must take special care to note whether apparent "facially neutral" regulations actually create an unfair burden for religious communities. Communities of faith contribute to public life in part by offering their adherents alternative modes of meaning and interpretation to the dominant secular culture. If that unique contribution is to be maintained, then the ability of these communities to practice their faith freely becomes especially important. Fourth, minority religions are particularly vulnerable to the "tyranny of the majority," and their freedoms must be guarded with especial care. This principle becomes even more important as religious diversity increases within America.

If the courts were to return to these fundamental values and principles, the disturbing trend toward restricting minority religious practice would certainly be reversed. Establishment adjudication, on the other hand, would probably not change significantly; however, the reasoning offered for such decisions would improve dramatically. Prayer in public school would still be prohibited because such prayer inevitably constrains the religious freedom of some students. Moments of silence could be approved, since each individual could freely engage in some form of reflection, meditation, or even daydreaming during this uncoerced period of time. Governments should be permitted to provide parochial schools with the same type of aid offered to nonreligious private schools, as long as such aid does not directly contribute to the advancement of the religious subject matter taught in the school. Additionally, governments would be prohibited from sponsoring religious observances of any kind, though they should take no steps to constrain the ability of communities of faith to display their own symbols on religious holidays. If the courts refocus their attention on the basic values and principles, they may not introduce dramatic new changes in establishment law, but their decisions and opinions could be reasoned with greater clarity and could achieve broader public accessibility. If the courts dismantle the tortured legacy of post-*Everson* adjudication and embark on a new appropriation of Madisonian reasoning they might contribute to the clarification of religion's proper role in public life. And that would be a gift not just to communities of faith but also to our common pluralistic democracy.

### DIVIDED LOYALTIES: RELIGIOUS COMMITMENT AND DEMOCRATIC RENEWAL

*"For here we have no lasting city, but we seek the city which is to come" (Hebrews 13:14).*

Pluralism inevitably creates a situation in which people have conflicting commitments and divided loyalties. We are members of multiple communities—families, nations, religions, ethnic groups, and the like—all of which contribute something to our identities. Each community calls forth a particular commitment from us, and each fosters a specific kind of loyalty. We seek, insofar as possible, to shape coherent personal identities forged from the multiple associations that claim our allegiance. We manage this process by finding complementary relationships among these commitments or by creating a hierarchy of loyalties. Family and work, for example, may exist in complementary relationship to one another until the prospect of a promotion or a job relocation creates a potential clash of loyalties. At such times, people must weigh conflicting values against one another and seek to decide which commitment lays the greater claim to one's definition of self. Sociologists have argued that this "pluralization of life-worlds" distinctively shapes modernity, creating persons who are capable of existing in many different worlds without feeling fully at home in any of them.[47] The modern self is open but conflicted, flexible yet divided.

The issue of divided loyalties also defines the relationship between religious commitment and democratic citizenship. I have argued throughout this chapter that religious commitment is compatible with the fundamental values of our constitutional democracy. Arguments grounded in religious warrants can meet basic democratic criteria for publicity, and religious believers can participate in public debate while fully respecting the values of liberty, equality, and mutual respect. Indeed, religiously based arguments can provide significant resources for justifying as well as criticizing public policy proposals, and such arguments are likely to be effective among the vast majority of citizens who identify themselves as religious. Further, these arguments can be broadened to engage and include those who do not consider themselves religious. Still, it is important to recognize that for people of faith, religious commitment takes precedence over all other loyalties. While one's dedication to democratic citizenship should always be serious, for the person of faith it is also always penultimate. Ultimate loyalty is owed solely to the object of religious devotion, to God.

The engagement of the religious citizen with a democratic regime is perhaps best captured under the notion of "pilgrim citizenship." Recognizing the penultimate character of the public realm, believers will not seek their final resting place in this sphere of power and persuasion.[48] Nonetheless, people of faith will often find the public realm to be a place of genuine hospitality and fulfillment, a place in which their own deepest convictions and beliefs are tested, criticized, confirmed, and reformed. Precisely because a pluralistic society requires conversation and exchange with those who are "different," public space provides a context within which faith seeks understanding in dialogue with persons holding diverse commitments.

Conversation makes a crucial contribution to understanding in the public realm because people of faith do not enter that realm with a divinely authorized program of policy prescriptions. Religious persons bring a set of fundamental convictions and orienting principles to public debate, but the specification and application of the resources of faith to particular situations can only be determined *in situ*. Thus the conviction regarding neighbor-love may be developed into a principle of justice like the "preferential option for the poor," but the application of that principle to a question like welfare reform requires careful attention to a range of social, political, and economic factors. Religious convictions and principles may provide a basic framework within which policy reflection takes place for the believer, but those resources do not determine choices in the public realm. Even believers who share the same orienting framework and basic principles may disagree regarding particular policy prescriptions. The underdeterminate character of religious beliefs provides another reason why people of faith should welcome the conversation and debate that characterizes a pluralistic democracy.

People of faith should function in a democratic society as "connected critics," persons committed to the fundamental ideals of democracy yet able to see the shortcomings of any particular democratic regime.[49] Connected critics engage in a form of "immanent" criticism that is available only to those who are fully engaged in the very enterprise being criticized. Because connected critics care so deeply about the values inherent in a particular venture, their critique serves to call a community back to its better nature. Connected critics recognize the ambiguity that clings to the life of every social organization, and seek to identify both the virtuous and the vicious dimensions of the common life in which they participate. Because people of faith share the fundamental values of democratic societies, they remain connected to public life even as they engage in criticism; because their commitment to democracy remains penultimate, they can appeal to transcendent ideals to critique current practice and to elevate the understanding of democratic values themselves. Two of America's greatest "public theologians," Abraham Lincoln and Martin Luther King, Jr., appealed to religious ideals to criticize the practices of slavery and segregation, and in so doing redefined the very meaning of freedom and equality for American citizens.[50]

Persons with deeply held religious and moral commitments can make important contributions to public debate in a pluralistic democracy. Religious warrants can be introduced into public argument in a way compatible with the fundamental values of democracy, congenial to the diversity of political and moral positions, and conformable to basic standards of publicity. Obviously some religious arguments will be more apt to persuade than others. Lincoln and King, for example, often appealed to notions of justice found in the Hebrew Bible, because that text is shared by Christians and Jews alike and because the words of the biblical prophets resonate deeply with basic democratic ideals. On some occasions, however, both leaders invoked biblical notions less common to the American tradition, for example, divine judgment and retribution (Lincoln) and the injunction to nonviolent love (King). Given the complexity of religious traditions and political life, it is impossible to develop a general theory about public religious reflection. Judgments about whether a religious argument should be introduced into public debate or about the kind of warrant that is appropriate are always situation-specific. The important fact to note here is that all moral reflection finds its natural home in particular communities of practice and discourse; in that regard, religious arguments do not differ from other kinds of discourse. Moral arguments are always "homegrown"; they take their rise from local contexts of interpretation and are then extended on specific occasions to engage the larger public realm. Agreement in the public sphere is the result of a genuine "overlapping consensus" or convergence among local moral arguments. Michael Walzer makes this point by distinguishing the "minimal" and "maximal" meanings of moral language.

> Morality is thick from the beginning, culturally integrated, fully resonant, and it reveals itself thinly only on special occasions, when moral language is turned to special purposes. . . . Minimalist meanings are embedded in the maximal morality, expressed in the same idiom sharing the same (historical/cultural/religious/political) orientation. Minimalism is liberated from its embeddedness and appears independently, in varying degrees of thinness, only in the course of a personal or social crisis or a political confrontation.[51]

Walzer's argument is designed primarily to help us understand how it is possible for people to experience political solidarity across international social and cultural boundaries. But given the increasing diversity within our own country, it applies with equal aptness to the question of whether we can reknit the fabric of commonalty within our own boundaries, whether we can discover an *unum* within our own *plures*. As we noted at the outset of this chapter, the fragile bonds that hold the American republic together are under considerable stress. The narrative that for more than two centuries provided a coherent framework for the aspirations of the American people now seems to many struggling citizens a story of exclusion and oppression rather than hope and opportunity.

While these strains on our common life are real, the consequences of these new efforts at recognition, the politics of difference, are often exaggerated by liberal commentators.[52] Liberal theory favors unity over diversity, harmony over dissonance, tranquillity over struggle. Classical liberalism urges us to view conflict as a threat to commonality rather than a necessary moment in the forging of a new consensus. Classical liberalism exalts the universal rather than the particular and values the achieved consensus more highly than the diverse communities that contribute to its achievement. That is why John Rawls, for example, asserts that the "political conception of justice" is a "free-standing" notion, conceptually distinct from the ideas of the good from which it is formed. Liberalism has fostered the dream that we can discover a moral life applicable to humanity itself, a form of moral reasoning detached from all particular communities.[53] In so doing, liberal theory has created expectations that no truly pluralistic society can fulfill, for liberalism has lost sight of the fact that moral communities

> are necessarily particular because they have members and memories, members with memories not only of their own but also of their common life. Humanity, by contrast, has members but no memory, and so it has no history and no culture, no customary practice, no familiar life-ways, no festivals, no shared understanding of social goods. It is human to have such things, but there is no single human way of having them. At the same time, the members of all the different societies, because they are human, can acknowledge each other's different ways, respond to each other's cries for help, learn from each other, and march (sometimes) in each other's parades.[54]

While we are surely not bereft of common memory, history, and culture, the narrative that tells the tale of our common experience as Americans is currently being rewritten. The new story will no doubt be recognizable as a version of previous stories, but we must also expect changes, perhaps substantial ones, as our national saga is enlarged to include those who have long been excluded. This moment of revision will appear less threatening if we remember that it has always been so, that the relation between unity and plurality, commonality and difference, is under continual reconsideration. As we seek to develop a new understanding of how commonality can emerge from diversity we need to conceive of the American republic not as an abstract expression of universal humanity but as a historically situated, constantly evolving experiment in constructing a pluralistic society from the many particular communities that constitute our national identity. At times of relative quiescence, our commonalities might appear rather "thick," broadly accepted and celebrated in national lore and ritual. At times of more fundamental change, our shared understandings will become "thinner," perhaps reduced to a simple acceptance of the democratic ideals of freedom, equality, and mutual respect, even as we disagree concerning the definition and application of those values.

As long as the basic commitment to those values remains intact, we should not fear the dynamic interplay in the dialectic between unity and plurality in the construction of our national identity. In particular, we should not adopt strategies of exclusion from public life to ensure or enforce an artificial unity. The attempt to exclude religion from the conversation regarding public policy is, I have argued throughout this book, intellectually unsupportable and practically unfeasible. As long as the cultural notion of "separation of church and state" dominates public consciousness about the role of religion, it will be difficult to engage in critical analysis of the proper role religion should play in our public life. Religion has always exercised significant influence in American public affairs—for good and ill. If we are to develop a more sophisticated understanding of religion's public role, we must begin by acknowledging the inevitable impact of religion upon public affairs. Then we will be able to devise appropriate criteria that should guide the involvement of religious individuals and communities within our constitutional democracy.

Religious voices should be welcomed into the pluralistic conversation of democracy as long as they agree to abide by the fundamental values of this republic: a commitment to freedom, equality, and mutual respect. When people violate those values—whether on religious or other grounds—we should not seek to exclude or coerce them but to refute their positions by reaffirming our common democratic heritage. By welcoming religious reflection in the public square we are not simply encouraging the voices of fanaticism; rather, we are seeking to devise the criteria by which citizens of all faiths and convictions might find common ground in this fragile but beloved democracy.

> Now there are varieties of gifts, but the same spirit; and there are varieties of service but the same Lord; and there are varieties of working, but it is the same God who inspires them in every one. To each is given the manifestation of the spirit for the common good. . . . If one member suffers, all suffer together; if one member is honored, all rejoice together. (1 Corinthians 12:4-7, 26)

## NOTES

1. The bitter battles fought over immigration policy during the 1994 elections in California illustrate the growing fear and anger over the presence of unregistered immigrants in the United States. The passage of Proposition 187 denied all state benefits and services to unregistered aliens. At the time of this writing, the implementation of the proposition has been stayed by the courts pending a decision regarding the constitutionality of the law.

2. Cf. Robert Hughes, *Culture of Complaint: the Fraying of America* (New York: Oxford University Press, 1993); James Davison Hunter, *Culture Wars: The Struggle to Define America* (Basic Books, 1992); Arthur M. Schlesinger, Jr. *The Disuniting of America: Reflections on a Multicultural Society* (New York: W. W. Norton & Co., 1992).

3. Schlesinger, *The Disuniting of America*, p. 17.

4. Ibid., pp. 13, 17.

5. Ibid., p. 138.

6. Alasdair MacIntyre, *After Virtue* (Notre Dame: University of Notre Dame Press, 1981), p. 207.

7. Ibid.

8. See, for example, Henry Louis Gates, Jr., *Loose Canons: Notes from the Culture Wars* (New York: Oxford University Press, 1992), and Cornel West, *Beyond Eurocentrism and Multiculturalism* (Monroe, Me: Common Courage Press, 1993).

9. Robert Hughes, *Culture of Complaint*, pp. 83-4.

10. Many authors from across the political spectrum have recently sought to address this question. See William Bennett, *The Book of Virtues* (New York: Simon and Schuster, 1993); R. J. Neuhaus, *America Against Itself: Moral Vision and the Public Order* (Notre Dame: University of Notre Dame Press, 1992); Jim Wallis *The Soul of Politics: A Practical and Prophetic Vision for Change* (Maryknoll, New York: Orbis Books, 1994); Cornel West, *Beyond Eurocentrism and Multiculturalism* (see note 8), *Keeping Faith: Philosophy and Race in America* (New York: Routledge, 1993), and *Race Matters* (Boston: Beacon Press, 1993).

11. Madison's argument has deep resonances within the Christian tradition. Similar positions on the nature of freedom and obligation have been developed by many theologians who have drawn on St. Augustine's original argument in *The City of God*.

12. I gratefully borrow this term from William A. Christian, *Meaning and Truth in Religion* (Princeton: Princeton University Press, 1964).

13. Three recent historical studies reveal the salutary effect that religion has had in democratic societies. See Evelyn Brooks Higginbotham, *Righteous Discontent* (Cambridge: Harvard University Press, 1993); Theda Skocpol, *Protecting Soldiers and Mothers: The Political Origins of Social Policy in the United States* (Cambridge: Harvard University Press, 1992); and Robert Putnam, *Making Democracy Work: Civic Traditions in Modern Italy* (Princeton: Princeton University Press, 1994).

14. See, for example, Seyla Benhabib, *Situating the Self: Gender, Community, and Postmodernism in Contemporary Ethics* (New York: Routledge, 1992);

Michael J. Perry, *Love and Power: The Role of Religion and Morality in American Politics* (New York: Oxford University Press, 1991); Iris Marion Young, *Justice and the Politics of Difference* (Princeton: Princeton University Press, 1990).

**15.** The role of voluntary associations in fostering a more compassionate society is documented in Robert Wuthnow, *Acts of Compassion: Caring for Others and Helping Ourselves* (Princeton: University of Princeton Press, 1991).

**16.** The dramatic Republican victories in the 1994 congressional elections were an example of this dissatisfaction within the American electorate.

**17.** Alan Wolfe, *Whose Keeper? Social Science and Moral Obligations* (Berkeley: University of California Press, 1989). Wolfe's work was brought to my attention in David Hollenbach's fine article "The Contexts of the Political Role of Religion: Civil Society and Culture," *The University of San Diego Law Review* 30, 4 (Fall 1993): 877-901.

**18.** Ethicists Gilbert Meilaender and Jeffrey Stout have also written about the "seepage" of influence from the economic sphere into other spheres of life. See Meilaender, *Friendship: A Study in Theological Ethics* (Notre Dame: University of Notre Dame Press, 1981), and Stout, *Ethics After Babel*, (Boston, Beacon Press, 1988).

**19.** Wolfe, *Whose Keeper?* p. 20.

**20.** This point has recently been argued by Stephen Carter in his widely read *The Culture of Disbelief: How American Law and Politics Trivialize Religious Devotion* (New York: Basic Books, 1993).

**21.** Hollenbach, "The Contexts of the Political Role of Religion," p. 885.

**22.** "Towards a Civil Society: Hopes for Polish Democracy," interview with Adam Michnik. Eric Blair, *Times Literary Supplement* (February 19-25, 1988). Excerpts from this interview are quoted in Hollenbach, "The Contexts of," p. 886.

**23.** Ibid., p. 887.

**24.** A deep tension lives within religious fundamentalism on this point. Fundamentalists accept a view of Scripture as inerrant and infallible, thereby protecting the basic sources of faith from external criticism. At the same time, they want to use those principles to provide a basis for policy proposals within our pluralistic democracy. It is not clear that fundamentalists can have it both ways. If religious principles enter the public fray, they must be open to critique.

**25.** I have written at length on this topic in two previous works. See *Revelation and Theology: The Gospel as Narrated Promise* (Notre Dame: University of Notre Dame Press, 1985), and *Constructing a Public Theology: The Church in a Pluralistic Culture* (Louisville: Westminster/John Knox Press, 1991).

**26.** The aspect of the parable that I will develop emphasizes the broadening scope of care for those in need. Thus I argue that this parable has an important contribution to make to communal, not just individual, ethical reflection. I disagree with Larry Churchill's claim that "the Good Samaritan ideal plays upon our sense of concern for the less fortunate but it does not, as usually interpreted, evoke our sense of interdependence and conviviality with the person who lies beaten on the road. . . . And arresting and powerful as this story is as a guide to individual acts of rescue, it is not clear how we are to interpret its meaning for anything beyond one-to-one neighborliness." Larry

R. Churchill *Rationing Health Care in America: Perceptions and Principles of Justice* (Notre Dame: University of Notre Dame Press, 1987), pp. 34, 36.

**27.** "Normative reflection arises from hearing a cry of suffering or distress, or feeling distress oneself. The philosopher is always socially situated, and if the society is divided by oppressions, she either reinforces or struggles against them. With an emancipatory interest, the philosopher apprehends given social circumstances not merely in contemplation but with passion; the given is experienced in relation to desire. Desire, the desire to be happy, creates the distance, the negation, that opens the space for criticism of what is. This critical distance does not occur on the basis of some previously discovered rational ideals of the good and the just. On the contrary, the ideas of the good and the just arise from the desiring negation that action brings to what is given." Iris Marion Young, *Justice and the Politics of Difference* (Princeton: Princeton University Press, 1990), pp. 5-6.

**28.** The defeat of the Clinton health plan was attributable to many causes, not the least of which was the inept way in which the plan's details were communicated to the American public. But the debate in Congress was a desultory affair, with little or no attention being given to the fundamental moral questions at stake in the health care issue.

**29.** For a thoughtful and challenging discussion of this problem, see Charlene Galarneau, "Undocumented Immigrants and Health Care Reform," *Dissent* (Spring 1994), 8-10. "The issue of health care for undocumented immigrants reflects a set of fundamental questions about who 'we' are as a political, moral and health care community. Who counts as members of this community and why? Are these distinct communities with distinct memberships? What benefits and responsibilities accompany membership? What is the nature of social justice in health care? Until 'we' pull together the political and moral will to address these deeper questions publicly, honestly, and wisely, we will continue to thwart health care reform efforts by believing, for example, that 'universal' means 'all but 3.2 million'" (p. 10).

**30.** While it is important to acknowledge religion's bellicose role in human history, it must also be remembered that communities of faith have made, and continue to make, an exceptionally positive contribution to American society. See Robert Wuthnow, *Acts of Compassion: Caring for Others and Helping Ourselves* (Princeton: Princeton University Press, 1991).

**31.** See, especially, James Davison Hunter, *Culture Wars*, and Robert Wuthnow, *The Restructuring of American Religion*.

**32.** Tensions between progressive and orthodox forces within traditionally conservative denominations (Lutheran Church—Missouri Synod and the Southern Baptist Convention) have recently led to schisms within those communities.

**33.** The conservative "backlash" has been particularly evident in the debates over sexuality within major Protestant denominations. The United Presbyterian Church in the U.S.A. and the Evangelical Lutheran Church in America recently produced statements on sexuality that have been soundly rejected because they were perceived as too "liberal" and out of touch with the mainstream membership of the churches.

**34.** *The Challenge of Peace; God's Promise and Our Response* (Washington, DC: U.S. Catholic Conference, 1986).

**35.** Nicholas Rescher, *Pluralism: Against the Demand for Consensus* (Oxford: Clarendon Press, 1993), p. 89.

**36.** This position rejects epistemological foundationalism. I have written at length on this topic in a previous book *Revelation and Theology: The Gospel as Narrated Promise* (Notre Dame: University of Notre Dame Press, 1985).

**37.** This nonfoundational position rejects the notion that good reasons necessarily possess causative force.

**38.** The phrase is Karl Barth's. "The Strange New World of the Bible," *The Word of God and the Word of Man* (New York: Harper and Row, 1957).

**39.** See my *Revelation and Theology: The Gospel as Narrated Promise*, pp. 71-91.

**40.** I have reflected on this issue at some length in "Radiance and Obscurity in Biblical Narratives." *Constructing a Public Theology*, pp. 45-62.

**41.** My thanks to Angela Carmella, Professor of Law at Seton Hall University and Visiting Fellow at Harvard Divinity School's Center for the Study of Values in Public Life, for her helpful guidance through these cases.

**42.** *Goldman v. Weinberger*, 106 S. Ct. 1310, 1313 (1986).

**43.** *Employment Division v. Smith*, 494 U.S. at 890.

**44.** Subsequent to this decision Congress passed the Freedom Restoration Act, thereby legislating the very freedom that the Court should have seen as inherent in the First Amendment. For an analysis of the significance of this act see Angela C. Carmella, "The Religious Freedom Restoration Act: New Roles for Congress, the President and the Supreme Court in Protecting Religion," *Religion & Values in Public Life* 3, 2 (Winter 1995): 5 - 7.

**45.** For another theological appropriation of the Madisonian tradition, one which I have just recently discovered, see H. Richard Niebuhr, "The Limitation of Power and Religious Liberty," *Religion & Values in Public Life* 3, 2 (Winter 1995): 1-4.

**46.** "The trouble with *Lemon v. Kurtzman* is that it is written as though the separation of church and state is meant to protect government against religion. It ignores the point that government is the enemy. You need *Lemon v. Kurtzman* to make sure that government stays out of the religion business, and that's really all that you need. I would delete from the test the excessive entanglement clause that causes nothing but trouble, so much trouble that in my judgment it causes religious groups to be discriminated against. It brings about a situation in which the Court reads the religion clause of the Constitution as though the Founders' intention was to treat religions worse than other entities in society. That is, on its face, patently ridiculous, but that's what happens." "A Conversation with Stephen Carter," *Religion and Values in Public Life: A Forum from Harvard Divinity School* 2, 1 (Fall 1993): 3.

**47.** See, for example, Peter Berger, Brigitte Berger, and Hanfried Kellner *The Homeless Mind: Modernization and Consciousness* (New York: Vintage Books, 1973).

**48.** Michael Walzer and I have had an interesting disagreement over the degree to which the civic realm serves as a place of "comfort." See "Conversations: Ronald F. Thiemann and Michael Walzer," *Religion and Values in Public Life: A Forum from Harvard Divinity School* 2, 2 (Winter 1994): 2-4.

**49.** Michael Walzer, *Interpretation and Social Criticism* (Cambridge: Harvard University Press, 1987).

**50.** Lincoln and King worked within the tradition of constitutional democracy but also brought a fundamental critique to bear on that tradition by drawing on theological principles. In so doing they considerably expanded the notions of freedom and equality beyond anything imagined by the framers of the Constitution.

**51.** Michael Walzer, *Thick and Thin: Moral Argument at Home and Abroad* (Notre Dame: University of Notre Dame Press, 1994), pp. 3 and 4.

**52.** A thoroughly sensible and balanced discussion of this issue is Charles Taylor, *Multiculturalism and "The Politics of Recognition"* (Princeton: Princeton University Press, 1992).

**53.** For a fascinating analysis of the racial biases inherent in liberal theory, see Robin W. Lovin, "Liberalism and Racial Justice, *Religion & Values in Public Life* 3, 2 (Winter 1995): 7 - 8.

**54.** Walzer, *Thick and Thin*, p. 8.

# Index